D1098121

Post-Exilic Judaism

The Baird Lecture for 1934

Post - Exilic Judaism

BY

ADAM C. WELCH, D.D.

EMERITUS PROFESSOR OF HEBREW AND OLD TESTAMENT,
EDINBURGH

William Blackwood & Sons Ltd.

Edinburgh and London

1935

PREFACE.

———

THE title of this volume has been chosen in order at once to define its aim and to mark its limitation. Its leading purpose is to trace the character of the new polity which was constituted by the men who rebuilt the temple and restored the cult at Jerusalem. In order to discover this, it has been necessary to submit the documents which bear on the period to a fresh examination, to seek to determine their relative dates, and thus to explore the factors which contributed to the development of the new community. But the ultimate end of this inquiry has been to bring to light, so far as possible, the ideals and the convictions of the men who guided the movement. For it was these, as embodied in the restored institutions, which strongly influenced, though they did not wholly control, the life of Jewry, both in Palestine and in the diaspora.

The title, however, also serves to mark the limitation of the volume. It has not been found necessary to include any discussion of the work of Nehemiah. That leader's chief contribution was the rebuilding of the city-wall, but he does not seem to have intervened in the work of reconstruction which was going on inside that wall. At the utmost he may have lent the weight of his authority as Persian official to the measures by which other leaders were restoring a Jewish polity. His Memoirs reveal a picturesque and vigorous personality, and serve to show the characteristic qualities of a devout Jew in that period. They are also suggestive to the historian in the glimpse they give of the Persian court and its relation to its provinces. But they contribute little to the understanding of post-exilic Judaism. That was well under weigh before Nehemiah arrived, and would have continued, although Jerusalem had remained an open town.

The author takes this opportunity to acknowledge his debt to the Baird Trustees who appointed him their lecturer. The discussion of an Old Testament question does not receive a ready hearing in a time which has so many and so urgent problems to face. When, also, a student's work departs widely from received opinion on its subject, he is apt to suffer peculiar neglect. For he must give in full the reasons which have driven him into dissent, and then he discovers that a discussion which necessarily involves some technical detail appeals only to those who desire more than results, even the reasons for these results. I am deeply grateful to the Trustees who have made it possible to publish a study which, without their confidence, would have been impracticable.

Yet this confidence implies a responsibility, since the Trustees administer a fund which was devoted to the purpose of maintaining the Christian faith.

The responsibility is no new one. It began when the author vowed allegiance to the Church of his baptism and his ordination : it was renewed when he was entrusted with the task of training Divinity students in the meaning of the Old Testament : it ends with the act of the Baird Trustees. When the author demits the task to which the Church commissioned him, he may not claim to have fulfilled his obligation, but he does claim never to have lost sight of it. The Old Testament is not merely one of the oldest and most influential religious manuals in the world : it is also one of the Church's final standards for faith and life. Unless these things are true, time spent in its study ranks with devotion to archæology. The time the author has spent with it has not been lived in the past. For the book remains alive, alive with the exultation and the agony of a great-hearted nation, alive with the voice of God, who through it speaks to men.

I have also to acknowledge the generous way in which my friend the Rev. Geo. S. Gunn, B.D., of Juniper Green, has come to my help, not for the first time, in the revision of the proofs. Mr Gunn's quick appreciation of the bearing of the discussion, as well as his exact mind, has been of great assistance.

ADAM C. WELCH.

Edinburgh.

CONTENTS.

POST-EXILIC JUDAISM.

CHAPTER I.

WHY ISRAEL SURVIVED THE EXILE.

THE eighth and seventh centuries saw the rise of one large question on the political and religious horizon of Israel : on the answer which the nation gave to this was to depend whether anything of its peculiar life was to survive its outward collapse as a State.

The force which had bound the clans into a federation after their escape from Egypt had been their religion ; the God to whom under the influence of Moses they gave their allegiance at Horeb was the God of the federation. The sense of unity derived from the religious bond enabled them to overcome the disintegrating influence of the conquest which, because it was sporadic, had threatened to bring back the old conditions. It had also enabled them to assimilate the clans which had not been in Egypt, and so had not directly received the new spirit of the Mosaic reform. Their next task was to create an institution which, while it maintained their national unity, also served to make Israel know itself one in a common destiny and in a common purpose. Without this there could be no security from the neighbouring peoples which sought to oust the invaders from the country they had won ; and there could be no order within, such as would enable the nation to develop its own distinctive life in morality and religion. Thus, all the elements in the national life combined to make the kingdom possible. Saul was at once the choice of Israel and the anointed of the Lord. In him the people found its protector against Ammon on the East and Philistia on the West. He also shared in the enthusiasm of the prophets who stood for the distinctive character of the national faith.

In its early period the kingdom vindicated the hopes of those who had founded it. David was able to do more than defend his territory, for he extended its frontiers on the East and North. The relations of Israel to the larger world were not of such a character as could directly affect its inner life or peculiar faith. Its relation to that world was through the successful wars in which David imposed his will on subject peoples, and through the trade begun in his reign with Tyre and extended by his son. The troubles of that period arose from within, and were due to the efforts to reorganise the nation : they sprang from the deep-seated resistance to centralised authority, and especially from the old division between Judah and Israel.[1]

But what had given Israel time and opportunity to consolidate itself round its new institution was a combination of circumstances which could not endure.

---

[1] On this period see ' Alt : Die Staatenbildung der Israeliten in Palästina.' 1930.

The brief glory of the united kingdom coincided with a period when the stronger powers of the West and East were too deeply engaged in their own affairs to be able to interfere in a border country, which neither of them could afford permanently to ignore. With the eighth century a change came over the situation, for Damascus began to press Westward toward the Mediterranean. Since this advance across Galilee was at the expense of Israel, and since a Syrian settlement on the coast threatened Tyre's trade-monopoly, it was natural that the two powers which found their interests in danger should unite. Omri was quick to recognise what was necessary ; he put an end to the running sore of the jealousy between Samaria and Jerusalem, drew all Palestine into a defensive league, and cemented the union by marriages between the royal houses. The kingdom needed a foreign policy in order to maintain its independence. The alliance brought Jezebel to Samaria, and in her dower she brought discord. On the one hand, it became necessary to show a new tolerance to the worship of the Tyrian Baal ; on the other, the new queen had the conception of the royal authority which she had learned at her father's court, and, bidding her " George be king," she incited Ahab to the outrage on Naboth. The new foreign worship and the new relation between king and subject were closely allied. Tyre, which set capricious force on the throne of heaven, could tolerate a king who was bound by no law in his relation to his people. The king of Israel was now to be neither the choice of his nation nor the anointed of the Lord. The two famous scenes in Elijah's life show how the situation appeared to the religious leaders of the

people. On the holy soil no other god might be acknowledged beside the God of Israel, and over the chosen
nation must reign the anointed of the Lord, not
another dreary Eastern despot like those who afflicted
the nations round about. Therefore in the theophany
at Horeb Elijah received the revelation of what must
befall his people. The nation itself could not perish,
for God had chosen it to serve His ends, and were there
not 7000 in Israel who had not bowed the knee to
Baal ? But the divine judgment was to fall upon the
royal house and to destroy the kingdom.

Already the question was mooted which was to
trouble Israel till the time of its fall as a State. Politically Omri's policy had been a brilliant success, since
it had preserved the national independence, and thus
might be said to have guaranteed Israel's peculiar
life and distinctive religion. But to the stricter
religious party it began to seem that these benefits
had been bought too dear, for they had cost a lowering
of their dearest convictions and so a breach of the
covenant between them and their God. The kingdom,
which they had helped to found for a larger end, was
being construed as an end in itself, and, in the effort
to maintain it, men were resorting to shifts and compromises which must result in the loss of the distinctive life it was meant to further. From this time we
begin to hear one voice after another among a school
of the prophets who take a new attitude towards the
kingdom. They all agree that the institution which
their predecessors had helped to set up was ripe for
judgment, and they all declare that this judgment was
to come from none other than the God of Israel
Himself. Now, since the same men unhesitatingly

believed and taught that its God had chosen Israel to be the sphere of the divine self-revelation, they could not have meant by their judgment of the kingdom a rejection of the nation itself. All that their God did was in furtherance of the purpose He had when He chose Israel to be His peculiar people, and His act in the ruin of the kingdom must serve this greater end. To preserve the nation's soul, He should break the instrument which had once been its defence, but had become a danger. We may well believe that only a few men were able to see the issue so clearly or had the courage to push their convictions to the inevitable end. Accordingly it is not surprising to notice that from this time we begin to hear of a certain type of ' false ' prophet, and to recognise that, from the time of Ahab until the reign of Zedekiah, these men were always welcome at the royal court. Alike at Samaria and at Jerusalem there were men who could not calmly see the kingdom go, and who believed that an institution which had been founded to preserve Israel's distinctive life must always be needed to protect and maintain its faith. Over against these men stands another succession from Micaiah ben Imlah through Amos to Jeremiah, who denounce the divine woe on the kingdom and who in consequence are frowned on by the court.

The question, however, seemed to be resolved at Samaria, when Jehu used the religious discontent to further his ambition, and, after slaughtering the house of Omri, included the Baal-priests in the massacre and defiled their temple. The kingdom was again to prove itself the defender of the faith and to serve its true end in maintaining loyalty to the divine head.

So it no doubt appeared to the Rechabites, those intransigent supporters of the ideals of a past which was dead, and so it may have appeared to the court prophets. But to the better minds in the nation it was clear that Jehu's methods had only served to smirch and debase the true religion. The God of Israel must alone be served by His people, but *non tali auxilio*. The Lord Himself would judge the royal house in the very place where it had seemed most devoted to His cause, said Hosea. Ahab had sinned by permitting another god than Yahweh to be worshipped at his court : Jehu had thought to honour Yahweh, and in his act had shown how little he understood the nature and will of the Lord.

What forced the question again to the front was the advance of Assyria instead of Damascus. During the period when the powers on Nile and Euphrates were struggling for the mastery of the border province, Israel was the pipkin between two ironclads. The situation of its kings was not of their own creation : all that was left in their power was to decide the attitude which they should take in the circumstances. The few pages of Hosea show the leaders of the nation, in the effort to maintain some shadow of independence, veering between the two great powers, which alternately courted and threatened them. The record of those troubled years is mirrored in the curt account of the fate which befell those who occupied the uneasy throne of Samaria : of the six rulers who followed Jeroboam II., four were assassinated and one died in captivity. Behind the meagre account it is possible to recognise the intrigue and counter-intrigue which brought about the tragedy, for a tragedy it remains, the story of a little people, caught in the net of untoward circumstances, which was struggling to maintain its independent life and which in the end went down fighting.

Through it all Hosea maintained one clear conviction. The measures by which king and court turned hither and thither, clutching at anything which promised to maintain a precarious independence, involved a fatal course of continual compromise which could only lead to the nation losing that which distinguished it from the grey mass of heathenism—it was " becoming mixed among the nations." It was better that Israel should keep its soul even at the cost of its kingdom. Therefore it was the will of God that the kingdom should go, and that Israel should return, a kingless and even a landless folk, to the wilderness out of which He brought it. But that should not be, or need not be, the end of the nation which God had chosen to serve His purpose and manifest His will in the world. For it was in the wilderness that He had chosen it first, and the years it spent there had been the years of its first love. Then it had been dependent on no one except Him, and had found Him sufficient for all its needs. What it had done once it could do again, and thus it should return to its first beginning.

The same situation presented itself in Judah. When Ahaz was faced with the choice between the coalition of Samaria and Damascus on the one hand and the power of Assyria on the other, he chose the more distant and the stronger ally. His prudence was vindicated when the league of the North was defeated, but he must pay Assyria's price and render homage both to the conqueror and to his god. He was able to maintain a shadowy independence, but in the temple the altar of Yahweh must yield place to the altar of Asshur. Therefore Hezekiah used the occasion of the Empire's weakness to assert his complete freedom and to purify the temple, with the result that the pages of Isaiah reveal the inevitable intrigues. In the narrow streets of Jerusalem appear embassies from Philistia, from the land of the rustling of wings which is beyond the rivers of Cush, and from distant Babylonia. The Gentiles were certainly seeking Zion and even bringing gifts, but they were seeking it to serve their own ends. So again Isaiah appeared with the old conviction which he framed in his own terms. When Hezekiah made a league with Egypt, the prophet bade him recognise that such help was futile, because the Egyptians were men and not God. Assyria was tumbling down men and their cities like packs of cards. Calno and Carchemish were already gone, for these were human, and between them and Assyria it was only a question as to which was the stronger. But when the Empire came up against Zion, it touched something which did not belong to its world and against which, therefore, a sword was helpless. God had laid its foundation in what did not belong to this world. When God had finished His work of judgment with the instrument which He had chosen, He should break Assyria and throw it aside. What should endure after that was the nation which had faith, and which He had chosen for a more enduring end than His temporary purpose of judgment. It was natural that men who saw Jerusalem alone survive when Sennacherib had wasted the land down to the border of Egypt should have concluded that the prophet believed the city and its temple essential to the divine purpose. It is not so pardonable that many interpreters of his teaching have drawn the same conclusion. What Isaiah counted essential to the divine ends was not stone walls, but faith ; and since only the souls of men can exercise faith, God's foundation-stone for the future was the remnant who trusted in Him. Those who lived by standards which were not of this world could overcome the world.

So long as the State continued, this courageous and high teaching produced little outward effect. Even devout men may well have hesitated to accept it, for it has never been easy to persuade men of the power that lies in the things of the spirit. For those who put faith in them have often distrusted their ability to continue in an untoward world, unless they are buttressed by outward force. As for the kings and their courts, they naturally identified the independent life of Israel with the institutions over which they presided, and did not hesitate to employ for its support what they counted the necessary means. Along the lines which such men followed there could be but one end. Sargon wiped out Samaria, as a man wipes out a dish ; and Nebuchadrezzar burned Jerusalem with its temple.

With the collapse came the vindication of the prophetic teaching. Israel was back in the wilderness, but it was still Israel and it still had its God. Judah was reduced to a remnant, but the remnant clung to its faith. In North and South the nation refused to die, because in its religion it found its common bond and its inspiration. Slowly and painfully it began to draw itself together again. Instead of sitting down to lament over what was gone and could never come back, it rallied on that which it could never lose except by its own choice. Its religion, which had been the nerve of its first beginning, gave it strength and hope to begin anew. History has many dramatic scenes and contrasts in its book of remembrance, but in all its long gallery there is no contrast so vivid as that between the fall of Nineveh and the fall of Israel. Assyria passed out of history in one swift hour of collapse, because it had nothing on which it could rally, for in this unstable world it is the unseen things which both abide and sustain. These came to the rescue of Israel which Nineveh had beaten to its knees.

The accounts which have survived from that time make it possible to trace how Israel took to heart the prophetic message and sought to preserve its distinctive life under wholly new conditions. Most of these, however, deal with only one side of that effort, the work of the men who restored the temple and the cult there. It is wise to recognise that there was another side, the work of the men who did not return from exile. Since these men remained Jews even in diaspora, they must have found a means, more intimate than the distant temple, for fostering their religious life. To them and to their needs the movement which produced the synagogue was due : and it is a remarkable fact that this other exilic institution should have silently stolen into life and left no record of its rise and spread. It is the more remarkable, because it has outlived the temple and has contributed so much to the Christian Church in its worship and its discipline. The men of the Return, on the other hand, were clinging to the past and eager to restore the one institution from that past which was left within their power. They were not prophets, but rather institutionalists, who sought to restore and maintain what they could rescue rather than to create a new thing. The work was done mostly by simpler and ruder natures, peasant-farmers in Palestine, exiles who returned from Babylonia, priests from both lands. The work they undertook limited their outlook, for it is one thing to see visions of what the faith may be and may do, it is another to set up on this stubborn earth a concrete thing which shall enshrine that faith. The actual conditions of their new life, as subjects in an alien Empire, contributed a share to the inevitable compromises the world constantly demands. But always they were inspired by a great ideal, the desire to restore a rallying-point for Israel, a home for the souls of their people, and a means by which they might preserve for the future the spiritual heritage of their race.

In one respect the task of a student who attempts to trace this work of restoration ought to be comparatively easy, because the period is unusually well documented. At three periods in the life of Israel our sources of information expand into more than mere annals : in connection with Moses, in dealing with David's accession, and in relating the time of the Return. The reason is not far to seek, since these three dates mark successive stages in the national life. Under Moses Israel received its distinctive bent through the adoption of its peculiar religion ; under David it reached national unity in the land it had won and threw up the institutions in Church and State which were to mould its future ; after the Exile it reconstituted itself round the only institution which was left to it and sought to make that the centre of a Jewry which was no longer confined to Palestine. The large attention which the leaders of the nation devoted to these three periods is the evidence of the significance which they saw to attach to the events which happened then. Yet no modern student could claim that the material which has gathered round the Exodus, the giving of the law at Horeb and the settlement at Kadesh, is equally reliable for the purpose of reaching a clear knowledge of the contemporary events. He must acknowledge that much of this material represents the view which later men took of what was the outcome of their great leader's work. They carried back to the past practices and laws of a much later date, and, by countersigning these with the name of Moses, seem to have insisted that they had not departed from his principles. The same thing, in a minor degree, is true of the material which has gathered round the name of David. There it is legitimate to recognise that we possess contemporary documents, which are not all of equal value, since they range from popular tales like those which relate the young leader's adventures on the hills of Judah to the inimitable record of Absalom's rebellion. But there also a comparison between the account of the reign in Chronicles and Kings respectively is enough to show that the same process has been at work as in the case of Moses. The author of Chronicles has carried back to the period of David regulations about the temple worship and the personnel there which clearly reflect a much later time.

In contrast with this situation it is possible to claim that the majority of the documents which have gathered round the time of the Exile and the Return are contemporary with the events with which they deal. Thus, in the books of Haggai and Malachi, in Zechariah, chapters i.-viii., and in certain sections of the book of Ezekiel, we possess collections of oracles from prophets who were speaking directly to the men of their time and who were active agents in the work which they and their fellows were carrying on. These are as valuable for the light they throw on the conditions at the Return as the utterances of Amos and Hosea have proved in connection with the kingdom. To recognise that there are no less than four voices bearing witness to the ideals and plans of this age is also to recognise how much more can be learned than from the solitary prophet under Jeroboam II.

There have also been handed down three longer documents, which have the form of history, but which are of a very different character and of quite different value. The first of these, the Book of Chronicles, relates the history of the nation from the time of David to the reign of Zedekiah, and accordingly deals only with the events which preceded the Exile. Directly, therefore, it offers nothing on the period which follows its record. Since, however, it was written at or after the Return, it recounts the history of the nation from the point of view of a man who lived then, and is capable of throwing valuable light on the attitude with which a section at least of the men who reconstituted Judaism were looking back upon their past. Its value for the present purpose can be compared with that of the prophets of the period, since it also reveals the attitude of the age which produced it. It may, however, do more, since the arrangements in the temple which the author ascribed to the initiative of David may really represent what he desired to see in the second temple. The second historical book bears the name of Nehemiah, and contains a number of contemporary documents, such as an extract from that leader's memoir, a somewhat mutilated description of the dedication of the Jerusalem wall, several lists of names, and the details of certain reforms which the governor introduced. All this material falls outwith the aim of the present study, but there are four chapters, vii.-x., which are generally recognised to belong to a different period and brought into relation to Ezra. Thus they open with the same list of returned exiles with which the editor of Ezra began his record, continue with an account of Ezra's and the people's relation to a law of Moses, include a long litany which has been prepared for some day of public repentance, and conclude with the terms of a pact into which certain members of the community entered at a date which is not defined. It is possible to distinguish there four, or five, original documents which have been set down together rather than brought into a continuous narrative. Accordingly scholars have been in general agreement in separating them from their casual connection with one another, and, while they have referred the pact of chapter x. to the period of Nehemiah, have attempted to bring the other three chapters into association with the activities of Ezra. The third historical

account is that which bears the name of Ezra. This
is entirely different in character from the other two,
since it presents a continuous narrative of the course
of events at Jerusalem from the time when the publication of Cyrus' edict made it possible for the temple
to be rebuilt and for the exiles to return, down to the
arrival of Ezra in the holy city. In contrast with the
book of Nehemiah it has been carefully edited by a
man who set himself to write the story of the גּוֹלָה
or the returned exiles : and we do not find in it the
want of connection which appears so clearly in the
other book. But, in the nature of the case, such a
document can only have been written at a later period
than the events which its author recorded. What it
offers is the official record of the course of events
which led up to the rebuilding of the temple and to
the reconstitution of Judaism round its cult. For a
long time it was accepted at its face value as the
reliable source of information on the period. But it
has become increasingly clear that the editor's dates
for certain events and the relative position in which
he set them are in hopeless disagreement with the
other documentary evidence from the Jewish records
and with the facts of Persian history. The recognition
of this, in turn, has drawn attention to the attitude
which dominates the book, according to which the
returned exiles were credited with the entire restoration of the polity at Jerusalem. We must recognise
in the editor of Ezra no more than the first author
who attempted to write the record of the restoration,
who certainly had the advantage over all who have
followed him of being nearer the events which he
recorded, but who also had the disadvantage that he

wrote with the bias which was inevitable in all who took part in that stirring time. It ought, however, to be added that the recognition of the character of the writer and of his narrative has often led to an undue scepticism as to the reliability of the material which he incorporated. Thus he has included the list of exiles, which appears also in Esdras and Nehemiah, an extract from the memoirs of Ezra, and a series of letters from the Jerusalem community to the Persian court with the imperial rescripts in reply. There has been at times an inclination, because we must question the time to which the editor assigned these documents and the interpretation which he set upon them, to doubt unduly the authenticity of his material. Yet we must count it possible, even *a priori* probable, that these are contemporary material of the highest historical value. At least the onus rests on those who reject them to prove them unreliable on other grounds than the fact that an early editor misused them.

Finally, there remains one source, which cannot be ignored, the law, both in Leviticus and in Exodus and Numbers. Since much of this came into force at the period of the restoration of the temple-worship, whether its original source was in Babylonia or in Jerusalem, its peculiar terms can throw light on the conditions and needs of the community which submitted to it.

The student who attempts to trace the history of the renewed cult and polity at Jerusalem may not complain of want of material. His chief difficulty is to bring the information which comes from so many varied sources into the form of a coherent account, and, when he attempts it, to ignore none of the material which lies at his hand.

CHAPTER II.

NORTHERN ISRAEL AFTER THE FALL OF SAMARIA.

THE position of the Northern kingdom had brought
it from the time of its foundation into close relation
to its heathen neighbours, and exposed it to Assyria's
first attack. Accordingly its people had the honour
of being the first to face the question as to whether
they could rally on that which was beyond the power
of any conqueror, or whether the collapse of Samaria
was to prove the prophets mere dreamers when they
declared that the final victory remained with the
spirit. Yet the situation of the nation might well
have appeared desperate. Sargon, convinced that the
older policy of maintaining native kings subject to
Nineveh had proved a failure, made the kingdom a
province and appointed a satrap at the former capital.
In order further to weaken the native resistance, he
had deported 27,000 Israelites, and in their place had
introduced settlers from distant parts of his Empire.
Thus, while the bulk of the population remained
Israelite, the men had lost with their independence
their native leaders, and the spirit of resistance was
broken, since the separate elements which now lived
together were never likely to make common cause
against their rulers.

B

The conditions in which the men were required to live are described in general terms in II. Kings, chapter xvii. The passage has received additions dating from the period when the relations between Samaria and Judah had been embittered by the schism, the purpose of which was to identify the native Israelites with the heathen settlers and so to discredit them and their worship. But the original narrator shows himself conscious of the distinction between the two sections of the population, and in his account appears to have aimed at more than a mere record of Sargon's conquest which brought about the collapse of the Northern kingdom. He rather intended to summarize a series of events spread over a longer period during which Israel had to suffer under its conquerors. The defeat by Sargon was the first, and may have been the severest, but there were other deportations of the native population, accompanied by the introduction of pagan settlers. Incidentally, however, the account not only proves the continuance of a considerable Israelite element in the province, but shows that the men preserved so much of their native temper as to compel active measures of repression on the part of their conquerors.[1]

The attitude and spirit of those members of the community who remained faithful to their religion can be learned from a number of documents which appear in the book of Deuteronomy. These serve to show that the men refused to accept defeat, to indicate the measures by which they sought to preserve

[1] For the evidence in support of this conclusion which can be gathered from the Assyrian records, cf. Montgomery, 'The Samaritans,' p. 51.

their national identity, and thus to supplement the Assyrian records by proving why the conquerors were compelled to take counter-measures against their stubborn refusal to amalgamate with the new neighbours among whom they were thrown.[1]

The men of Northern Israel were not made dumb under a calamity which might well have stunned them. For they have left a vivid description of the horrors which attended the siege of Samaria and a no less poignant description of the condition to which they were reduced under their new masters, Deut. xxviii. 47-57, 27-37.[2] In themselves these passages would merely prove how keenly the people felt the loss of their independence, and that there was found among them a master of terse phrase who could express his people's agony in memorable and moving terms. As such, they form a human document, which serves to explain why Nineveh fell without one to regret its fall. The connection, however, in which these passages occur is more significant than their content. For they form part of a long litany in which the people acknowledged that what had befallen them had not

[1] The paragraphs which immediately follow summarize conclusions which have already been advanced in my earlier book, ' Deuteronomy : the Framework to the Code.' In that volume reason was given for assigning several passages in the introductory and final chapters of Deuteronomy to the Israelite community after the fall of Samaria. Here the further step is taken of separating these sections from their present connection and weaving them into their true historical relation. In the case of each such passage reference has been made to the relative pages in the previous volume, where a reader may find the proof that the passage derives from Northern Israel. A reviewer of that volume pointed out with justice that it passed too lightly over the period between the Exile and the Return. The reason for the omission was that, in order to fill the gap adequately, a separate study was needed.

[2] Cf. *op. cit.*, pp. 134 ff.

been unmerited on their part, but was a just chastisement for their sin. Men who face defeat after this
fashion are unbroken in spirit : so long as they retain
that temper, they are indomitable. When a nation
faces the shattering blows of fate with grave self-
discipline, and has humility and courage enough to
confess that its failure has been largely due to its
own perversity, it reveals its native sincerity of outlook and toughness of fibre. And when it unites with
this the conviction that even defeat has a meaning,
since it does not come from blind chance but from
One who has the world in His keeping, it has not
surrendered its soul into the power of things. To
remember the past after this wholesome fashion is at
once to believe in a future and to prepare for it. There
have been men who became very sorry for themselves
in such circumstances, who counted repentance futile
because they blamed their world and not themselves,
and who wasted their strength in whimpering over an
untoward universe where fate and circumstance had
been too strong for them. These have lost alike their
faith and " the stalk of carle-hemp in man." Israel
kept both.

That on which Israel rallied was its religion. How
greatly the faith, which had made and controlled the
people's past, could sustain them in the time of their
defeat is the burden of what is called the Song of Moses,
Deut. c. xxxii.[1] In it one of the religious leaders
of the humbled people reminded himself and them
that the message of the prophets, as it had been their
sharpest rebuke in the days of their prosperity, could
bring them in their adversity the profoundest com-

[1] Cf. *op. cit.*, pp. 141 ff.

fort and heartening. It could do both, because it was not the outcome of time and circumstance, but contained the revelation of the divine purpose. God had chosen Israel and made it the sphere for the manifestation of His will ; and His purpose with it could not be defeated by Assyria.

Only a faith which thus held by what was not of this world could support men whom their world had defeated. The men had lost their independence and with it the outward forms of their worship. But they had not lost the faith which had made them a nation and had built their shrines ; and in this dark hour of their history they could begin again where their fathers had begun.

Some of the men, probably many, gave way under the strain and were absorbed in the heathenism by which they were swamped. To these men Jeremiah at a later day addressed one of his most moving oracles, iii. 21 to iv. 1. They had tried, he said, to forsake the Lord their God, and to satisfy their religious needs by taking part in the wild frenzy of the pagan rituals round them. It was idle for them to imagine that they could cut loose from their past, for into their very blood had entered the moral judgments and sanctions of the faith they were trying to ignore. Let them not, he pleaded, go on in a way which could only end in the death of all hope : let them return unto the Lord, for He would pardon.[1]

The first help which came to the loyalists is related in the incident found in II. Kings xvii. 24-28, according to which the local authorities, troubled by the ravages of lions in the country and believing that

[1] Cf. my ' Jeremiah : his Time and his Work,' pp. 57 ff.

these were due to the anger of the *numen loci,* sent a petition to the Assyrian court with the request for a priest who might restore the necessary sacrifices. The worship of Yahweh was renewed at Bethel. It would be unwise to rate the influence of this restoration of the old cult too high. So far as the pagan settlers were concerned, that influence would be nil. With their ideas of those sacrifices forming a solatium to the wounded dignity of the local deity they would conclude that what they had done was all that was needed. As for the Israelite community the direct influence of the restored shrine must have been largely confined to those in the South of the province, for, while the local satrap had sanctioned the cult at Bethel, he was not likely to permit the renewal of the annual festivals. These could not have failed to quicken the national sense among the native population, and, by bringing them together for religious ends, would only have served to strain the relations between the two sections of the community he must control.

The indirect influence of the restoration, however, must have been real, for it meant that the worship of Yahweh had received a certain measure of recognition from the imperial court. The God of Israel was acknowledged to have His place among the gods to whom the men of Babylonia, Cush and Hamath were offering their sacrifices. It became possible for the Israelites to take measures for maintaining their faith. Local leaders, men of the type of the author of the Song of Moses, could venture on cautious but more overt efforts to draw together those who were like-minded with themselves. In our ignorance of the conditions which prevailed in the Northern province after Sargon it would be foolish to claim that such action is proved, and even more foolish to venture on any description of what may have been attempted. It must be enough to claim that the recognition of the Yahweh-worship by Assyria made such action possible, and to add that the possibility helps to throw light on the next development.

This came from the side of the sister nation, Judah, and is described in the account of Hezekiah's effort to institute a joint celebration of passover at Jerusalem. When Hezekiah, after the lapse under Ahaz and Amon, instituted his reform, he did not confine his efforts to his own kingdom, but sent messengers throughout the North with a view to drawing the Israelites there into closer relations to the still independent South. Montgomery has pointed out that the royal action was not prompted solely by religious considerations or by Hezekiah's sympathy with his co-religionists. It corresponded with his political ambitions, because Sennacherib's Prism makes it probable that the king of Judah attempted the rôle of a conqueror in South Syria during a temporary weakness of Assyria before the rise of Sennacherib.[1] Hezekiah's action will then be similar to that which was later followed by Josiah. In both cases a purification of the temple went along with an effort at rapprochement with the North, and in both cases these efforts coincided with a period when Nineveh was weak. Now when Hezekiah made these overtures, he met with a varying reception. According to II. Chron. c. xxx., he sent messengers through Ephraim

[1] Cf. Montgomery, ' The Samaritans,' pp. 51 ff.

and Manasseh and into lower Galilee. Certain of Asher, Manasseh and Zebulun were favourable, v. 11, and many in Manasseh, Ephraim, Issachar and Zebulun actually took part in the celebration at the temple, v. 18. Evidently, however, from the terms employed all Israel was not of one mind in its attitude to the Judean proposals. In our ignorance of the situation it is impossible to say why the people were divided. Some of the men approached may have realised the gravity of the step proposed and hesitated to take part in what could be considered overt rebellion against Nineveh. Some may have been governed by jealousy of Hezekiah and Judah. But the account serves to make one thing clear, which is exactly what might be expected in the conditions which have been sketched. There was no central authority which could speak in name of the whole community of Northern Israel. Instead of this there were scattered bodies of loyalists acting under local leaders, whose influence was personal. All these men naturally did not take the same view of the situation when Hezekiah approached them with his overtures.

What appeared possible to the loyalists was a step which served to consolidate them and to mark off their distinction from their heathen neighbours. They enacted for their own guidance the law against inter-marriage with the heathen, which is found in Deut. c. vii.[1] This regulation, which went beyond the terms of any previous law governing the relations between Israel and the outside world, was of grave significance for the future. It meant, on the one side, that the

[1] Cf. for a full discussion ' Deuteronomy : the Framework to the Code,' pp. 69 ff.

loyalists were convinced of the distinction between themselves and the heathen world in which they must henceforth live, and were resolved to maintain this distinction. Israel was Israel and was resolved to continue such. It meant, on the other hand, that the men were quick to recognise that new measures were needed to maintain this distinction, and were prepared to take them. Once the outward polity of a kingdom and a religious organisation had served to mark them off from their world. When these outward aids were gone, they were prepared to frame new ones ; and they did, as soon as conditions made it practicable. It might have been impossible to take such an overt step in the days of Assyrian vigour ; but the temporary weakness of their conquerors made it possible to venture on action which served to confirm their corporate life, while it did not go so far as to lay them open to the charge of rebellion, if Assyria should recover.

The actual religious life of the Northern loyalists, however, could not have been maintained by the exiguous measures which have been sketched. The existence of a single centre at which sacrifice was offered to Yahweh, though there had been added to it the opportunity to take part in an annual passover at Jerusalem, could not have done much to keep alive the faith in the scattered homesteads among the glens of Samaria and Galilee. Even the refusal to inter-marry with their heathen neighbours merely served to prove that the men realised how separate was their outlook on life and duty : it could not foster or sustain this outlook in itself. At a later period a prophet realised the truth of this when the exiles in Babylonia wrote and asked for his advice in their case. He knew they could not build the humblest place of sacrifice, but he also believed that they did not need to plot for their return to the temple. So he bade them pray to their God and discover a new means of maintaining what was their very life. Without realising what he did, he began the movement which resulted in the institution of the synagogue.[1] It is possible that Jeremiah learned the suggestion which he passed on to the Judean exiles from the practice of the remanent Israelites, for there have been preserved three litanies which were clearly intended for a form of worship in which altar and sacrifice had no place. The longest of these is to be found in Neh. c. ix. It is also the most instructive for the present purpose, partly because it is introduced by a few sentences which describe the occasion for which it was employed, partly because its terms are of such a character as to throw light on its date and its source.

The litany, which consists of a confession of sin and a prayer, follows a simple, closely connected line of thought. Like several similar litanies in the Psalter, it gives an epitome of Israel's history, beginning with the deliverance from Egypt, passing on to the reception of the law, describing the wilderness journey and the conquest of East Jordan, and ending by the arrival of the people in Canaan. It refers to the conduct of the nation during this period, and dwells throughout on its failure to respond to the divine mercy ; thus it prepares for the conclusion, which consists in an act of penitence for the sin which has brought the men to their present condition.

[1] Cf. my ' Jeremiah : his Time and his Work,' p. 247.

The text is in good order and appears to be homogeneous in character. Only in one place, vv. 7 f., does the late usage of *waw* consecutive with the perfect to express a perfect, rouse suspicion that the sentence may be an addition. The context lends some support to the suspicion, since the mention of how God, in faithfulness to His promise to Abraham, gave Palestine to Israel, rather anticipates the final conclusion. Yet it is impossible to pronounce definitely on the question, since we do not know when the peculiar usage crept into Hebrew syntax, and since the writer, by his early introduction of the promise to Abraham, may have wished to emphasise that the divine grace brought the nation into being. Israel owed its existence to the purpose of God.

The most obvious feature of the litany is the extent to which it is steeped in the language and ideas of Deuteronomy. The confession opens in v. 6 with a description of God as Yahweh alone which is reminiscent of Yahweh אֶחָד in the *shema* at Deut. vi. 4 ; it calls Him maker of heaven, even the heaven of heavens, in a phrase which is peculiar to Deut. x. 14 ; like Deut. xxxii. 39, it declares that He is the maintainer, מְחַיֶּה, of all living creatures. In the same way the prayer of v. 32 employs about God two deuteronomic phrases, naming Him הַגִּבּוֹר, the mighty, Deut. x. 17, and the One who keeps covenant and mercy, Deut. vii. 9. The confession shows the same character when it develops the record of the divine dealing with Israel. Yahweh showed signs and wonders on Pharaoh, v. 10, as in Deut. vi. 22. He led the people by cloud and fire as in Deut. i. 33. He came down on Sinai and yet spoke from heaven, v. 13,

which is the description of the theophany in Deut. iv.
36 ; and there He gave them excellent statutes, for,
says Deut. iv. 8, what great nation is there, which
hath statutes and judgments so righteous as all this
law which I set before you this day ? In particular
He appointed to them the Sabbath at this time, v. 14.
But it is the deuteronomic decalogue which connected
Sabbath with the Egyptian bondage, Deut. v. 15 :
the decalogue in Exodus associated the institution
with the divine act at creation. On receipt of the law
the people, v. 16, dealt proudly or הֵזִידוּ, which is their
sin in Deut. i. 43, xvii. 13 ; they stiffened their neck,
which is another description of their conduct in Deut. x.
16, cf. the similar language in Deut. ix. 6, etc. Despite
their sin, God bade them, v. 15, go in and inherit,
לָבוֹא לָרֶשֶׁת, the land in another favourite deuteronomic phrase, *e.g.*, Deut. ix. 5, where also, as in this
case, the national success at the conquest was based
on the divine oath. In the wilderness it is only
Deuteronomy which in viii. 4, cf. xxix. 4, describes
how the people's clothing did not waste and their
feet did not swell, as in v. 21. Again, it is Deuteronomy
in i. 4, ii. 24, iii. 4 f. which dwelt, as in v. 22, on the
victory over Sihon and Og, of whose land they took
possession or יִרְשׁוּ in another favourite word of
Deuteronomy, cf. i. 21, etc. In spite of the long
wilderness journey and these wars Israel, v. 23,
multiplied like the stars of heaven, cf. Deut. i. 10,
with the result that Yahweh subdued the land before
them, with v. 24 cf. Deut. ix. 2. How well the people
fared in the new land, winning there towns, vineyards
and wells, v. 25 describes in terms similar to those
used in Deut. iii. 5, vi. 11—for עֵץ מַאֲכָל or fruit-

bearing trees, cf. Deut. xx. 20. Yet they rebelled, וַיַּמְרוּ, with v. 26, cf., *e.g.*, Deut. ix. 24. When finally the litany described how the increase of the land, תְּבוּאַת הָאָרֶץ, went now to maintain the kings whom God had set over Israel because of its sins, the writer had in mind the happier days when, according to Deut. xiv. 22, this increase went to serve their God, and especially the joyous festival of tabernacles when the people rejoiced at harvest over the fresh proof of the divine bounty and brought this increase to Him, Deut. xvi. 15. It made their present situation peculiarly bitter that men could no longer tender to their God His due acknowledgment. What makes this list more remarkable is not merely the number of words and ideas common to the litany and Deuteronomy, but the number of cases in which the litany employs phrases which are peculiar to the earlier book.[1] The connection between the two documents is beyond question. It is, accordingly, natural to discover that the men who are said to have presided on this occasion and to have guided the people in their act of devotion were the levites, vv. 4 f. The text of those verses is somewhat confused and uncertain, but at least it leaves no doubt as to this general conclusion. Now the levites were the religious leaders of the nation throughout Deuteronomy, and in particular they appear in chapters xxvii. f. of that book,

---

[1] The above comparison in language and ideas between Neh. c. ix. and Deuteronomy was published in an article in the Z.A.W., 1929, pp. 130 ff. So far as the mere comparison between the two is concerned, there is nothing to add to it. So far, however, as the conclusion based on the comparison—viz., that the litany derives from N. Israel—is concerned, it gains in weight through the proof offered in ' Deuteronomy : the Framework to the Code,' that the book of Deuteronomy is almost entirely a North-Israelite product.

charged with the duty of reading the sacred law in the audience of the people.

The litany, however, refers, or may refer, to other books of the Pentateuch besides Deuteronomy. Thus, v. 9 has a similarity to Ex. xiv. 10, which is generally assigned to E. In v. 10 the Egyptians הֵזִידוּ or dealt proudly with Israel : the verb is used in the qal with the same sense by Jethro, Ex. xviii. 11 JE, in the hiphil with a general sense, Ex. xxi. 14 E. Verse 11 resembles Ex. xiv. 21 f., which is variously ascribed to P^g or E. Verse 12 more closely resembles Ex. xiii. 21, which is derived from J, but it is also present in Deut. i. 33. Verse 17 may be compared with Num. xiv. 4 E ; the description there of Yahweh as merciful and gracious is similar to Ex. xxxiv. 6 f. JE. Verse 18 can be paralleled in Ex. xxxii. 4 E : verse 20*a* has a certain analogy to Num. xi. 17, 25 f. E, verse 23*a* may be compared with Gen. xxii. 17 JE, but is much nearer Deut. i. 10. The list is somewhat exiguous, and the parallels are not always convincing, especially when they are compared with the parallels to Deuteronomy. But what it does give is a few parallels to passages which derive from E and a few others to passages which can be called JE, but the precise source of which cannot be determined. In no instance is there a reference which compels the conclusion that the writer of the litany was acquainted with or dependent on the Judean account of the origins of the nation.

More direct evidence of the source from which the confession has been derived is to be found in its author's description of the condition of his people. Because of their sins their God has delivered them into the power of the peoples of the lands, v. 30 ; and this has been their situation from the time of the kings of Assyria unto this day, v. 32. The humiliation of the nation began with the domination of Assyria in Palestine, has continued since that time, and has resulted in its subjection to ' the peoples of the lands.' Two features in this statement call for special attention. The first is that there is no mention either of captivity or of a return. The writer indeed excludes both, since he makes his people acknowledge that their God did not make a clean sweep, nor did He wholly forsake them, v. 31. The natural sense of this description is that, while the nation has been and remains humbled and weakened, it is suffering in its own land. In order to realise the precise force of the writer's description, it is only necessary to contrast his terms with those of a similar confession which is put into the mouth of Ezra in Ezra ix. 7 f. " For our iniquities have we, our kings and our priests been delivered into the power of the *kings* of the lands, to the sword, to captivity and to spoiling and to confusion of face, as it is this day. But now for a little moment grace has been shown from the Lord to leave us a remnant to escape and to give us a nail in His holy place that our God may lighten our eyes and grant us a little reviving in our bondage." Both confessions acknowledge that the people have lost their independence and are subject to alien authority. But the one which is put into the mouth of one of the leaders of the returned exiles, cannot ignore captivity as an element in the penalty, nor partial restoration as a proof of the divine mercy. It can also see a gleam of hope in the fact that Yahweh has extended mercy in the sight of the kings of Persia to set up the house of our God, Ezra ix. 9. The other confession finds its only hope in what God has always been to His people, and in the fact that He has not made a complete end of them. For the present they are in bondage to the *peoples* of the lands, they have received no relief from any kings and they say nothing about the house of their God. Such a description of the condition of the people is not appropriate to Judah before the captivity, since then it was not subject to the peoples of the lands, nor does it suit the attitude of Judah after the Return. On the other hand, it corresponds with the condition of Northern Israel after the fall of Samaria, when the people were living among the alien settlers under an Assyrian satrap.

The other feature of the litany is that the condition to which the men have been reduced is dated from the time of the rise of Assyria to domination in Palestine. In itself such a date for the calamity is enough to create a presumption that Northern Israel is intended, since it was on Samaria, not on Jerusalem, that the weight of the Assyrian attack fell. But this presumption is confirmed, when it is recognised that the divine chastisement for the national sin is said to have appeared first in the triumph of Assyria and to have continued ever since. There is no suggestion of any other conqueror, and there is also no suggestion that the penalty had been mitigated. The yoke of the Empire is still heavy on the nation's neck. Now Judah also considered its loss of independence to be the evidence of the divine chastisement. But it did not date this foreign domination from the time of the

Assyrian kings. On the contrary, it counted Sennacherib's failure to capture Jerusalem the proof that
Yahweh had intervened to protect His city. Judah,
which related that an angel had destroyed the invad-
ing army in a night, would never have written or used
a litany which dated the beginning of its overthrow
from the period of the Assyrian wars. Instead of
seeing in Nineveh the origin of the collapse of Jerusalem, it consistently derived that calamity from
Babylon and made Nebuchadrezzar the divine instrument for chastising the sins of Manasseh. Again a
comparison between the two litanies in Ezra and
Nehemiah brings out the differing situation. After
the Return Judah could say in Ezra ix. 7, that it had
been delivered into the power of the kings of the lands.
The phrase adequately describes how the people had
been at the mercy, now of Babylon, again of Persia.
But that described the past, for now God has had
compassion and has given the men favour in the eyes
of their conquerors so that they may restore their
worship. The litany in Nehemiah confines itself to a
dreary present. That began with the Assyrian
victory and still continues. This phrase, in turn,
accurately sums up the situation of the remanent
population in Ephraim after the destruction of Samaria.
Their God had not made a full end of them, but He
has delivered them into the power of the heathen
colonists and their heathen governor.

To recognise this source for the confession gives
additional point to one minor feature in it. It has
already been noted that verse 6 speaks of Yahweh
Who made the heaven, even the heaven of heavens.
But the author has added to the deuteronomic phrase

C

the remark that the Lord made the heavens with their host and that this host worships Him. The man was living among heathen colonists, many of whom practised the astral cults of Assyria, and he made his protest against that lower worship.

After examining the language of the litany and the historical situation which it describes it is necessary to turn to the introductory verses. There we find a description of the people who took part in this act of worship which contrasts strongly with similar descriptions in the passages round the chapter. Those who gather together are not the whole people of viii. 1, nor the קָהָל or community of viii. 2, nor yet the heads of families of viii. 13. They are בְּנֵי יִשְׂרָאֵל, the children of Israel and the seed of Israel, and these two phrases mean exactly what they say. They are the men of North Israel who remained faithful, but they are not constituted into a community, nor can they call themselves the whole people. It is also said about them that they separated themselves from בְּנֵי נֵכָר, or all strangers, and again the words mean exactly what they say—*i.e.*, foreigners. It is not necessary to give the term the forced explanation of proselytes. Such an explanation requires an interpretation of נֵכָר which is otherwise unexampled, and it fails to show why proselytes should have been debarred from an act of worship, since they joined Israel for the sake of its worship. The foreigners are the heathen settlers, from whom the faithful had separated themselves by their regulation which forbade connubium. Again, the people acted on their own initiative and did not, as in Neh. c. viii., ask for guidance from Ezra as to their ritual. The scattered sheep of the flock of Israel needed to create their new methods and institutions, since Assyria had deprived them of their accustomed forms. Part of the day they devoted to reading the law, as was their custom on solemn religious occasions, Deut. xxxi. 9-13 ; another part they devoted to fasting and prayer.

To recognise that the litany had its origin in North Israel implies that originally it had no connection with the chapter which immediately precedes it. That chapter relates how, on the first day of the seventh month, Ezra read in the book of the law of Moses to the assembly in a plaza before the water-gate at Jerusalem. It continues with the description of a celebration of the festival of tabernacles, and concludes by stating that the law was read during this celebration which ended with a solemn assembly on the eighth day. Since Tabernacles began on the fifteenth day, that brought the account down to the twenty-second day. Now, since ix. 1 begins " on the twenty-fourth day of this month," it was natural to conclude that the day of fasting and prayer fell on the second day after Tabernacles. It was equally natural to conclude that the solemn rite had nothing to do with the Day of Atonement, which fell on the tenth day of the seventh month. It must have been a special occasion.

But the effort to find a connection between the successive events has long given rise to difficulty. As Torrey remarked, " the sudden transition from feasting to sackcloth and ashes, without any statement of the reason why, is at least very noticeable." [1] He might have added that the spontaneous action of the

---

[1] Composition, etc., of Ezra-Nehemiah, p. 31. 1896.

people in coming together for fasting and prayer contrasts curiously with the way in which the heads of families came to Ezra in viii. 13 to learn the right way of celebrating Tabernacles. Apparently the men were more familiar with the method of conducting a special service than with the ritual of their leading national festival. The surprise is only increased when it is noted that Ezra had no part or function in the novel form of worship, and that the levites appear instead of him. Bertholet has attempted to meet Torrey's difficulty ; " this fast day is not the Day of Atonement, but appears to be no more than the official expression of the feeling, which already manifested itself in viii. 9, but was repressed because of the intervening festival of Tabernacles." [1] The explanation seems at least artificial in view of the terms in which the people were forbidden to mourn, viii. 10, and of the express mention of the great joy which attended the celebration of Tabernacles. Besides, a day of repentance might well be appointed to prepare the people for the public reading of their law and for the following celebration of their leading festival : it was scarcely appropriate after these two events.

Kosters earlier had drawn attention to the fact that the day of fasting and prayer was associated with a separation between the worshippers and the heathen, and had asked for a reason why such a separation was needed then, and apparently had no place at the reading of the law and the celebration of Tabernacles.[2] Had the heathen been permitted to take part in the festival ? Haller sought to meet this objection by

[1] K.H.C. *ad loc.* 1902.
[2] Wiederherstellung, etc., pp. 64 ff.

translating " the children of the foreigner " of ix. 2
as proselytes, and thought that these adherents to
the faith were refused admission to the solemn pledge
to adhere to the law which he finds in Neh. c. x.[1]
Apart, however, from the difficulty of translating
בְּנֵי נֵכָר by proselytes and the larger question as to
the meaning of chapter x., such an explanation does
not satisfy. Haller must be supposed to consider that
these proselytes had already been permitted to hear
the law and to take part in the celebration of Tabernacles. After that there seems to be no reason for
their being refused the opportunity to take upon them
the acceptance of the law, even if chapter x. describes
such an acceptance. Wellhausen very early drew
attention to this peculiar situation of the litany
between chapters viii. and x., but was content to
acknowledge its inexplicable character.[2]

In order to improve the present impossible order of
events, various suggestions have been made. Kosters
believed that all which was necessary was to place
the litany of confession before the incidents recorded
in chapter viii. Then the separation from the heathen
and the day of fasting preceded and prepared for the
hearing of the law and the celebration of Tabernacles.
Torrey, however, insisted that it was impossible to
separate the segregation mentioned in ix. 2 from the
effort of Ezra to enforce a law against inter-marriage.
Accordingly he transferred the two chapters of Nehemiah to the close of the book of Ezra, and made them
the conclusion of the leader's work. It cannot be said

---

[1] ' Schriften des Alten Testamentes,' *ad loc.* 1925.
[2] ' Israelitische und Jüdische Geschichte,' p. 135, note : " wun-
derlich an seiner Stelle ist der erste Satz von Neh. ix. 2."

that this improves the situation, for it forces on the attention that, while Ezra is, in Torrey's opinion, the chief agent in connection with the law forbidding inter-marriage, he disappears from the act of repentance and confession which was associated with that lapse. The more closely, also, the litany is brought into connection with Ezra's prayer, the more difficult does it become to explain the difference in the language and the historical attitude.

The perplexities into which the ordinary interpretation of the chapter has brought scholars serve to support the conclusion which was based on the examination of its contents. It had no connection originally with the chapter which at present precedes it.

What must next be noted is the resemblance between this litany and two other national prayers of confession which have been included in the Psalter and which have plainly been associated with a fast day. The first of these is Psalm lxxx. It is not necessary to give here the reasons which have led some scholars to ascribe the psalm to a North Israel source, for Gunkel in his Commentary has left no more to be added. What is necessary is to recognise the condition to which the people, according to the terms of this psalm, have been reduced and what is the burden of their petition. The writer spoke of the divine election and protection of Israel, and likened the nation to a vine which its God brought out of Egypt. He dwelt on how it was planted in Palestine, where it took firm root and filled the land. But that was in the past, for now Yahweh had broken down all the fences of the vineyard and left the vine defenceless. All who pass by may pluck its grapes at their will, and the wild beasts may feed upon it. The people are still in their own land, but are exposed a helpless prey to all who choose to ill-treat them. They are at the mercy of others, or in the power of the peoples of the lands, Neh. ix. 30 : but there is no mention of captivity. And as there is no mention of exile, so there is no reference to a possible or actual return in the prayer with which the psalmist concludes. All for which he pleads is that God would have mercy on His people and keep them loyal to Himself.

Psalm xliv., again, is best understood when it is recognised to derive from the same period and to depict the same situation. While that psalm is generally acknowledged to be intended for a national fast, it has frequently and confidently been assigned to a Maccabean date. On that question it is again sufficient to refer to Gunkel's discussion, since he has stated with force and care the reasons which make such a date for the confession inadmissible. While, however, Gunkel rejected the Maccabean reference, he confessed himself unable to suggest another locus or period which was appropriate for the peculiar language of the psalm. Especially did he feel puzzled by the claim to have remained loyal to the ancestral faith in the heart of a penitent confession of sin. Yet, if the psalm be compared with the other two confessions, it becomes natural and appropriate that men who were seeking at some cost to maintain that faith should have inserted, in their confession and even as a plea for the mitigation of their merited chastisement, such an utterance as : in spite of all this our heart has not turned back, neither have our steps declined from Thy way, xliv. 18. Such a plea is peculiarly appropriate on the lips of men who in Psalm lxxx. prayed that their God would keep them loyal to Him. It was natural for men who had made some sacrifice for their faith to pray for help that they might not fail in their difficult obedience.

It is possible, then, to recognise three liturgies, consisting of confession and prayer, the character and content of which show that they were intended for use in connection with a day of fasting. Two of these were taken into the Psalter and accordingly are provided with no introduction : the third, which found its way into a historical book, has been equipped with a suitable introduction. From this it is possible to learn that the men who took part in the public act of repentance combined with it the reading of parts at least of their law and that this duty was performed for them by levites. They had also constituted themselves into a separate community by segregating themselves from the peoples of the lands. The condition of the people in all three liturgies is the same. They are conscious of having lost their independence as a nation, so that they are servants where they were once masters, for they are suffering harsh treatment at the hands of their neighbours. Yet the men were not in exile, but were still in their own land. They did not pray for return to Palestine, nor did they refer to exile in evidence of the divine chastisement for their sins. What they asked was that God should grant them relief from the worst features of their present condition, or should give them help to remain faithful under the penalty which they confessed themselves to have merited. One of the liturgies speaks about the means by which they have reached their condition, for it dates their distress from the period when the Assyrian armies arrived in Palestine. Now it has been possible to show that chapter xxxii. in Deuteronomy proves that one result of the condition to which North Israel was reduced was to rouse a repentance which was evidence that the men refused to renounce their own faith. Again, chapter vii. in the same book proves that some at least resolved to segregate themselves from their heathen neighbours by rejecting connubium with them. The fast day, with its confession and prayer and the public reading of the law, served in turn to strengthen their hold on the faith which was their one common bond.

One feature in such a form of worship deserves attention. Since it did not involve sacrifice, it could be carried out without priest or altar and might therefore spring up in the spontaneous way which is suggested by the opening clause of the chapter in Nehemiah : the children of Israel came together. It could appear wherever a faithful few found themselves, especially wherever a body of men had accepted the direction of their leaders and segregated themselves from the heathen. Thus, the practice may well have been the background for Jeremiah's letter to the first exiles in Babylonia. The synagogue may have had its dim origin in Samaria. It sprang up to answer a human need, and it appeared first as soon as that need arose.

The date at which the practice began is not easy to determine. One thing, however, seems clear. It was not likely to have been tolerated at the time when the power of Nineveh was at its height. An act of worship of so public a character, combined with a movement for segregation from the heathen, could not have been ignored by the Assyrian authorities. From the book of Ezra it is evident that the Persian governor at Samaria watched any similar movement at Jerusalem with jealous care, and was quick to take the alarm, should the Jewish community venture on any step which served to accentuate their peculiar character or strengthen their position. It is not likely that an Assyrian official was less careful to note anything which was calculated to trouble the peace of his province. The movement must rather be assigned to some period when the hold of Assyria over the West had become weaker ; that is, it must date either in the reign of Hezekiah or in that of Josiah. Two facts serve at least to suggest the earlier of these two dates. On the one hand, Josiah's action rather tended in the direction of discouraging independent action on the part of North Israel. He centralised the cult at the temple and in that interest destroyed the Bethel altar, so that all the tendency of his policy was in the direction of making Jerusalem the religious centre for the whole nation. On the other hand, if the movement in the North sprang up during a temporary weakness of Assyria in the time of Hezekiah, this date would serve to explain why men there took action along their own lines. It would further serve to give time during which the new worship developed into more regular form. For the three liturgies which have been preserved witness to the existence of a ritual which had consolidated itself. They are all carefully prepared forms of worship, so that there is a history behind them. Especially is this apparent in the litany of Nehemiah, c. ix. The spontaneous act of the faithful in gathering for their fast day, the mention of their having separated themselves for that purpose, the presence of the levites in order to read the law— all these features witness to a formal act which had become a practice.

There is further evidence that the practice took root and continued with some tenacity in North Israel. For the existence of the fast serves to explain an obscure oracle in Zech. vii. 1 ff. The occasion of this oracle is stated to have been the appearance of certain men from Bethel, at Jerusalem. These formed a delegation from North Israel, deputed to consult the priests and prophets of the capital as to whether the community which they represented were at liberty to discontinue a practice of weeping in the fifth month, separating themselves as they had done for a number of years. Unfortunately, the oracle sheds no light on the attitude which was taken to the petition, or on the answer which was returned to the men's request. Zechariah, who was presumably one of the prophets consulted, did not even, at least so far as this oracle was concerned, address his reply to the delegates from Bethel, but spoke to the men of Jerusalem and to the priests there. Again, while the delegates asked about one particular fast in the fifth month, the prophet dealt with fasts in the fifth and seventh months. These last fasts are generally considered to commemorate events in the past of the Judean community, which were not of peculiar interest to the men of Israel. Nor does either of these Judean fasts, so far as is known, appear to have been associated with separation on the part of the worshippers in the way in which the delegates reported their fast to have been in the North, and in the way in which Nehemiah, ix. 2, reports its service to have been observed. Whether Zechariah deliberately evaded giving any answer to the question which was put to him it is impossible to say : what is certain is that he did not answer it. He rather used the opportunity in order to preach a little sermon on the purpose and efficacy of fasting in general, which he addressed to his own people. In one respect the fact was fortunate, for it may have been the general reference of the oracle which led to its preservation. The decision of the particular case may have been omitted, but the address it called from Zechariah led the Jerusalem community to preserve his oracle.

But the fortunate preservation of the oracle has retained also the description of the circumstances which gave rise to it. This reveals the existence of a community in the Northern kingdom, who had organised themselves for religious purposes, for they could formally depute certain members to consult the religious authorities at Jerusalem. The question on which they asked for a decision was whether they were now at liberty to discontinue a practice which was peculiar to themselves. They had for " these so many years " been fasting in the fifth month, and separating themselves for this purpose. Such a practice must have been regulated and must have given rise to a certain amount of devotional literature which was novel in its character, since it served to guide a non-sacrificial ritual. The three litanies, which have been examined, answer these requirements and suit the conditions in which the men of Northern Israel found themselves.

It deserves to be noted that the time when these delegates appeared in Jerusalem was at the period of the restoration of the temple. By that time a change had come over the situation in Samaria. The loyalists there had been drawn into closer relation to the community at Jerusalem. The movement began under Josiah, but, as will be pointed out later, continued during the Exile. It had resulted in making the temple the centre of worship for all Israel. Naturally, therefore, a practice which was peculiar to the North began to lose its *raison d'être*. It had served a useful purpose in keeping some Israelites loyal to their faith and separate from their heathen neighbours. Now it threatened to perpetuate a distinction between Judah and Israel for the North to continue practices which were wholly their own.[1]

[1] Sellin has recognised the significance of the situation which forms the background in Zechariah's oracle, and has discussed it at some length, ' Geschichte des Israelitisch-Jüdischen Volkes,' II., pp. 117 f. His method of dealing with it, however, suffers from serious disadvantages. He has realised the importance of the fact that the delegates from Bethel belonged to Northern Israel, though he has not quite seen what the existence of an organised religious community there at such a late date implies about conditions in Samaria. But he takes it for granted that their fast in the fifth month must have been in commemoration of a disaster which befell Jerusalem then. Yet he makes no attempt to explain why the men in the North should have been peculiarly interested in the fall of Jerusalem, why they singled out one particular event in that fall from among the four which were commemorated by the Judeans, cf. Zech. vii. 5, viii. 19, why they combined with their fast a peculiar practice of separating themselves for the purpose and why they desired to discontinue the rite and in connection with this desire consulted men who presumably continued it. Hence, one must demur to his conclusion that the passage in Zechariah proves that throughout the Exile fasts in remembrance of the fall of Jerusalem were held at Bethel. The passage proves no more than that fasts were celebrated by Northern Israel, probably at

Bethel, and it associates with these a feature which was peculiar to the North. The verse, Jer. xli. 5, which Sellin has adduced in proof of his view, does not support it.

Again, Sellin considers that the prophet showed a certain dexterity in avoiding the question put by the delegates, and compares his action with the refusal of the leaders at Jerusalem at the same period to permit men from Samaria to take any part in the building of the temple, Ezra iv. 1-3. But there is no real parallel between the two incidents. The men from Bethel were not, like those who came from Samaria, asking for permission to take part in the work at Jerusalem. They were asking whether they were at liberty to discontinue a practice of their own. Indeed, if the leaders at the rebuilding of the temple refused Samaritan help, lest they should draw upon themselves the suspicion of a watchful satrap, they were the more likely to permit the men at Bethel to drop their fast day commemoration, since that ritual in Sellin's view drew them into closer relation to their co-religionists at Jerusalem.

CHAPTER III.

JUDAH BETWEEN THE FALL OF SAMARIA
AND THE EXILE.

THE fall of Samaria brought with it a change in the relations between North and South Israel. The old jealousy between the sister kingdoms disappeared before the sense of a common peril. The first result has already been recognised in the overtures made by Hezekiah, but this movement was brought to nothing through Sennacherib's invasion, which reduced Judah to impotence. The Judean king was indeed permitted to see a comparative success during his lifetime, since he preserved his capital and a nominal independence, II. Kings xx. 16-19. But the doom fell, when Assyria returned to the attack on Egypt, for Jerusalem was in no condition to resist, and Manasseh's counsellors saw no way of saving the State except by submission to the inevitable. The consequence was that the heathen emblems were again set up in the temple and in connection with religion matters reverted to the situation which had existed before Hezekiah's reform. Evidently, however, the court policy roused strong opposition, for it is said that Manasseh shed innocent blood very much, till he had filled Jerusalem from one end to another, II. Kings xxi. 16. Since this accusation follows immediately on a description of a violent denunciation of the royal measures by certain prophets, it is a natural conclusion that this harsh treatment was directed against the Puritanic party in the city. Circumstances were forcing on Judah the recurrent dilemma, whether the State was to maintain itself at the price of compromise in matters of religion or whether men must keep the faith even at the cost of their independence. The strength of the opposition which evoked persecution proves that thoughtful men in the religious party were being driven to consider the fundamental issue which was involved. The ground was being prepared in Judah for the conviction which Jeremiah voiced, that it was the divine purpose to destroy the kingdom by the power of Nebuchadrezzar.

During the long reign of Manasseh no effort could be made in the direction of drawing closer the relations between North and South. Instead, both sections of the nation appear to have suffered under the recovered power of Assyria. For it is probably to this period that we may assign the renewed deportations from Samaria and the additional settlement of alien colonists, of which Montgomery believes he can find mention in the Assyrian annals. Both the little States were also required to supply contingents to the army which their suzerain led on his invasion of Egypt. To this return into Egypt reference appears to be made in Deuteronomy xxviii. 58-68.[1] Their common suffering was the only bond between the two peoples.

Closer relations, however, were resumed under

[1] Cf. ' Deuteronomy : the Framework to the Code,' pp. 138 ff.

Josiah. During the period of weakness which preceded Nineveh's collapse the king seized the opportunity to set on foot a scheme which combined a
reform in religion with an assertion of national
independence. Palestine was purged of every emblem
of heathen worship. The temple was erected into the
one centre at which sacrifice might be offered and the
festivals might be celebrated. All Israel was to gather
at the sanctuary which Yahweh had chosen out of all
the tribes to make His name dwell there.[1] The old
united kingdom was to be restored under the representative of the divinely chosen Davidic house. This
event of the reunion of Israel under its own dynasty
at its old capital was inaugurated by a celebration of
Passover at Jerusalem. The nation was reborn after
another Egyptian bondage, and the rite which had
been associated with the birth of the people was
solemnly renewed. The author of Chronicles, who has
given a full description of the ceremony, recognised
its national character, for he described the priests of
Judah and the levites of Israel officiating together in
connection with it. To this time also we may ascribe
the amalgamation of the religious literature of the
divided kingdoms.[2] There is no other period when
such a momentous step was conceivable. For a time
Israel ceased to vex Judah and Judah to vex Israel.

The scheme was bold, large in its conceptions, and
generous in many of its aims. But it had a fatal
weakness in its political implications. The dream of
a united and independent Israel under a scion of the

[1] In an article in the Z.A.W., 1925, pp. 250 ff., I collated the
evidence which proves that this description of the Temple dates
from the time of Josiah.

[2] Cf. my ' Jeremiah,' pp. 23 ff.

house of David had become an impossibility in the absence of the conditions which had combined to make it real for a brief hour in the national life. Politically Josiah's plans ended on the day when his servants brought their master's body from Megiddo to his capital. On their religious side, however, they continued to control the life of the people until the Exile. In particular, no effort was ever made to go back on the principle of centralisation of the cult at the temple. That remained as the unquestioned place to which all sacrifice must be brought, for Northern Israel made no attempt to restore the sanctuary at Bethel which Josiah had desecrated. It was easier for North and South to continue their worship at Jerusalem, because Palestine had now passed into the power of Babylonia. Had the change been made at an earlier date, the Assyrian governor in Samaria would have viewed with suspicion the introduction of a practice which brought the native Jews of his province into closer relation to their neighbours in Judah. His Babylonian successor, who found these Jews sacrificing at a distant shrine, may have tolerated this, as he tolerated the rest of their peculiar customs. It is one thing to allow a novel practice to spring up : it is another to accept something which already exists.

What helped to such tolerance was that, so far as is known, the Babylonians do not appear to have interfered with the worship of their subject kingdoms as the Assyrians had done. Nowhere in the historical account of the kings who succeeded Josiah do we hear of heathen emblems being introduced into the temple or set up in the land. Nor is any of these kings charged with having encouraged foreign customs among the people or having attempted to promote apostacy in their nation. It is true that all these rulers are said to have sinned against the Lord. But the charge is uniformly colourless, and contrasts vividly with the long list of enormities which Manasseh introduced into the capital and the temple, the chief feature about which was that the practices derived from Assyria, II. Kings xxi. 2 ff. So colourless are the charges against the later kings that one cannot avoid the suspicion that they were a stereotyped formula, the purpose of which was to explain the misfortunes which befell each of them. Thus, when the historian came to deal with Jehoiakim, he found nothing worse to say about him than that he did evil in the sight of the Lord, as all his fathers had done, xxiii. 37. Yet the same charge is made against Jehoahaz in verse 32, who during the three months of his reign before he vanished into Egypt, had no great opportunity to do either good or evil. Also the common charge against the two brothers of having followed the pernicious example of all their fathers has at least an odd sound when it is remembered that their father was the pious Josiah. It deepens the suspicion of the stereotyped character of the accusation to notice that the historian, after describing the treatment Jehoiakim received at the hands of Nebuchadrezzar, added that this calamity was due to the sins of Manasseh, xxiv. 3. In the same way, before he related the death of Josiah at Megiddo, he stated that the Lord turned not from the fierceness of His great wrath wherewith His anger was kindled against Judah, because of all the provocations that Manasseh had

provoked Him withal, xxiii. 26-30. Evidently the
writer felt in both cases that something more than the
personal conduct of the two kings was needed to
account for the fate which befell them. Jehoiachin,
again, is said to have done evil like his father, Jehoiakim, xxiv. 9. Yet he also reigned for a brief three
months, before he was carried away into exile, and
that on account of a rebellion for which he was not
responsible. If the king had led, or even continued,
a reaction against pure Yahwism, it is difficult to
understand the evident sympathy with which the
later records dealt with him, or the hopes which
gathered round his memory. Especially difficult is it
to explain why the men of the Return dwelt upon the
fact that Zerubbabel derived through him from the
old royal line. As for Zedekiah, all the records show
him to have been a ready hearer of the message of the
prophets, and only to have hesitated with a pardonable uncertainty between their conflicting advice as
to the policy he ought to follow.

As a supplement to the meagre record in the book
of Kings, we possess a peculiarly valuable witness to
the religious conditions which prevailed in Jerusalem
during this period, for Jeremiah lived then in the
capital. In his earlier years under Jehoiakim he
appeared in the temple-court during a festival. The
sanctuary was thronged with worshippers, many of
whom had come up from the country. When the
prophet addressed them, he had nothing to say about
an alien worship there which was devoted to another
god than their own. What he severely blamed was
the undue value which the men set upon ' the temple
of Yahweh ' and the place they gave it in their re-

ligion. They were capable of stealing, murdering, committing adultery, swearing falsely and burning incense to Baal ; and from deeds like these they came into the sanctuary in the confidence that everything could be put right there. By their conduct they were turning the temple into a den of thieves, so that God must judge them for their false worship. But it was a worship which was being offered to Him. The prophet must have spoken in wholly different terms, if another god had been acknowledged there. He bade the people add their burnt-offerings to their sacrifices and eat flesh. The reason he gave was that Moses had issued no commands on these matters. A man who spoke in such terms was conscious that his people were making too much of their own cult and were seeking to satisfy the demands of their own God by an abundant ritual. His rebuke has no meaning, if another god than their own was acknowledged there.

In the prophet's later period, again, we still find Jeremiah about the temple, and still in opposition. But his debate was no longer with the worshippers, nor was the subject of debate connected with questions as to the form of the cult or the place it ought to occupy in men's lives. He rather appeared in close relation to the court and engaged in discussion with other prophets who were also called prophets of Yahweh. These men were consulted by, and were in high favour with, the royal counsellors. There were so many of them, and they received such consideration, that Duhm questioned the authenticity of certain passages in the book of Jeremiah, merely because, as he stated, they made it appear as though Zedekiah's court swarmed (wimmelte) with prophets. Yet none of these supporters of the faith had a word to say about any leaning towards apostasy on the part of the king or his advisers, nor did Jeremiah even accuse them of indifference to the cause of religion as they understood it. The constant subject of discussion between Jeremiah and the rest of the prophets was the bearing which the national faith, to which they were all devoted, ought to have on their political action. No one proposed to cast off allegiance to their own God, but they were deeply divided over the question of what they might expect Him to do, and what course the nation ought to follow because of their faith in Him. Fundamentally, the issue between Jeremiah and his fellow-prophets was the same as that between him and his fellow-worshippers ; it concerned the character and the demands of Him whom they all acknowledged and served. In a particular case Jeremiah and Hananiah appeared before the Court with widely diverging counsel. Men's minds in Jerusalem were strongly stirred over the fate of certain temple-vessels which had been carried away into Babylonia with the early company of exiles. Hananiah declared his conviction that the God of Israel should bring these back, and to this end should destroy Babylon. Jeremiah asserted that it was the divine will to send the remaining temple-vessels after their predecessors, because only this would convince men that the sanctuary was not essential to their relation to Yahweh. But men who could believe that their God would intervene in order to restore certain temple-vessels to their true use were, after their own fashion, zealots for His undivided honour.

It has been necessary to marshal the historical evidence as to the conditions which prevailed in Judah after Josiah's reform in some detail, because it is so generally asserted that the reform was followed by a strong reaction. The main evidence for this assertion is drawn from those early chapters in the book of Ezekiel which contain a vehement denunciation of the holy city and predict its fall on the ground of the abominations which were being practised in the temple. All these oracles are carefully supplied with dates, which refer them to the period following the reign of Josiah. But to accept these dates and on the basis of them to reconstruct the history of the time is to run directly counter to the method of criticism which is applied to every other prophetic book. Wherever a book like Hosea or Joel or Micah is under consideration, no absolute reliance is placed upon the headings which indicate its origin or its date. Instead of this, the oracles themselves are sedulously examined in order to discover any reference to contemporary events. The date of the oracles and the possibility of their having been written by the prophet under whose name they appear are then determined by whether they do or do not correspond with the facts of history. But for those facts of history the historical records are made the final criterion, because it is recognised that the headings to the prophetic books may be the addition of later collectors of the oracles, and that these men may have been guided by nothing higher than tradition. In the case of the early oracles in the book of Ezekiel, the opposite procedure has been followed, and on the authority of their dates and their ascription of authorship the description of Jerusalem which they contain has too often been forced upon the historical records. It might appear as though the precision of that dating, where day and month and year are exactly stated, instead of rousing hesitation because of its unusual character, had hypnotised the critical faculty of many scholars.

There are three leading characteristics of several of the early Ezekiel chapters which denounce judgment on Jerusalem. In them the writer assailed the beloved city with a virulence which is unexampled elsewhere, and which occasionally descends to scurrility. To him the holy city sprang from bad stock and has produced shameful issue, so that now Jerusalem was worse than Samaria, worse even than Sodom which God destroyed. Even after full allowance has been made for the Eastern's love of invective, there is a note in this invective which demands another and more intimate explanation. Jerusalem had done more than offend against the man's deepest convictions : it had made him suffer for them. This, in turn, falls into line with the second feature in the attitude of those chapters. The recurrent charge is hurled against Jerusalem that it has become a city of blood. Instead of watering down the expression into a metaphor, or seeking a more recondite explanation, it is at once simpler and more natural to take the words literally. For, when they are taken in the sense that the leaders in the capital did not hesitate to use force in order to reach their ends, they serve to explain the violence of the writer's language. He has been one of a proscribed party, and, though he has escaped himself, he has seen his friends suffer perse-

cution from those who controlled affairs. Other men
besides Jonah have believed that they did well to be
angry when they were called to suffer for their convictions. Sometimes their anger has been more
uncontrolled, because they knew themselves to be
impotent and could find no other vent for their
outraged feelings.[1]

The third feature of these passages is the description
they contain of certain superstitious rituals which
were being practised in the temple. The fulness and
precision of the details as to these rites show the
intimate knowledge of a man who had witnessed
them. They could not have been supplied at second
hand by a messenger to a man in distant Babylonia
and have retained the sharpness of outline which
appears in his description of them. Nor is it easy to
see why a prophet should have entered into such
detail when he was addressing himself to his fellow-
exiles who had never witnessed them. On the other
hand, a devoted worshipper of Yahweh, who was
himself perhaps a priest in the temple, would naturally dwell on the enormities which were being practised
in the beloved sanctuary, because they gave the reason
for the horror and disgust which they produced in
him and in all who were like-minded with him. To
this have the rulers in the city brought their temple,
and they have added to their sin by proscribing the
men who ventured to oppose their policy. Jerusalem
has become vile with a vileness which has no parallel
except that of Sodom.

[1] My fellow-Scotsmen will understand why I find a certain
resemblance between passages in those chapters and some utterances of the Covenanters during ' the killing times.' Oppression
has often driven good men and wise men mad.

There is nothing in the historical record of the condition of affairs at Jerusalem between the reform of Josiah and the fall of the city which can justify the reference of such a description to that period. On the other hand, the chapters can be referred to the reign of Manasseh.

They reproduce the vehement protest of the Puritan party of that time, which was the more shrill and bitter because the men were reduced to impotence by the measures which the Court took to repress them. They supply, too, the reason why the destruction of the holy city and of the temple was so often explained to be the result of the unexpiated guilt of Manasseh. The memory of such deeds having been permitted by authority in the holiest shrine of the faith, and of their having been associated with persecution of those who opposed them, lived in men's minds and awoke such horror that they saw in the fall of Jerusalem the inevitable retribution.[1]

---

[1] Since the above was written, I have secured Herntrich's valuable contribution to the Ezekiel question in his Beiheft to the Z.A.W.: Ezekiel probleme. He has accepted Hölscher's position as to the late and artificial character of the exact dating in the book, but has drawn from this the obvious conclusion which Hölscher missed, probably because that scholar has a bias for stuffing the most incongruous materials into the exile. Yet the deliberate way in which these oracles have been assigned to Babylonia and to the period of the exile suggests at once that they belonged originally neither to the one nor to the other. A student must then examine these oracles with an open mind, and see whether they do not give evidence of the place in which, and the date at which, they were uttered. This is what Herntrich has done, and he has had no difficulty in proving that the majority of the materials in chapters i.-xxxix. belong to Judah in the time of the kingdom. I confess to a bias toward accepting his proof, for this was the conclusion to which Hölscher's book had already driven me.

Unfortunately, however, Herntrich has stopped there in his examination of those early oracles. He has somewhat hastily taken it for granted that all this material must belong to the same period, must have been addressed to the same situation and must

Whether this date and origin for the chapters in
Ezekiel be accepted or rejected is relatively of little

have been uttered by one prophet. This has led him to ignore the
force of Hölscher's evidence for a good deal of eschatological
material among the oracles. But it has led to a more serious
omission : he has failed to recognise the divergence of attitude
which appears in these oracles. They differ in their theological
outlook, and in their representation of the situation. It is impossible here to enter fully into that question, but one example of
this divergency may be offered. Thus chapters xvi. and xvii. agree
in denouncing doom on Jerusalem and on its governing class. But
chapter xvi. pronounces the city's doom because of its idolatry
and because of its alliance with the heathen powers which brought
with it apostasy. It is thus in agreement with Hosea and Isaiah in
tracing the end to a religious failure. Chapter xvii. finds the cause
more in a want of political judgment. The writer there was favour-
ably inclined to Babylonia and also inclined to see in Judah's habit
of making itself a great nation a mere form of megalomania. He
put his finger on one result of this : it had led the governing class
to play fast and loose with ideals of national honour and to be
disloyal to their promises. Now, when we further note that the
author of chapter xvi. included Assyria among the heathen powers
with which Jerusalem had allied itself, and remember that
Nineveh disappeared in the reign of Josiah, the conclusion to which
I am driven is that the two oracles derive from two different
situations. Chapter xvi. refers to Manasseh : chapter xvii. to
Zedekiah.

Herntrich has not recognised the possibility that the original
oracles in chapters i.-xxxix. which he has sifted out may contain a
collection of pre-exilic material, belonging to different dates and
deriving from different authors, which has been edited in Jerusalem after the Return. His contribution is a monograph rather
than a complete study. It deals with one aspect of the problem
admirably, since he has succeeded in proving how much of the
prophetic book demands an earlier date than the exile, and a *Sitz im
Leben* other than Babylonia. But his study has not been done
' in the round.' That is one great service he has done to future
students. He has also made it clear that certain of the weird
phenomena connected with Ezekiel, such as his having been
carried away bodily to Jerusalem, are not merely due to the late
editor, but were introduced by him to explain how a prophet living
in Babylonia could show such intimate knowledge of events in
Jerusalem. Now these are the grounds on which has been based
much speculation as to Ezekiel's mental condition. He has been
called a psychopath, a neurotic, and has been endowed with
telepathic powers. Since there emerges from Herntrich's monograph a figure worthy to be set alongside his predecessors in moral
dignity and intellectual power, we may hope to see an end put to
this kind of thing.

importance for the present subject. What it is important to recognise is that the canons of criticism do not warrant their being used to prove a reaction in Judah after the Josianic reform. The historical records in II. Kings do not bear evidence to such a reaction, and the book of Jeremiah testifies to the fact that the effect of the reform was to invest the temple and its cult with a new and dangerous significance in the minds of the people. Against this undue value set on the sanctuary and the worship there the prophet needed to enter a solemn protest in his temple address. Hananiah founded the policy of rebellion, which he urged on the Court, on the dogma that the due performance of the sacrificial ritual was so essential to the relation between Yahweh and Israel that He would never suffer Jerusalem to be destroyed. The first exiles in Babylonia were in despair, because their inability to continue the old means of grace meant to them their rejection by God. As soon as the edict of Cyrus made a Return possible, the Jews in Babylonia began to trickle back in a steady stream to the holy land. Their readiness to make considerable sacrifice and to run large risks for this purpose is the sufficient proof of the place which the cult held in their minds. They went back, because the Josianic reform had made it illegitimate to practise that cult at any other sanctuary than the temple.

What the early exiles under Jehoiachin thought about themselves was the conclusion which their brethren in Jerusalem were equally bound to draw. Men on whom the divine judgment had fallen so signally that they were cut off from relation to God were rejected, except their God through some signal act of mercy brought them back to Himself; they were the rotten figs of Jeremiah's parable, c. xxiv. The verdict was inevitable to all who accepted the principle of the Josianic reform. As for themselves, those who escaped the exile claimed to be the שְׁאֵרִית, the 'residue' or 'remnant' of the R.V. Jeremiah applied the expression to them at xxiv. 8, and showed the sense in which it was understood. For he told his hearers in the capital that God, who had sent Jehoiachin and his retinue into exile, would mete out the same fate to them by scattering Zedekiah, his princes and the 'residue' of Jerusalem among the nations. Those who had escaped from, or had been spared in, the first judgment should suffer from the second. The word שְׁאֵרִית which the prophet employed does not mean the rest of the people of Jerusalem, the common people, in contrast with Zedekiah and his princes, or the ruling classes there. It has a special, almost a technical, sense, and is used for those who survive, in particular those who survive from some divine act of retribution. Even in its earliest and rather secular usage the word bears this sense, when the woman from Tekoa declared that, if nothing was done to stay the avenger of blood, he would leave to her house neither name nor 'remainder' (or survivor) upon the face of the earth, II. Sam. xiv. 7. In a few cases the word is employed merely to mean others in addition to a class which has been already described, Ezek. xxxvi. 3, 4, 5; Jer. xxxix. 3; I. Chron. xii. 38; in three other cases it is used ambiguously, II. Chron. xxxiv. 9; Jer. xli. 10, 16; once the text is too bad to permit the drawing of any conclusion, Ps. lxxvi. 11; but in general it is applied to those who have been spared on the occasion of some divine judgment, II. Kings xxi. 14, xix. 4, 31 ; Gen. xlv. 7 ; I. Chron. iv. 43 ; II. Chron. xxxvi. 20. Hence, it is a favourite word with the prophets in connection with their descriptions of what God was about to bring about and had brought on Israel [1] or on other nations.[2] The specific sense which attached to the word is brought out by the fact that it appears as a parallel to הַפְּלֵיטָה, ' that which escapeth ' or survivor,[3] and again as equivalent to ' her that was cast off.' [4]

The expression was not confined to those who escaped from the early captivity under Jehoiachin, but was used to describe the Judeans after Nebuchadrezzar had destroyed Jerusalem. Thus, it appears in the historical account of conditions in the country which has been included in the book of Jeremiah,[5] as well as in the record of Jeremiah's dealings with the men who went down to Egypt ; [6] and it is employed by the two prophets who belonged to the remanent population after the captivity.[7] Elsewhere in the material which deals with the Return it appears in two cases which deserve to be isolated and noted,

---

[1] Amos v. 15 ; Isa. xiv. 22 (in the form שְׁאָר), xxxvii. 4, 32 = II. Kings xix. 4, 31 ; xlvi. 3 ; Jer. vi. 9, xv. 9, xi. 23, viii. 3, xxiii. 3, xxxi. 7 ; Ezek. ix. 8, xi. 13, v. 10 ; Micah ii. 12, iv. 7, v. 6 f., vii. 18 ; Zeph. ii. 7-9, iii. 13.

[2] Amos i. 8, ix. 12 ; Isa. xiv. 30, xv. 9 ; Jer. xlvii. 4 f., xxv. 20, l. 26 ; Ezek. xxv. 16.   In one case, xliv. 17, Deutero-Isaiah employs the word of the wood which the carpenter has not needed for his other purposes.

[3] II. Kings xix. 31 = Isa. xxxvii. 32 ; I. Chron. iv. 43 ; Isa. xv. 9.

[4] Micah iv. 7.

[5] Jer. xl. 11 (contrast the use of הַנִּשְׁאָרִים in xli. 10), xl. 15.

[6] Jer. xlii. 2, 15, 19, xliii. 5, xliv. 1-12, 14, 28.

[7] Hag. i. 12, 14, ii. 2 ; Zech. viii. 6, 11, 12.

because they will require special attention later.[1] No translation can quite adequately render an expression which is so peculiarly and closely related to the prophetic teaching. All that can be said in favour of the rendering which is employed here, viz., the remanent Judeans, is that it is more colourless than remainder or residue, which suggests the leavings or the others. What the proposed rendering fails to bring out is that these men conceived themselves more privileged than their fellows in exile, because they had been spared in the day of the divine anger, and were, therefore, since they remained in the holy land and within reach of the temple, in constant relation to God. So far from counting themselves inferior to the exiles, they believed these men their inferiors, because they, through the divine wrath, had been driven out into a land which was unclean. The privileges which belonged to the true Israel with the responsibilities remained their possession.

[1] Neh. vii. 72 ; Ezra ix. 13 f. In connection with these cf. p. 137.

CHAPTER IV.

LITTLE is known about the outward conditions which prevailed in Palestine after the fall of Jerusalem. In certain respects it would appear that Nebuchadrezzar dealt with Judah much as Sargon had dealt with Samaria. His experience with Zedekiah had apparently convinced him that a native prince in control of a subordinate kingdom could not be trusted. So he too 'changed the government of the country,' and placed it, for a time at least, under the control of a military governor ; but whether this was a permanent arrangement cannot be determined. He may have combined all Palestine under one satrap with his residence in Samaria and so originated what prevailed under Persia, when the governor beyond the River had authority over the whole country. Jerusalem certainly could not even have housed a governor, for the capital had been dismantled, its walls broken down and the temple with many of the greater houses burned. A number of the leading citizens were also carried into captivity. But there the resemblance ceased, for the new conqueror did not follow the Assyrian practice of planting the province with alien settlers. Instead, he issued orders to the governor whom he left to settle the country that fields and houses should be allotted to the peasantry, and even appointed a Jew, Gedaliah, to act as intermediary between this governor and the local population. Evidently, therefore, the bulk of the inhabitants of Judah remained Jewish. But beyond such a general statement it is not possible to go, for we cannot reach a definite estimate of the number of the exiles. The evidence in the Hebrew records is very conflicting, and Nebuchadrezzar, unlike Sargon, has left no statement on the subject. The attempt has been made to reach some conclusion by calculations based on the numbers of those who returned, as these appear in Ezra and Nehemiah. But the basis for such an estimate is precarious. Thus we do not know whether the exiles were accompanied by their wives, nor whether their condition during the forty or more years of their captivity admitted of the natural rate of increase in their numbers. Nor is it certain whether those who returned were all descendants of those who were carried away with Zedekiah : they may have included members of the earlier Judean captivity or even exiles from Northern Israel. We are equally ignorant as to the relative numbers of the men of the Return and those Jews who elected to remain in Babylonia.[1] But the probabilities of the case, as well as the few facts which have come down, warrant the conclusion

[1] Guthe in his ' Geschichte des Volkes Israel,' pp. 255 ff., has advanced good reasons for estimating the number of the captives as one-eighth of the population. For other estimates the histories of Sellin and Kittel may be consulted, where full references are found to the relative literature.

E

that Judea, even more than Samaria before it, remained in the hands of the Jewish peasantry.

The province did not settle down at once after the confusion produced by the conquest. Marauding bands, led by wild leaders, had taken to the hills and were prepared to plunder wherever loot could be won. For some unknown reason the Ammonites interfered, and used one of these brigands to bring about the assassination of Gedaliah. But the strong hand of the Babylonian governor would make short work with these guerillas and would not tolerate Ammon's interference beyond its frontiers. In his task of restoring order he could count on the support of the decent farmers of Judah. In a little oracle which can be assigned to this period, and which has been ascribed to Jeremiah, xii. 7-13, it is possible to catch a brief glimpse of the condition to which the country had been reduced ; and it is also possible to overhear the disgust which many felt at these " brigands who roam on the bare heights in the wasted land . . . no flesh hath peace." Once these men were assured of the fair treatment which their conqueror meted out to them, they went back to the farms and crofts where, according to Jeremiah, c. xxxii., they had ploughed even when Nebuchadrezzar was battering down the walls of their capital. The condition of that capital was at first more deplorable than the state of the rest of the country, according to the evidence of chapters i. and ii. of Lamentations. The walls and strongholds had been dismantled, i. 4, ii. 2, 5, 8, 9, and many of the houses in the city had been burned down. The king and his leading men had disappeared into captivity, i. 6, ii. 2, 9, along with

many of the young women and young men, i. 18.
There was such distress that it was hard for the inhabitants to maintain life, ii. 11 f. The memory of
the horrors of the siege was still present in men's
minds, ii. 19-22. Yet, though men were finding it
hard to live, there were inhabitants in the city, and
these must have had houses of some kind. There
were even elders left, though they were overwhelmed
by the disaster, ii. 10 ; and priests were present,
though their chief occupation was to lament over the
desecration and ruin which had befallen their beloved
sanctuary, i. 4.

The first effect of the calamity was to stun and
bewilder. Beyond a curt acknowledgment that the
fate of the city had not been unmerited, i. 18, the
chapters in Lamentations contain nothing but a wail
over desolate Jerusalem, with a description of the
condition to which it had been reduced. In this
respect the two litanies contrast strongly with the
Song of Moses in Deuteronomy, c. xxxii., where before
a similar disaster the author set himself to remind his
people of that which remained inalienable by any
conqueror, and even treated with contempt the people
who had won a temporary victory. The contrast was
natural. For the Judeans had entered the war with
Babylonia in the confident expectation that God must
protect Jerusalem and the temple, since these were
essential to the continuance of His people. It needed
time and thought before men could recover from what
appeared to them a betrayal of their faith in Him.

Yet, though the men were thus bewildered, they
clung to the rites of their worship and continued these
on the site of the ruined altar. It is one enduring

power in life's routine that it helps men to rally from a disaster which has threatened to leave them naked of all hope. Even during Gedaliah's short term of authority eighty men arrived in Judah on their way to Jerusalem, bringing offerings to be presented in what was still called the house of the Lord. The men were drawn from certain districts of North Israel, Jer. xli. 5 f. Evidently, therefore, the altar-site was being used for sacrifice, though the temple had been burned, for the incident took place after Nebuchadrezzar had withdrawn to Babylonia. Men who brought offerings from Israel must have known that the temple was in ruins. Clearly, too, it was not the Israelites who had resumed the practice of sacrifice at the sacred site, for the men could count on finding an altar and officiants in Jerusalem. The principle of the Josianic reform had struck very deep roots when this could happen, and it had come to govern not only Judah but Northern Israel. Men from the North, who persisted in bringing their offerings to Jerusalem even during the troubles of such an unquiet time, were clearly continuing a habit which had become part of their religious life. They valued it so highly that they were prepared to run, and did run, serious risks rather than forgo the privilege. The measures of the reformers had succeeded in uniting North and South in a common devotion to the cult at Jerusalem.[1]

[1] The reported incident supplies another proof that no reaction followed the reform under Josiah. If the temple had become the centre of a semi-pagan cult like that described in Ezekiel, it could not have retained the allegiance of Israelites, who had enough pagan cults in Samaria to satisfy them, and some of whom, *teste* Jeremiah, had given way to their seductions. Only men devoted to the purer worship would have continued to ' go up to Jerusalem.'

The priests at the capital had thus other duties besides that of lamentation over the desolate altar. The altar-fire was rekindled, and they must tend it. But, as soon as life resumed its more ordinary course under the Babylonian régime, it became necessary to regulate this restored worship and to provide for the men who conducted it. In my judgment we possess in chapter x. of Nehemiah, the chapter which immediately follows the Israelite litany, the terms of an אֲמָנָה or pact, which was intended to serve this purpose. Since, however, this view of the chapter is somewhat revolutionary, and since the text is in considerable confusion, it is necessary to discuss the document at some length.

The first question is to determine the connection of the list of names in verses 2-28 with the rest of the document or with its subject. As the list stands, it begins : " now over those who were sealed was Nehemiah the tirshatha " ; and this is followed by a list of priests in verses 2-9, of levites in verses 10-14, and of lay leaders of the people in verses 15-28. In the M.T. this list is preceded in verse 1b by a heading or docket : " concerning the sealing, our leaders, levites, priests." [1] Similar headings are to be found in connection with other documents. Thus, Jer. xxiii. 9-40 consists of a series of oracles on true and false prophecy, and the section is headed by a curt docket " concerning prophets." [2] The natural suggestion in

[1] I have translated literally. The character of these words, which contain no verb, is missed by English readers, since the translators have turned it into a complete sentence and so given it an apparent connection with the preceding clause.

[2] In this case the R.V. has recognised the character of the two words and left them without any connection.

both cases is that the words formed the heading to a
document which once existed in an independent
form, but which was later incorporated into a larger
collection. To find such a document with its formal
docket in association with the pact of chapter x. does
not prove their original connection any more than the
fact of chapter ix. following directly on chapter viii.
proves the litany to have been written for the celebration of Tabernacles. Further, the natural sense
of החתום in verse 1*b* and of החתומים in verse 2 is that
these men were sealed for some reason, not that they
sealed anything.

The suspicion thus roused that verses 1*b*-28 are an
intrusion and have nothing to do with the pact is
confirmed by the examination of verse 29. This reads :
and the rest of the people, the priests, the levites, the
door-keepers, the singers, the nethinim and everyone
who separated himself from the peoples of the lands
to the law of God, their wives and their children of
suitable age. After this follow several clauses descrip-
tive of the attitude of these classes, but without a
principal verb. It is impossible to construe or to make
sense of this passage as it stands. If we attempt to
connect this new body of people with the document
about the sealed, it becomes necessary to suppose
that ' the rest of the people ' means the rest of the
laity, as contrasted with their leaders in verses 15 ff.
It then becomes necessary to suppose that the priests,
levites, door-keepers, etc., mean all the lower clergy
in contrast with their leaders in verses 2-9 and 10-14.
But, in order to express such a sense, Hebrew syntax
requires the repetition of ' the rest ' before mention
of these lower clergy, and who then are the men who

separated themselves from the peoples of the lands ?
These words do not describe ' the rest of the people,'
but form a class by themselves. Even if the men
described in verse 29 be closely joined to the list of
the sealed, this only serves to raise a greater difficulty
as to the sense. The only purpose in selecting certain
representatives of the clergy and laity to be sealed
was that these men acted in name of the whole community. Yet, on this construction of the passage,
these men did not so act, for all the rest of the
community were sealed as well as their leaders. Why
then should a list of the leading clergy and laity have
been selected, and why should it have been carefully
preserved ?

The matter only becomes more complicated if, as
Haller seems to imply,[1] those leaders were not sealed,
but affixed their seals to the agreement of verse 1a in
token of their acceptance of it and as a pledge of their
fulfilment of its terms. This interpretation of החתומים
is rather forced, and the suggestion leaves the docket
of verse 1b hanging in the air : but, what is more
serious, it only makes the difficulty about the sense
graver. Where the signature of an agreement that
involves a community is concerned, it is obviously
necessary to have this done by representatives. But
one hardly sees why, after that obvious step was taken,
the whole community, clerical and lay, even women
and children, should have been required to affix their
seals. One may even question whether the whole
community possessed seals.

If the section 1b-28 is recognised as an independent
document which has been intruded by mistake or

[1] In ' Die Schriften des Alten Testamentes,' *ad loc.*

by a copyist's blunder, and if verse 1*a* be read in direct connection with verse 29, the sense and the situation become clear. What remains is another document which begins : in connection with all this, or because of all this we enter into an agreement committing it to writing. The connection has been lost, so that it is impossible to say what conditions led to the men's action. But the agreement into which they entered was not a covenant ; it was, as in Nehemiah xi. 23, a provision to meet a particular case— in chapter xi. the case of the singers. The men who thus realised that circumstances required such an agreement are defined in verse 29, and, since the two classes mentioned constituted the ' we,' there was no need for a finite verb. They are called שְׁאָר הָעָם or the rest of the people with their clergy,[1] and everyone who separates himself from the peoples of the lands unto the law of God. The last group are identified for us by the litany of chapter ix. They were the loyalists in Northern Israel, who had been delivered into the power of the peoples of the lands, v. 30, who separated themselves from these, v. 2, and who associated a public reading of the law with their act of separation, v. 3. Naturally this group is less clearly defined than ' the rest of the people,' since they formed a looser community, consisting of those who separated themselves from the heathen settlers. It is a suggestive, though minor confirmation of this view of their origin to note how, not merely in this verse but throughout the agreement, constant use is made of the divine name Elohim, even in such significant

---

[1] The list of minor clergy may have been expanded by adding a familiar list of such officials.

phrases as the law of Elohim and the house of Elohim.[1]

As for the ' rest of the people,' when the document about the sealing has been removed, it becomes clear that the words are dependent on nothing which precedes them, and cannot, therefore, be understood in the sense of the rest of a community in contrast with others who have been previously mentioned.[2] The phrase is employed independently as a sufficient description of a definite group, as it is used in Nehemiah xi. 1 and as שְׁאֵרִית הָעָם in Haggai i. 12, ii. 2. These men were the remanent Judeans of pp. 60 ff. *supra.* When it is recognised that these were the Judeans who had not gone into exile, the statement in verse 30 gains its full significance. The loyalists in North Israel separated themselves from the heathen settlers in order to keep the divine law, and cast in their lot with their brethren in Judah. The outcome of their common effort was the pact.

It may serve to show the comparatively early date of the passage if its terms are compared with the somewhat similar language used in connection with a celebration of passover which the editor of Ezra, chapter vi., ascribed to the men of the Return. It is stated in verse 21 that the children of Israel who had returned from the captivity and all who had separated themselves from the filthiness of the heathen (גּוֹיֵי not עַמֵּי) of the *land* took part in the celebration. To

[1] In Haller's opinion this body of men consisted of proselytes; but, besides the clear references to c. ix., v. 30 describes these men as adhering to, or casting in their lot with, their brethren. ' Their brethren ' is not a natural expression to define the relation between native Jews and newcomers from heathenism : on the other hand, it is appropriate as between North and South Israel.

[2] To express this sense, Neh. iv. 19 uses יֶתֶר, not שְׁאָר.

that writer there were also two classes in the community who were capable of uniting in Jewish worship, the men of the Return and all other native Jews. Since he ascribed the entire work of the restoration to the returned exiles, the rest of the community did no more than support them, and, before they were worthy of the task must separate themselves from the filth of the heathenism of Palestine in order to cast in their lot with the true Israel. Hence it is said that they separated themselves unto the returned exiles. In the account of the pact there are also two classes, but we hear nothing about returned exiles, and the men who separate themselves do so from the peoples of the lands unto the divine law. It was a subordinate element in their act that they also cast in their lot with their brethren. The difference between the two accounts underlines the change produced by the Return.

It remains to test the terms of the pact, and especially to test whether these agree with the late date after chapter xiii., to which it is commonly referred, largely because of the mention of Nehemiah among the sealed. Bertholet [1] and Haller [2] may be cited as representative of this view.

The first clause of the pact forbids all intermarriage with the peoples of the land, v. 31. It thus goes a little further than the Judean legislation of Exodus xxxiv. 16 on the subject, for it stiffens up the earlier law by forbidding any Jew to give his daughter in marriage to a heathen : on the other hand, it is in accord with the step taken by the loyalist Israelites

---

[1] ' Hand commentar zum A.T. : Ezra und Nehemia.'
[2] ' Schriften des Alten Testamentes.'

in Deuteronomy vii. 3.[1] The aim was to constitute
the people into a separate community on the basis
of their religion, as the men of the North had already
done. A minor feature shows the scope of the regulation. While one section of those who united in the
pact are said to have separated themselves from the
peoples of the *lands*, v. 29, the joint body resolve to
refuse intermarriage with the peoples of the country :
the regulation was meant to apply to all Palestine.
The law against intermarriage is also set into a position
of peculiar prominence, since it is made the first
clause in the pact : in Exodus it forms a mere item in
a longer code, in Deuteronomy it is a novel addition
to an earlier code. The reason for this lay in the
condition of the people at the time. They were
constituting themselves into a separate community,
who were bound by the terms of the pact ; and,
since the question before them was the maintenance
of their cult, they were defining the men who were
capable of taking part in its services.

In Bertholet's view this regulation was the outcome
of Nehemiah's action in Nehemiah xiii. 23-28, and,
therefore, very late. This implies that the governor,
after having excommunicated the high-priest's son
for marrying a heathen woman, passed a law to forbid
such marriages. The Borders of Scotland are charged
with an ancient custom which has received the name
of Jeddart justice, and which consisted in first hanging
a man and then judging him. The custom is not one
of which my countrymen are peculiarly proud, but
they may at least congratulate themselves that their
forefathers did not go quite so far as Bertholet's

[1] Cf. p. 24 *supra* and the reference there.

Nehemiah, who first condemned a man and then passed the law which brought him in guilty. The governor's action in expelling the high-priest's son is only explicable if this law was already in existence. He enforced, he did not create it. Further, the received view of the course of events regards the segregation of the community at Jerusalem by refusing all intermarriage to have been the special work of Ezra in virtue of his authority from a Persian king. If, then, Nehemiah's acts in chapter xiii. followed Ezra, he dealt with the erring son of the high-priest on the acknowledged basis of his predecessor's enactment. Why, then, did he pass a law which was already in existence ?

Having thus constituted themselves into a separate community, the men proceeded to maintain among themselves the distinctive features of their religion. Their first act was to set a hedge about the holy days by forbidding all trade with foreigners on those sacred occasions, v. 32*a*. Here they went a step further than had been the recognised practice in one part at least of the nation, for Amos viii. 5 shows that business dealings among the people were forbidden in the Northern kingdom on new moon and Sabbath. In that earlier period either the temptation to trade with foreigners did not exist, or it may have been counted lawful to buy from men who broke no law of their own by selling, as it was legitimate to sell the carcase of an animal which had died to men who, unlike the Jews, had no scruples about eating it, Deut. xiv. 21. This liberty, if it had previously existed, was to cease.

Again, Bertholet thinks that this law was the out-

come of Nehemiah's action in refusing to admit
foreign traders into Jerusalem on the Sabbath, xiii. 15 ff.
In reality the act of the governor and the clause of
the pact are entirely different in character. In
the one case we see a community which had no power
to prevent the foreigner from becoming a danger to
their religious customs : if they were to protect
themselves, they must do it by voluntary action.
In chapter xiii., on the other hand, the civil governor,
in virtue of his authority as such, took action which
removed the temptation. The men of the pact
passed a law in favour of total abstinence : Nehemiah
went further and enacted prohibition. But no one
passes a law of total abstinence in a country where
the distilleries and breweries have been abolished,
and Nehemiah did not trouble to forbid purchase
from the foreigner, after he had made sure that no
foreigner was there to sell. As for the governor's
treatment of his fellow Jews in xiii. 15, he merely
enforced among them their own Sabbatic law.

In pursuance of the same purpose, the two parties
in the pact took steps to protect the sanctity of the
seventh year. They resolved to forgo the crop of
that year, adopting thus a regulation from the Judean
law of holiness in Leviticus xxv. 4, and the exaction
of debt during the period, a similar regulation from
the Israelite code, Deut. xv. 1 ff. They thus combined
in verse 32*b* the legislation on the holy year which
had governed the conduct of the two sections of the
people. Whether the intention was to bring the whole
people under the same law by making what had once
belonged to only one kingdom binding also on the
other, or whether the clause merely enforced in each

section of the community its own specific legislation,
it is impossible to say. But it is significant to notice
the curt terms in which the earlier laws are sum-
marised and the fact that in each case the exact
terms used in the originals are quoted. Men who
thus referred to terms of their older legislation must
have been very familiar with its language.

No one will accept such a view of the situation except those who hold that the Law of Holiness and the
Code of Deuteronomy derive from Judah and Israel
respectively. But all who reject the offered explanation ought to recognise that this does not
exonerate them from producing an alternative which
will account for this remarkable clause. If both
Leviticus and Deuteronomy were once intended for
the same community of Judah, whence arose the
divergence in the method of celebrating the seventh
year ? If Deuteronomy was the Code which was
made authoritative under Josiah, did the exaction
of debt then take the place of the forgoing of a crop,
or was it superadded on the other without any reference to its existence ? If, on the other hand, Leviticus
xxv. 4 formed part of the Priestly Code, what led
the men of the Return to add the burden of forgoing
a crop for a year at a time when the community were
in sore economic distress ? Why did they enact it
without any reference to the exaction of debt ?
Finally, what was there in the conditions of Nehemiah's
time, which led the governor for the first time to
combine the two enactments in a common law ?

The men of the pact had thus laid down regulations
on the subject of the sacred seasons, where an adjustment of the terms of those regulations was recog-

nised to be necessary. They then proceeded to take order about the essential feature of their common life, the maintenance of the cult. The first necessity was to maintain the essential elements in their communal worship : the shewbread, the daily burnt-offering and the sin-offering. Since these were continuous, not occasional, since also they were for the benefit of the community, not of individuals, the community, which had constituted itself on the basis of its religion, made itself responsible for them. The men agreed to an assessment of one-third of a shekel for this purpose, vv. 33 f. Their regulation, accordingly, had no connection with Exodus xxx. 11-16, where the sum of half a shekel was required from every male Israelite above the age of twenty. For that is not said to have been an annual charge : it was made at a particular time when the people were numbered, and it was an assessment *ad hoc* for the purpose of defraying the cost of the tent of meeting. The writer of II. Chronicles xxiv. 6-9 so understood it, for he relates that Joash, when he restored the temple after the confusion under Athaliah, laid the tax of Moses upon the people for this special purpose, but for this special purpose only.

Bertholet has also pointed out that the terms in which the clause is framed prove it to have been a novelty. He has, however, failed to recognise that a novel clause of this character disagrees with the late date under Nehemiah. The *terminus a quo* for the introduction of such a regulation is clear. The communal and continuous offerings at the temple had been a charge against the royal exchequer so long as the kingdom existed. But, when Babylon forcibly disestablished and disendowed the Church, the charges had to fall on the voluntary gifts of the faithful. The *terminus ad quem* is equally clear. For, as soon as the temple was restored, the cost of the daily sacrifices, according to the terms of Darius' rescript in Ezra vi. 9 f., was defrayed from the imperial exchequer, on condition that prayers were then offered for the imperial house. The period when such a regulation became necessary was between 586 and 520. Naturally, therefore, no reference to it appears in chapter xiii. : it had already fallen into desuetude.

There follows a regulation about bringing to the temple the necessary wood for the altar fire, v. 35, the first-fruits of the ground, v. 36, the firstlings of men and cattle, v. 37. These verses are generally regarded as two, or even three, regulations ; and לְהָבִיא to bring in verse 35, where it refers to the wood, is subordinated to the main verb ' we cast lots ' in the same verse, while in verses 36 f. the same word is referred back to the main verb ' we made ordinances ' in verse 33. Yet it would appear more natural to connect the three construct infinitives with the same principal verb, and conclude that the men cast lots to decide all the three ' bringings.' Such a construction would make better Hebrew, since, if the intention had been to connect the bringing of first-fruits and firstlings with verse 33, we should have expected ' we made ordinances ' to be repeated before the two infinitives. Further, xiii. 31 mentions the transport of the wood-offering and of the first-fruits, and thus brings the two together.

The men met the charges of their continuous and communal sacrifices by the new assessment of one-third of a shekel. But this tax did not cover all the expenses of the cult : the altar-fire must be maintained and the priests needed to be supported. Nor was the new assessment intended to do away with the old regulations of the law common to both sections of the community which served these ends. First-fruits, firstlings and apparently the supply of wood for the altar[1] had always been supplied by the faithful. Accordingly the men did not find it necessary to mention either the amount or the method of raising or using these offerings : they did not even re-enact them. These questions were already determined by their law. The only matter with which they dealt concerned the regular transport of the gifts to the temple, and recourse was taken to the lot in order to determine it. What particular purpose the lot served in this connection I do not venture to suggest ; and unfortunately no commentary which I have con-sulted on the passage even seems to recognise the need for an explanation. That it was, however, a temporary arrangement to meet the difficulty is clear from xiii. 30 f., where regular מִשְׁמָרוֹת or wards were instituted over the altar-wood and the first-fruits. Since a permanent arrangement naturally follows a temporary one, the comparison of the two passages again indicates that the pact of chapter x. preceded chapter xiii.

There follows in verses 38-40*a* a regulation which, it is generally recognised, has received later additions. Thus, verse 38*a* cannot be translated as it stands :

---

[1] In verse 35 the provision of this wood is expressly said to be in obedience to an older law, though no such regulation appears in any of the early codes.

and we shall bring the first-fruits of our עֲרִישׂוֹת [1] and
our heave-offerings and the fruit of every tree.
Obviously it was not the fruit of every tree, but its
first-fruits, which were dedicated to the temple service,
so that the fruit of every tree must be subordinate to
the first-fruits. But this implies that the heave-
offerings, like the two other nouns between which
the word stands, must also be subordinate to the
first-fruits. Yet this again is impossible, since it
was the heave-offerings, not merely a part of them,
which were dedicated. Accordingly the ' Biblia
Hebraica ' and Haller follow the LXX^{BAℵ} and omit
the heave-offerings.

The same two authorities are at one in omitting as
a homogeneous gloss verses 38*b*-40*a*. With this position I cannot entirely agree, because the rejected
passage is not homogeneous, but deals with two different subjects. Thus the sentence at the close of
verse 38 and that with which verse 39 begins—for
they, the levites, take the tithes in all the towns of
our tillage and a priest the son of Aaron shall be with
the levites when the levites levy tithes and the levites
shall bring up the tithe of the tithes—deal with one
question, that of levying the tithes. They gloss the
original, since, in supplement to the undertaking of
the people to *bring* their tithes, they expressly direct
the levites to levy these offerings, order a priest to
accompany the levites at the levy and add that a
tithe of this tithe must be set aside for the priests.
This expansion is complete in itself ; it corrects,
rather than supplements, the original ; it is also

---

[1] So uncertain is the exact sense of this word that it seems wiser
to leave it untranslated.

clearly later in date. For it uses עִשֵּׂר to tithe in the sense of levying tithe, while Genesis xxviii. 22, Deuteronomy xiv. 22 employ the verb for paying tithes; and the expression, the priest, the son of Aaron, belongs to a later period.

On the other hand, verse 40 begins with an entirely different subject—viz., that of the use which was made of certain chambers in the temple. It reads: for the children of Israel and the children of Levi were in the habit of bringing heave-offerings of corn, wine and oil to the chambers in which vessels of the sanctuary were kept. This has nothing to do with the way in which the tithe was raised or with the devotion of the further tithe to the priests. If the sentence was a gloss, it has been added to some other sentence or phrase than that which dealt with the tithes. Its point of attachment is found in the final clause of verse 39, to the house of our God to the chambers at the treasury; and it serves to prove that those words are original.

If, now, the glosses are removed from the text, the original regulation in the pact will run: we undertake to bring the first-fruits of our עֲרִישׂוֹת and of the tree fruits (wine and oil) to the priests at the temple-chambers, and the tithe to the levites to the temple at the treasury-chambers. It deserves to be noticed that this undertaking in its amended form agrees with the rest of the regulations and differs from the two major glosses in the employment of the first person plural and in the retention of the house of our God as a description of the temple.

It would have been unnecessary to labour this minor detail in the exegesis of the passage did it not serve to throw light on the origin of two of the glosses, and so on the relation between chapter x. and chapter xiii. For xiii. 4-13 describes the act of Nehemiah in expelling from a temple-chamber Eliashib who had appropriated the room for his personal ends. This account mentions that the chamber had been previously employed for accommodating sacred vessels and offerings, and speaks about heave-offerings. Probably the heave-offerings for the priests in x. 38 (cf. xiii. 5), and the description of the use to which those chambers were put in x. 40*a*, were glossed on the original by someone who wished to bring out that the governor was not acting arbitrarily, but was carrying into effect a regulation which Eliashib ought to have recognised and obeyed. His act will then serve to show his opinion as to the relative age of the documents.[1]

The pact closes with the solemn undertaking : we will not forsake the house of our God. The pledge does more than close the document : it shows the purpose for which it was drafted and reduced to writing. The men, whoever they may have been, began by constituting themselves into a separate community on the basis of their religion. They proceeded to take steps to safeguard the outward observances of their common faith, they assessed themselves to meet the expenses of their communal sacrifices, undertook to continue their former offerings for the maintenance of the altar-fire and its officiants, and promised to bring their offerings to the priests and levites at their respective chambers. The purpose

[1] I may be allowed to add that the relation between chapters x. and xiii. may have some light to throw on the question of the date of Nehemiah's governorship : but that is beyond the scope of this study.

of all this was to continue the cult at the temple, which they did not mean to forsake.

Reason has been shown for rejecting the usual date of this agreement, according to which it was placed after chapter xiii., and therefore during a supposed second visit of Nehemiah to Jerusalem. With the modern swing of opinion in the direction of placing Nehemiah before Ezra,[1] the date and even the fact of a second visit have become problematical. It has become necessary to find, if possible, a new date and with it a new occasion for such an agreement, for we must be able to show that at the date selected there was something in the conditions of the time which demanded this formal act. In my judgment the document is one of the earliest of those bearing on the period which we possess, and it shows the first effort at the reconstitution of the temple-cult to have been made by the remanent Judeans and the loyalist Israelites in combination. The men deliberately resolved to continue the unity which had been the outcome of the Josianic reform on its religious side. In no circumstances shall they go back to their old separation, and in no circumstances shall they go back to the local sanctuaries. The one centre of their national and religious life, their common centre for sacrifice and festival, shall remain their continual care.

The document thus supplies an additional proof that one part of Torrey's contention was justified. There was no absolute break with the past in 586, and there was no blank period between 586 and 520. The altar-fire continued on the old site which David had

[1] Thus Dr Oesterley inclines to date Nehemiah a generation before Ezra, ' History of Israel,' II., p. 117.

chosen, though the temple lay in ruins round it. There were, instead of the temple-buildings, such simple chambers or לשכות as even a village in old Israel had been able to supply, when Samuel received Saul as an honoured guest at a sacrifice. The priests still found a task in ministering to the faithful, though they might mourn over the departed glories of the temple. Beside them were levites, and, though the relation between the two bodies of clergy is left undefined, the document appears to regard them as on an equal footing.

CHAPTER V.

SHESHBAZZAR AND THE EDICT OF CYRUS.

BETWEEN the sack of Jerusalem, 586, and the accession of Cyrus, 538, lay forty-eight years. The fact that the book of Chronicles closes with the one event and the book of Ezra opens with the other is apt to suggest that nothing happened during those silent years. Yet much can happen in the life of a nation in a generation, especially when the nation, after a time of disquiet, has passed under the control of an Empire which guaranteed stable order and peace. The life of the peasants in both parts of the province resumed its usual course, the more readily because Nebuchad-rezzar's attack had been directed against Jerusalem and the rulers there. Even the capital must have begun to recover from its ruin. The chapters in Lamentations which can be dated in this period show that the city was still occupied. Its citizens must have had houses to live in, and by the time of Haggai in 520 were reproached by the prophet with caring more for their homes than for the condition of their temple. Some of the reasons which had led to the original prominence of Jerusalem under the kingdom made its recovery certain. The Babylonian governor could not ignore the natural centre of his Southern province. Though he himself may have resided in Samaria, he must have recognised the advantages of this second centre of administration. He could much less pass it by, since it remained the centre of worship for most members of the community which he controlled. The restoration of the cult at the old altar must further have helped in the recovery of the city. Not only did the pact bring back the priests and levites to the house of the Lord : it brought back the worshippers from all Israel and those who supplied their wants. The restoration of Jerusalem may have been slow, but by 538 it had had forty-eight years of settled order to become apparent.

What brought a change in the situation was the accession of Cyrus in 538. In outward matters this merely meant that Palestine passed from being a province in the Babylonian Empire into the same condition under Persia. But shortly after his victory the new king issued an edict which granted liberty in religious affairs to all his subject kingdoms. The decree was the evidence of the wholesomer relations between ruler and subjects which were introduced by Cyrus. Hitherto these relations had been that the dominant power had exploited the conquered. The Assyrians, and even the Babylonians, had failed to make the nations which they incorporated into their Empire feel as though they had gained something through entering into a larger community. These Empires rather resembled a steam-roller which flattened out everything over which it passed. The Persians would seem to have been the first who attempted a different policy. It is not necessary to suppose that the change was due to a higher or more civilised conception of the art of government on the part of this conquering race. One scarcely sees how Cyrus could have hoped to maintain himself by any other method than that which he followed. The two tremendous blows by which he struck down Lydia and Babylonia had been so theatrical in their swift suddenness, the extent of territory which passed under his control was so vast and its constituents so varied, that he could not have held together by mere force what he had thus won. Besides, if he had attempted to rely on the support merely of his native Persians, the reservoir of men on which he could draw was too small to supply a force sufficient to hold down and administer a territory which stretched from the borders of Egypt to the shores of the Levant. He was compelled to appeal beyond the central authorities which he had struck down to the smaller nationalities which had been swallowed up by the large Empires. It is clear that he followed such a policy in his relations to Babylonia. Even before his victory he gave himself out to the inhabitants of the capital as having been summoned to his conquest by the tutelary deity, in order to avenge the insults which the last king, Nabonid, had shown to that deity. He also enlisted into his service leading Babylonians whom he had thus won over to his side, and, since he had been largely supported by the local priests, he showed peculiar favour to their forms of worship.

In his volume on the discoveries at Ur, Mr Gadd sums up the view of Cyrus' policy which he has gained from the inscriptions there. "Harassed by the gathering danger (from Cyrus) Nabonid now sent to

gather into Babylon the gods of all the cities in his
land, if perchance they might avail him, or perhaps
with the view of protecting them at least within his
impregnable walls. . . . Whatever his motive, the
king's action was most bitterly resented by priests
and local patriots, and the first, most popular, act of
Cyrus was to send back the gods to their several
homes." Again, "after his victory, gained as much
by the efforts of his supporters in Babylon as by his
own military conduct, it was at least wise, if not
indispensable, to maintain the character of champion
of the true worship against the alleged heresies of
Nabonid, particularly as the strength of his faction
was undoubtedly the malcontent priesthood. This
gesture was perhaps the easier to make since it is not
certain that Cyrus himself was ever a Zoroastrian.
However that may be, his first action was to undo
all the work of Nabonid. The gods which had been
collected to Babylon were sent back to their own
cities, and the new reformer complacently records
the gratitude which rewarded his zeal.

There can be little doubt that the Moon-god of Ur
now returned with pomp to his city, for on a broken
cylinder found there, Cyrus says : Sin, the illuminator
(?) of heaven and earth with his favourable sign
delivered into my hands the four quarters of the world
and I returned the gods to their shrines. But there
is even more material evidence than this, for under
Cyrus and doubtless in his first year, as preparation
for the god's return, the last building operations of
which any trace remains were undertaken at Ur. The
southernmost of the gates in the north-east side of
the wall round the sacred enclosure was renovated

and fitted with new doors by Cyrus, who stamped his inscriptions upon the bricks with which the hinge-stones were surrounded. He declares that the great gods have delivered all the lands into my hands, the land I have caused to dwell in a peaceful habitation. Such an inscription, couched in general terms, would be equally suitable for every god and city, so that it is conceivable that similar bricks were used for a like purpose in every place which received back its god. The words of the proclamation and of this brick inscription may in fact be abbreviated and modified versions of a general edict from the chancellery of Cyrus." [1]

The Hebrew records have preserved two accounts of the way in which this edict reached Jerusalem : the one forms the opening chapter of Ezra, the other is found in v. 13-17. It is important to recognise the different purpose, and so the different character, of the two documents. That in chapter v. forms a plain, official statement inserted in a document prepared by the Jewish authorities and intended for the Persian court, when Tattenai, their local governor, requested to know the authority in virtue of which they were building the temple in the reign of Darius 520. The men confined themselves to a brief account of the events which happened when Cyrus issued his famous edict, and were content to state the facts without elaboration. On the other hand, the first chapter of Ezra forms the beginning of the story of the restoration of the temple by the men of the Return, written by a Jew for the information of his fellow-Jews. The

---

[1] C. J. Gadd, ' History and Monuments of Ur,' pp. 348 ff. Cf. also Woolley, ' Ur of the Chaldees,' pp. 205 f.

author began with the event which made that Return possible. But he did not confine himself to a bare record of facts : he elaborated it, giving it the aspect under which it appeared to him and to men who thought like him. His account could not fail to have a strong Jewish colouring.

This Jewish colouring appears most clearly in the opening verses of the chapter. The author did not fail to recognise that Cyrus' edict concerned the whole Empire, but he has left the impression that the act of grace was confined to the Jews and was merely issued for the information of the rest of the nations. The reason lay in his desire to insist that the king's act, which led to the restoration of Judaism through the rebuilding of the temple and the return of the exiles, was no mere human scheme of policy, but was ultimately due to the purpose of Yahweh. Thus he recast the terms of the inscription which Mr Gadd discovered in Ur. Instead of writing " the great gods have delivered all the lands into my hands," he wrote, " all the kingdoms of the earth hath Yahweh the God of heaven given me." In the same interest he stated that Yahweh stirred up the spirit of Cyrus to make the proclamation, and showed his attitude very clearly, when he added that thus the divine word through Jeremiah was fulfilled. To him Cyrus was a mere instrument in the hands of One who had purposed this of old time and had made it known through a prophet. Further, since his interest was chiefly in the history of the returned exiles, he devoted much more attention to that part of the edict which permitted this return than to the permit to rebuild the temple. Indeed, he rather slurred over any share

Cyrus might claim in this restoration, for he continued with the statement that liberty was given to such as chose to return themselves to undertake this work. It need, then, cause no surprise to find that the Jerusalem authorities in chapter v. made no reference to the permission given by the edict for the return of the exiles. Tattenai was challenging the right of the community to rebuild the temple, not the right of certain members of that community to be in Judah. Naturally, therefore, the men confined themselves in their reply to the terms of their governor's inquiry, and dealt only with the edict, so far as it bore on that question. What, however, is significant is that the community of 520 not only stated that Cyrus gave authority to rebuild the temple, but added that his governor, Sheshbazzar, actually laid the foundation of the sanctuary. Their reason for including this statement is obvious. It was plainly in their favour to be able to say that the Persian satrap who brought the edict began the work which they were only carrying to completion. So obvious is it that one might suspect the men of having inserted this statement without authority, were it not that the author of chapter i. did acknowledge that Cyrus was charged to build a house for Yahweh in Jerusalem, v. 2. The writer, as has been pointed out, supplemented his statement by the remark that, so far as this was concerned, Cyrus gave the men of the Return authority to rebuild. Further, when he came to write about conditions in Jerusalem seven months after the arrival of Sheshbazzar, he went a little out of his way to remark that the foundation of the temple of the Lord was not yet laid, iii. 6. There is a certain anxiety to make it clear that the sacred work owed nothing to the hands of a heathen : only the returned exiles were worthy of such a pious task. Mr Gadd's description of the foundation-brick at Ur, if he should be right in his suggestion that it was the model for what was done elsewhere, throws light on the writer's motive in the matter. It was intolerable to him that the central shrine of his people should be reared over a foundation-stone which bore a pagan inscription.

Again, both our accounts emphasise the fact that Sheshbazzar brought back the sacred vessels which had been carried away by Nebuchadrezzar. That fact was of grave significance to the author of chapter i., since he belonged to the party who had been most deeply distressed by these sacred implements having been transferred to a Babylonian temple in the time of Jehoiachin's captivity, cf. Jer. xxvii. 12-22, xxviii. 1-6. He said nothing, however, of the word of the Lord to Jeremiah the prophet in connection with these vessels, for obvious reasons. It was equally important for the community of 520 to dwell on their return, for, since their only use was in connection with the temple-worship, Cyrus' restoration of them was a clear indication that he purposed the rebuilding of the sanctuary. Now, Cyrus' act in this matter was in line with his conduct in Babylonia after the passing of his edict. In other places he sent back the images of the gods to their respective cities and temples, but, since the temple contained no image of Yahweh, he sent back the holy emblems to Jerusalem.

Dr Oesterley has recently questioned whether Cyrus ever gave permission for the temple to be

rebuilt, and has advanced the opinion that the pro-
ject did not take shape until the time of Haggai and
Zechariah. In his judgment a permit which originally
applied to the building of the walls has been, by
mistake or design, made to refer to the restoration of
the temple. He finds a support for this in the fact
that Tattenai required the community at Jerusalem
to give their authority for building this house and
finishing this wall.[1]

In order to prove his point, he must also prove
the unreliable character of the two documents on
which the other view is based. Accordingly he
points out that in vi. 2-5, where the original permit
from Cyrus is said to have been discovered at Ecbatana,
there is mention of a roll on which it was written.
Now, the Persians did not use rolls, but clay tablets,
for their official documents. It must, however, be
noted that the sentence is no part either of Tattenai's
letter to Darius or of Darius' reply : it is part of the
material into which a later writer incorporated those
two original documents. It is legitimate to suppose
that a Jew, who was writing for his fellow-countrymen,
was not pedantically accurate in his description of the
Persian archives, but used language which was understood by his own people. Personally I should even
count it possible that the man did not know the Persian
practice in this matter, but took it for granted that
they employed the material with which he was
familiar.

Again, Dr Oesterley doubts whether such a decree
would have specified the precise size of the temple
which is set down in vi. 3 f. Yet if the decree stated,

[1] ' A History of Israel,' II., pp. 75 f.

as at present it does, that the building was to be restored at the cost of the imperial fisc, which presumably means that the expenses were to be charged
against the revenues of the province, it was a natural
precaution to order that the Jewish community were
not to be given *carte blanche.* Unless some such
general limits as appear in the decree were clearly
defined, the Persian authorities must have been very
bad economists.

What may appear a more vital objection is found
in vi. 3, where it is said : in the first year of Cyrus the
king, Cyrus the king made a decree. In this case the
statement is in the decree itself, not in the preface.
There is force in Dr Oesterley's objection against the
likelihood of Cyrus or his scribes dating the reign of
the king by the year of his accession in Babylon, as
though he had not reigned in Persia before that year.
Yet nothing can decide a question of this character
except actual knowledge of the practice of the Empire
in its communications to the provinces which came
under its authority after the fall of Babylon. Since
no evidence is offered as to the court practice in these
matters, the objection rests on nothing stronger than
a probability.

When Dr Oesterley turns to the account in chapter i.,
he notes that the writer who credited Cyrus with having
returned the golden vessels of the temple evidently
forgot the statement in II. Kings xxiv. 13, where it is
said that Nebuchadrezzar, at the time of the first
captivity, cut in pieces all the vessels of gold which
Solomon had placed in the sanctuary. Yet it is equally
necessary not to forget that verses 13 f. in that chapter
have long been questioned independently of their

relation to the passage here. The devastation which attended the captivity of Jehoiachin could not have been on the scale which these verses represent. Thus a captivity of all Jerusalem is an exaggeration, when it is compared with what succeeds, v. 14. The 10,000 leading men, plus all the craftsmen and smiths, cannot be reconciled with the 8000, including craftsmen and smiths, of verse 16. When it is said that none were left except the poorest sort of the people of the land, the description of Judah has a suspicious resemblance to the condition of the province after Zedekiah was captured. As for the sacred vessels, the statement that they were all cut to pieces in the time of Jehoiachin contradicts the description of what happened at the final catastrophe, xxv. 15 ff. There is also mention of the spoliation of the temple-treasure under Jehoiachin in Jeremiah xxvii. 18 ff., but, instead of this having been complete, it is there stated that the king of Babylon had carried away certain of those vessels, and the prophet added that those which were left should be carried away in turn. In view of these difficulties connected with the verses, all of which are independent of the present question, Stade long ago suggested that II. Kings xxiv. 13 f. are a fragment from some account of the final ruin of the temple, which has been inserted in the wrong place. To relegate the passage to the later date serves to explain why in verse 13 the sacred vessels are said to have been destroyed as the Lord had said. The writer may then have seen in their fate the fulfilment of Jeremiah's prophecy. What he meant by the words, if the reference is to the first captivity, it is not easy to see. Nor is it possible to explain the deep interest which men in Jerusalem continued to take in the fate of those vessels, unless they were still in existence and known to be. The number returned under Cyrus, which is set in Ezra, chapter i., so high as 5400, may well be exaggerated. But, when Dr Oesterley has to deal with the large number of priests who are said to have returned from Babylon, in chapter ii., he has no hesitation in suggesting that the writer who included that list increased the numbers for the sake of glorifying the temple ministrants. The same interest in all matters connected with the cult may well have led to an exaggeration of the number of the vessels.

It is possible to sum up the general situation on this question. There is reliable evidence that Cyrus initiated the policy of permitting his subject provinces to restore their national forms of worship. There is no evidence that Darius, though he was an able organiser of his ill-settled Empire, anywhere initiated reforms in matters of religion. When, therefore, the Jewish records ascribe the permit for the temple-restoration to Cyrus, and the continuation of this to his successor, it may well appear that better proof than has yet been led is required to overturn their authority.

When, however, it is recognised that the edict was not issued on behalf of the Jews alone, but formulated the policy of Cyrus in connection with the government of his whole Empire, a further conclusion follows. Sheshbazzar did not come to Jerusalem to bring the edict or the temple-vessels or even to escort a body of returned exiles. He came in the capacity of a Persian governor to take over the administration of the province in place of the local representative of the defunct Babylonian Empire. As such, he bears a Babylonian name, for he may have been one of the numerous Babylonians whose accession to his cause helped the conqueror. Cyrus could safely reward him with an appointment to a distant province, where he was removed from the neighbourhood of his friends in the old capital. The edict was an important part of the general instructions which the Court had given him in order to guide him in the conduct of his new administration. Accordingly, it is not surprising that the leaders of the Jewish community did not show Tattenai a copy of the imperial edict, when he demanded their authority for rebuilding the temple. Sheshbazzar never gave them such a copy; but, acting as governor, he gave them authority in virtue of his instructions. In virtue of the same instructions he laid the foundation-stone of the temple. When the representative of the new government took this definite action, he did what he was commissioned to do, but he could not anticipate that the men at Jerusalem would fail to carry on the building which he had begun, and so give one of his successors a good reason for asking as to their right to begin again after the lapse of eighteen years.

It must even remain uncertain whether Sheshbazzar took up his residence in Jerusalem. Apparently two later governors, Zerubbabel and Nehemiah, lived there, but both these men were Jews who naturally chose to reside in the sacred city. Besides, from the fact that Zerubbabel was challenged as to his action by Tattenai of Samaria, it would appear that the Northern governor had the right to do this and was therefore superior in authority. On other occasions, when

there is mention of intervention from Samaria, the
impression left is that the governor there was administering directly or was responsible for the affairs
of the Southern province. So far as the Hebrew records
go, our information about the methods of the Persian
government in Palestine is not precise or full. From
them, indeed, it might be possible to infer that these
methods varied from time to time. Scholars who
deal with the Persian sources agree that Darius
introduced changes in the direction of a more efficient
administration of the Empire, and he may therefore
have altered Cyrus' original arrangements for the
government of Palestine. Even there, however, the
information appears to be vague and incomplete.
Accordingly, no one may venture to be dogmatic on
the subject. Yet one must recognise that Sheshbazzar's appointment and arrival in Palestine followed
closely on Cyrus' conquest of Babylon. It is a natural
conclusion that the new governor was sent with a
strong force to take over the control of what is called
elsewhere the whole province beyond the River. If
so, the seat of his authority would naturally be
Samaria, since that town was more central and had
already been the seat of an Assyrian and a Babylonian
governor. His action in Jerusalem, as it is described
in the book of Ezra, was one part of his work on a
visit he made to the Southern province. What is
known about the condition of the Judean capital
serves to confirm this view. As has been pointed out
above, the city cannot have remained in the state of
ruin to which it was reduced by Nebuchadrezzar, but
any restoration which had taken place during the
forty-eight years must have been of a modest character.

It may well be doubted whether it contained a building fit to serve as an official residence for the governor. In all such respects Samaria was in a very different case.

Such a view of the function of Sheshbazzar explains at once why he disappears entirely from the later history of Judaism and from the records in the book of Ezra. The man, so far as his later story was concerned, was of no more interest to the community than any other governor whom Persia might choose to send. They were as indifferent to his further fortunes as they were to those of Tattenai. What they reported about both was the account of the men's acts, so far as these affected the life and history of their own people, but after that they reported no more. The author of Ezra, chapter i., was less likely to enlarge on the later acts of the governor, because he slurred over his initial deed in laying the foundation-stone of the temple.

Another question, however, emerges here. There must evidently have been some responsible authority in Jerusalem, when Sheshbazzar arrived ; the men whom the new governor authorised to rebuild the temple, in whose presence he laid the foundation-stone, to whom he delivered over the sacred vessels, and to whom, if the record of Ezra, chapter i., may be trusted in this respect, he handed over the gifts sent by the exiles in Babylonia. He could not make his proclamation in an empty plaza of the ruined city, or deposit the vessels on the temple-site. On this point the two Hebrew accounts are not in entire agreement. Thus the men who replied to Tattenai were content to say that the recipients were their predecessors.

They could count themselves the representatives of the men who were in Jerusalem at the time of the first governor's arrival, but they did not feel it necessary to add more. From other sources, however, it is known that the men who began the restoration of the temple under Darius were composed of Judeans who had never been in exile, and of those who had returned with Zerubbabel and Joshua. On the other hand, chapter i. says nothing about remanent Judeans. So far as this account is concerned, the city, when Sheshbazzar arrived, might have been unoccupied. Instead of saying anything about conditions in Judah, the author related the effect which Cyrus' edict produced among the exiles. He wrote as though the edict authorised these men to return in order that they might undertake the restoration of the temple. He continued with a statement about the eagerness with which they bestirred themselves to take advantage of the opportunity thus put within their reach. He described how many, who could not yet leave Babylon, sent gifts to help on the sacred work. Finally, he followed the account of Sheshbazzar's mission with chapter ii., which contains the list of exiles who at once returned. The position in which he set this list long produced the impression that these men came up with the new governor.

It will be necessary later to attempt to determine both the character and the date of this list.[1] Meantime, it must be enough to state that its position here is at least highly disputable. But it is legitimate to point out even here that the list is peculiarly improbable in the position in which the writer has placed it.

[1] Cf. pp. 126 ff.

The preparation of such a thoroughly equipped caravan needed time ; time for the scattered exiles in Babylon to hear of the new policy of Cyrus, time for the men to settle their affairs before transferring themselves to a country which they had never seen. Yet the administration of Palestine, even of Judah alone, could not wait on these men's arrangements. An author who wrote as though Cyrus' edict was a special grace shown by Cyrus to his own people, can be pardoned for so regarding the new governor's action. But, when the edict is set in its true historical perspective and recognised to have dealt with the affairs of an Empire, the whole outlook must be changed.

When Sheshbazzar came to Jerusalem, the Return was still in the future, so that the new governor had to deal with the men who had never been in exile. Now, the pact of Nehemiah, chapter x., shows these men to have been so far organised round their sanctuary that they could represent the Jewish community in matters of religion. There was an altar in the city ; some rude buildings had sprung up round it ; above all certain priests were officiating there. The Persian official dealt with these men in terms of the instructions which he had received from his Court. He laid the foundation-stone of the temple in their presence, and he handed over to them the vessels with which he had been charged. More formally and explicitly than had been the case when the Israelite priest was restored to Bethel, the Jewish worship at Jerusalem was declared to be *religio licita* in the new Empire, and the worshippers were permitted to restore their temple. When the situation is construed along those lines, it becomes possible to understand the peculiar terms in which the men at Jerusalem quoted the governor's permit to Tattenai. They represented him as having been empowered to " take these vessels, go, put them in the temple that is in Jerusalem, and let the house of God be builded in its place," v. 15. At the first glance this might appear like a contradiction in terms, since it seems to imply that the temple was already in existence and yet needed to be restored. But, only a few months after the sack by Nebuchadrezzar men were still using the old name of ' the temple ' about the ruined site, Jer. xli. 5. They could and did continue to term it the sanctuary, and the men who made the agreement of Nehemiah, chapter x., pledged themselves to maintain the house of our God. Over that sacred place they were now permitted to rear a house of God.

But this was all which Sheshbazzar did for the Jewish community in their religious capacity. In every other respect they were simply subjects of the Empire. How he dealt with them and with his province there was no need to say. Neither the author of chapter i. of Ezra nor the community under Darius were interested in his future activities. He came and went like any other governor, but during the short or long period of his rule, he, acting in the name of Cyrus, gave a legal status to their first tentative efforts after the renewal of Judaism. How they might use their new power depended on themselves.

It is not possible here to enter fully into the tangled questions which have come to be connected with the person of Sheshbazzar : yet these cannot be altogether ignored.

At first it was supposed that the governor should be identified with Zerubbabel. That was a natural supposition, since the editor of Ezra has made Zerubbabel contemporary with Sheshbazzar. Now Zerubbabel is also styled governor, and it is not easy to believe that Persia sent two governors to Judah at the same time. The question, it will be noted, is intimately related to the other question as to whether the list of returned exiles in chapter ii. can be dated so early as is done in Ezra : that matter will require later discussion. If the list is wrongly dated here, then Zerubbabel and Sheshbazzar need not have been contemporaries. What weighs heavily in my judgment against the view that the two names refer to the same man is the different way in which the editor regarded them. As has been pointed out, he slurred over all connection between Sheshbazzar and the foundation-stone of the temple : he even denied that the stone was laid by him. On the other hand, he agreed with Zechariah in insisting that Zerubbabel laid that foundation, and appeared to recognise a peculiar fitness in the fact that a descendant of the house of David restored what the first king had planned. Further, it must be noted that the leaders of the community at the time of Darius, of whom Zerubbabel was one, refer to Sheshbazzar as a person somewhat remote from their date, Ezra v. 14-16.

Ed. Meyer again suggested the identification of Sheshbazzar with Shenazzar, a descendant of David who is mentioned in I. Chronicles iii. 18, and several scholars have supported this view. The latest of these is Sellin, who has devoted a good deal of attention to the question and built somewhat large consequences on the conclusion.[1] Thus he has adopted Rothstein's conjecture that the true reading in I. Chronicles iii. 18 is ‏ופראיה הוא שנאצר‎—*i.e.*, Shenazzar must next be identified with Pedaiah, the son of Jehoiachin. Probably, adds Sellin, Pedaiah was the Hebrew name, while Shenazzar was that by which the man was known in Babylon. Probably again he was the eldest son, who was born to the deposed king after his thirty-five years of imprisonment, and thus in 538 he was perhaps twenty-two years old. Pedaiah= Shenazzar=Sheshbazzar who was appointed governor of Judah by Cyrus. The reason for the new king choosing a Jew for this office was that he found the family of the exiled Jehoiachin in high favour at the Babylonian Court. Amel-Marduk had already lifted up the head of the father, and, according to Sellin, had even made him prince or ‏נשיא‎ of the Jews in Babylonia. To please the Jews, Cyrus made this descendant of the Davidic house satrap at Jerusalem. Since Zerubbabel was also derived from the royal line, this succession of Davidic governors served to rouse and foster strong Messianic leanings in the community at Jerusalem, which resulted at last in a certain clash with the Empire.

Now it may be that I have an undue dose of Scottish caution. But this glittering fabric of conjecture piled on hypothesis leaves the impression of great ingenuity rather than of discovering the sober basis of history. The initial identification of Sheshbazzar with Shenazzar cannot be said to be proved, for the two names cannot be called alike, and the effort to

---

[1] Cf. ' Geschichte des Israelitisch-Jüdischen Volkes,' II., pp. 82 ff., with the relative literature.

equate them by calling in the LXX in order to help out the MT is far from convincing. If the two were the same, and Sheshbazzar boasted Davidic descent, the distaste of the author in chapter i. in Ezra to connecting the governor with the temple is left unexplained. Again, when Sellin and Rothstein take the further step of identifying Sheshbazzar with Pedaiah and attempt to explain how a son of Jehoiachin could be satrap of Judah in 538, the ' probables ' rattle about one's ears like hailstones. Conjecture follows conjecture in a somewhat bewildering succession. The reason for Cyrus having sent one of the Davidic line to Judah—viz., that he continued the Babylonian confidence in that house and that he desired to propitiate the Jews in Judah, is scarcely convincing. The new king was more likely to trust those who had come over to him from the old regime than the men whom the Babylonians had favoured, and there was no obvious reason why he should propitiate the inhabitants of a small and outlying province. In the situation in which Cyrus was placed he needed to act promptly. He had to provide for the staffing of the local administration of his vast, far-flung and newly won Empire. The first consideration with him and his advisers would seem to have been that they should send men whose loyalty was assured. They were not likely to select for a distant province a man whose descent was calculated to recall to a proud race the days of their independent kingdom, and whose arrival according to Sellin did stir those ancient memories.

CHAPTER VI.

FROM SHESHBAZZAR TO ZERUBBABEL.

THE arrival of the new Persian governor had brought no accession of strength to the Judean community. The edict of Cyrus gave the men full liberty of worship and permission to rebuild their temple, but no more : it remained with them whether they would make any use of this permit. As a matter of fact, nothing was done for the eighteen years between the date of Cyrus' accession and 520 in the reign of Darius. The editor of the book of Ezra felt it necessary to give an explanation of this delay, the more so, because he represented the exiles as having returned in large numbers under the escort of Sheshbazzar. These men, who were zealots for the cult, must have had a grave reason for calling a halt in the main purpose which had brought them to Jerusalem. He has offered such a reason in chapter iv. of his book, for there he has gathered several cases of interference with the Judeans on the part of certain Persian governors in Samaria. The suspicions of these authorities, however, were roused by the native Jews of the Northern province, so that their intervention was really due to the animosity of men who afterwards formed the sect of the Samaritans. But for the opposition of these jealous Israelites, the returned exiles would have proceeded without delay to the supreme task of restoring the temple.

Now it has already been pointed out that this editor's initial position in dating the list of returned exiles of chapter ii. so early as the arrival of Shesh-bazzar is very open to question, and demands careful examination before it can be accepted. It must further be recognised that chapter iv., where he has combined a number of cases of interference from Samaria, has given rise to grave difficulty. The difficulty is not as to the truth of the records which he has quoted, or as to the probability of those Persian governors in Samaria having been suspicious of the activities of the Jerusalem community. It largely turns round the date to which the editor has assigned their action. We must consider it possible that, in the interests of his theory of the course of events at the Return, this editor has pre-dated certain documents which he has incorporated in his narrative.

It will be necessary to examine the list of returned exiles in chapter ii. with special reference to its date, and to test the contents of chapter iv. again with special reference to their date and to the purpose which their collection in this period was meant to serve. For the sake of clearness in a discussion which abounds in side-issues, I have postponed both in-quiries, and propose to ignore the testimony of the editor of Ezra, and, on the basis of results already gained and of the other documents we possess, to set out the course of events between the edict of Cyrus and the beginning of the temple-restoration. The later discussions will show whether this distrust of the editor of Ezra is justified.

There is no need to seek for an external cause in connection with the delay of eighteen years in undertaking the building of the temple. The reason is to be found in the condition of the community. Most of the Judeans were simple farmers, who could not venture without hesitation to set on foot so serious and costly a task. Further, as Haggai acknowledged, the men had had a succession of bad harvests which made matters more difficult. Nor was the provision of the new temple so urgent. By the terms of the pact with their Israelite neighbours they had secured the necessary means for their cult. They had already made some sacrifice in order to meet this charge, and may have counted that they had done enough. The equipment at the old altar-site may have been poor enough and very inadequate. But the men were, for the most part, simple peasants, and content with humble forms. They had provided what they did out of their poverty, and what men give to God out of their poverty often sits nearer to their hearts than what is offered from their superfluity.

Two events combined to rouse the community to action. The first was the appearance of two, in my judgment, of three prophets who were dissatisfied with the religious condition of their people. They appealed for a quickening of the religious life, and two of them flung themselves eagerly into the work of the temple-restoration as one means for bringing this about. The other new factor was the arrival of a body of exiles from Babylonia, under the leadership of Zerubbabel and Joshua. The mere fact that these men had left their homes and come back to Judah was the proof of their zeal for the temple-cult. They counted it essential for themselves and for Israel. The newcomers also were of a different type from the peasant-farmers of Judah. Since they were able to leave Babylonia and undertake the long journey to Palestine, they must have been in comparatively good circumstances. Men of this type were not likely to remain satisfied with the somewhat haphazard method in which they found the worship was being conducted in Jerusalem.

Accordingly, we find Haggai, when he addressed Zerubbabel and Joshua at i. 1 f., saying to them : this people keep saying, the time has not yet come for the house of the Lord to be built. The prophet could not have reproached the two leaders of the returned exiles for neglect of duty on the part of those who accompanied them. The sufficient proof of the interest the men of the Return took in the question of the restoration was the fact that they were in Jerusalem at all. Haggai was setting over against the eagerness of these men the apathy of the community among which they had arrived. By ' this people ' he meant the remanent Judeans who kept saying that matters were very well as they stood. The terms of the reproach which he hurled against some of those to whom he referred, and the promise which he made to others, serve to show that this was the case. Thus he charged some of them with being more interested in the condition of their own homes than in the decent appointments for their worship. One need not press the reference to the ' ceiled houses ' as though the words implied any degree of luxury in the men's houses, but they do

prove that by this time the restoration of the city was
real and that some part of Jerusalem had been renewed. That could not have been the work of the
newly-arrived exiles, who had not had time to carry
out such a task. Further, the prophet did not speak as
though there were no sanctuary in the city. There
was a house of God, but, in comparison with the care
the men devoted to their homes, it was receiving
scant regard. Again, Haggai recognised that some of
' this people ' had a better excuse for apathy than
undue interest in their own comfort. The country-
farmers could plead that they had been suffering from
bad harvests and therefore could not afford the time
and money needed for the work at the temple. With
these men the prophet dealt differently, for he assured
them that the true method of bringing about better
conditions was a deeper devotion to their religious
duty. If they would show a worthy zeal by setting
about the work at the temple, God should reward
them by sending better seasons. But a prophet who
spoke in these terms was addressing men who had
been settled long enough in the province to be able to
point back to several lean years in their farming. He
could not have addressed the returned exiles in these
terms.

The description of Haggai's activity which appears
in his first oracle agrees in certain respects with the
situation described in Ezra, v. 1 f. There the initiative
in the work of restoration is ascribed to the men of
the Return under Zerubbabel and Joshua, who are
said to have been supported by the two prophets in a
vigorous propaganda among ' the Jews who were in
Judah and Jerusalem.' The propaganda was so

successful that the local community supported the newcomers, and a beginning was made. When, therefore, Tattenai sent to demand the authority in virtue of which the men were acting, the heads of the community or the elders at Jerusalem took full responsibility, v. 5. What was being done was not due to the irresponsible zeal of a few newcomers from Babylonia. Zerubbabel and Joshua discreetly retired into the background, since they could not have claimed that the terms of Cyrus' edict applied to them. On the other hand, the local community, through its elders, could claim that this edict had been directed to them, and gave them ample right for that which they were doing. The terms in which Haggai addressed his countrymen do not justify the conclusion that the Return was necessary to revive a Judaism which would have collapsed without it. The only reproach which the prophet addressed to the Judeans was that they were careless about the duty of rebuilding the temple. Had the men, during the sixty-six years which elapsed since the destruction of the sanctuary, made no effort to restore their cult, he could not have been so mild in his censure.

A clearer view of the condition and temper which prevailed in Northern Israel can be obtained from the collection of oracles which bears the name of Malachi. For I am now compelled to assign this book to the period which preceded the restoration of the temple.[1] The date of this collection has long presented grave difficulty to scholars. Thus Wellhausen did not fail to recognise the constant dependence of the author on

---

[1] Now, since at one time I accepted a later date in the article Malachi in H.D.B.

Deuteronomy, both in language and in teaching. There was no reference to the peculiar legislation or principles of the Priestly Code, so that the prophet must have been acquainted only with the Deuteronomic Code. On the other hand, his supposed allusions to the question of mixed marriages and even to the consequences of legislation on the subject seemed to prove conclusively that Malachi must have followed the return of Ezra, who, according to Wellhausen, introduced that new law. Thus, the situation emerged that on Wellhausen's principles of criticism the law which governed the community at the time of Ezra's arrival was still the Deuteronomic Code. There was only one way out of this difficulty. It drove the great scholar to conclude that the Priestly Code must post-date Malachi and the arrival of Ezra. Indeed, the date to which he assigned Malachi was one of his strong proofs for the late date of the Priestly Code. But this in turn ignored an objection which was fatal to the whole reconstruction. For here was a prophet who not only followed the Deuteronomic Code in general, but who, in agreement with that Code, described the priests as the sons of Levi and ascribed to these sons of Levi the functions of administering the law and of bringing sacrifices to the altar. Yet, according to Wellhausen, the levites had long been debarred from exercising these functions, for in his view it was not the Priestly Code, but Josiah, who had relegated the levites to a lower position than that of the regular priests.

So far as this question is concerned, the matter becomes clear when Malachi's activity is placed in the transition period before the temple-restoration, when Judah and Samaria were living under the pact of Nehemiah, chapter x., according to which both priests and levites were officiating at the altar. Whoever the prophet may have been, he was addressing that part of the community to which Deuteronomy was possessed of peculiar authority. Therefore he based his appeal and his rebuke on the Code which they acknowledged. Whatever Judah might do, and by whatever forms it conducted its life, Northern Israel must recognise its obligation to the law which Moses gave it at first, and needed to be recalled to its own worthier and more heroic past. So the conclusion of the book is a demand on the people to remember the law which Moses received at Horeb, statutes and judgments, iv. 4. That is Deuteronomic in language and Deuteronomic in conception.[1] God, he said, was to come in His day a swift witness against those who oppressed the hireling, the widow and the fatherless, and who ill-treated the stranger or גר, iii. 5. Sellin has remarked that the mention of hired servants throws a sidelight on the social condition of the Jews of the period, since it implies that the men were in a position to employ labour. He has failed, however, to note the more peculiar introduction of 'the stranger' in this place. Who were the גרים in Judah under the Persian Empire, and why were the Jews likely to defraud or maltreat these men? A 'stranger,' ac-

[1] The verse has been set aside as a later addition. But the later it is placed, the more difficult does it become to explain its peculiar terms. If Malachi wrote later than Haggai, so much later that the religious quickening which followed the restoration of the temple had had time to grow weak, and if Ezra's P.C. was introduced in order to revive the zeal of the community, it is at least remarkable that a late annotator introduced a reference to the law which Ezra had superseded.

cording to Old Testament ideas, was a man with no civil rights, who was consequently liable to be ill-treated by the full burghers among whom he happened to live. Naturally, so long as the Israelites were the rulers in their own country, they needed a warning against taking advantage of men who could not appeal for protection to the laws of the country. But the situation was changed, so soon as all who lived in Palestine were subjects to Persia, and equally subject. The Jew had no advantage over the alien then. In reality, the prophet was using the familiar language of the Deuteronomic Code, which set the widow and the fatherless, the stranger and the hireling under the peculiar protection of Yahweh. Speaking to men who were familiar with their law, he was not careful to consider how far its terms corresponded with the conditions of his own time.[1]

When the prophet spoke of and spoke to certain members of the community who were inclined to surrender their religious faith, he represented them as asking what profit they had gained through walking in mourning attire before their God, iii. 14. The language is peculiar and cannot be explained by a general, vague reference to the custom of fasting and repentance, which is said to have become more prevalent after the exile. Evidently the practice is emphasised as characteristic of the men ' who feared the Lord ' and who were strict in their observance of their law. The laxer party revolted against this mark of outward devotion. The selection of this feature as an

---

[1] The treatment men mete out to the גּר is more markedly characteristic of Deuteronomy, because it is no feature of the Law of Holiness.

evidence of peculiar loyalty to the old faith recalls how the loyalists in the North had separated themselves from their heathen neighbours, fasting and mourning before the Lord. Incidentally, the reference here may serve to mark the weakness of every such form of Puritanic strictness. Whenever the distinctive note of any religious movement has become negative, whenever men have been asked to show their loyalty to their faith by abstinence rather than by action, the result has been to produce that cleavage between the older and the younger generation which Malachi noted and deplored in his time.

Again the prophet sharply rebuked his people for having failed to present their offerings, and in particular for having turned their tithes and heave-offerings to their own use, iii. 8. In describing these, he employed the peculiarly Deuteronomic phrase המעשר והתרומה. That Code also was peculiar in requiring its adherents to make a solemn assertion that they had not diverted their tithes from their true destination, Deut. xxvi. 12-15. As this demand was followed in the law by the promise that God would bless His people with abundance, so the prophet ended his rebuke with the assurance that amendment would be followed by a like blessing. The difference between the law and the prophet was that Deuteronomy devoted those tithes to the needs of the poor and to the levites within the homestead, while Malachi rebuked men for not having brought them to the storehouse. For the prophet was addressing men who had entered into the pact of Nehemiah, chapter x., and who, in view of the need to maintain the temple-worship, had agreed to bring

their tithes to the treasure-chamber at Jerusalem for
the support of the levites. They were adding to their
original sin of diverting sacred gifts to their own use
by failing to maintain their solemn promise.

There are two leading reasons which have led
scholars to date the book certainly later than the
restoration of the temple, probably later than the
arrival of Ezra. The first of these was that Malachi
had so much to say about the neglect of the sacrificial
worship on the part of the people, and about the careless way in which the priests were conducting that
worship. There must, therefore, have been an altar
in regular use at his period, with a community which
acknowledged their responsibility for maintaining it,
and there must have been a priesthood in charge of
the ritual which was being carried on there. But
the recognition that there was an altar in use before
the time of Darius and that such an altar demanded
both worshippers and celebrants has already invali-
dated this conclusion.

There is, however, an oracle in which Malachi fore-
told that the Lord should suddenly come in His temple,
iii. 1, and another in which he told the priests that it
would be better to close the doors altogether rather than
continue a perfunctory worship which only served to
show their want of interest in the service they were
required to offer, i. 10. While it is true that in the
latter case he did not actually mention the temple,
there can be little doubt from the connection in which
he used the expression that he was referring to it.
Language of this character seemed to involve that
the temple of Darius' time was already built. Yet
the Israelites of Gedaliah's date could be described as

bringing gifts to the temple only a few months after the sack of Jerusalem ; and even the reference to closing the doors cannot be held final, since the expression might be used in the general sense that it would be better to shut the place up altogether. Those who, while they recognise that the prophet spoke in verse, demand that he should have maintained a prosaic literalness and that, when he spoke about doors, he meant doors, may also consider that, as soon as matters had settled down and the altar was continued for its old use, the worshippers were not likely to leave the sacred enclosure open to all the pariah dogs in Jerusalem. Again, the view here presented of the pact in Nehemiah, chapter x., serves to confirm this conclusion, since the chambers for the levitical tithes could not have been left open. Even the author of the book of Ezra did not contemplate an unenclosed space, since the temple-vessels had been brought thither.

The principal cause, however, which led students to assign a late date to Malachi was the conviction that, especially in ii. 10-16, he referred to the question of mixed marriages with the heathen, against which Ezra was supposed to have introduced legislation.

This conclusion implied that Ezra was the first to issue a law which forbade all Jewry to contract connubium with the heathen. But evidence has been led to show that a regulation on this subject was introduced among the loyalist Israelites in self-defence against being submerged among their heathen neighbours, and that a similar regulation formed the first agreement in the pact in Nehemiah. In a later chapter evidence will be brought to prove that Ezra's concern with this law was to enforce it among the returned exiles.¹ Even if Malachi in the cited passage was referring to the law against mixed marriages, this would not prove him to have followed Ezra.

It must, however, be added that it is far from clear that the prophet in those difficult verses was referring to mixed marriages at all. This is not the place to enter fully into the meaning of a very debatable passage, but one thing is clear in connection with it. The text is so corrupt and the sense so uncertain that the verses cannot form the basis of any sure conclusion. To base a large decision about the date of the whole prophecy on a doubtful interpretation of a notoriously corrupt passage is to build on sand. The clause which has often appeared to give the key to the general sense—Judah has married the daughter of a strange god—does not naturally bear the sense which has been put upon it. For " the daughter of a strange god " is unexampled as the description of a woman who worshipped a foreign deity. To quote in support that Hosea called Israel the son of Yahweh is merely inept, since there the reference is to the nation, while here it must be taken to refer to individual women. Indeed, the reference to Hosea merely emphasises that in Malachi the defection to which the prophet referred was national. Judah hath dealt treacherously ; Judah hath profaned the holiness of the Lord ; Judah hath married the daughter of a strange god : in each case the transgression is that of the people, not of individuals. The vehemence also of the curse which Malachi denounced against the people can be understood, if he was referring to

¹ Cf. pp. 247 ff. *infra.*

some national defection : it is too strong in its terms,
if it referred to a by-law which had only a few years
before been promulgated by Ezra, and even more
exaggerated, if it be supposed to refer to such a by-law
before it had been adopted by the community. Again,
it is said that the statement in verse 13—ye cover
the altar of the Lord with tears, with weeping, and
with sighing—refers to the divorced women who
lamented the infidelity of their husbands there. Yet
it demands a powerful imagination to believe that
heathen women would have carried their complaint
to the altar of a God whom they did not worship,
or that the priests, who were supporting their divorce,
admitted them to this altar.

To the prophet the condition of his people appeared
very grave. Many among them had lost heart, so
that they were tempted to cast off the restraint of
their religion. These rebels [1] were finding it to their
personal advantage to cast off the trammels of the
past. Even more seriously-minded members of the
community were asking whether the sacrifice involved
in the maintenance of their faith was worth the effort.
Men who took a different way were prospering, and
there was no evidence of the divine disapproval of
their conduct. Where was the God of judgment ?
There was a danger that the people might fall into
two sections. On the one side were those who feared
the Lord and who walked in mourning attire before
Him : on the other were those who were at least
indifferent. The conditions of the time were making

---

[1] He used about them the term זדים, iii. 15, which recalls the verb
הזידו which Deuteronomy and the litany of Nehemiah, chapter ix.,
employed for the conduct of Israel.

it peculiarly hard to maintain a united testimony and an undivided loyalty.

Against the hopelessness which asked for any evidence of the divine care for Israel the prophet recalled the old story of the past which told how Yahweh chose Jacob and rejected Esau, i. 2 ff. But he also found in the actual condition of the two nations evidence that the initial choice of Jacob was still active. The proof did not lie in the mere fact that Edom's towns were ruined and its country desolate. So far as that was concerned, the same thing could be said about Israel. What Malachi insisted on was not that Edom was ruined, but that its condition held no hope for the future. Even if the people were to rebuild their ruins, the effort would be futile, for God should not suffer them to renew their State. The obvious contrast was that Israel, however it might be destroyed, had hope, since any effort it might make at restoration was not foredoomed to failure. The prophet was there giving his own interpretation of the new liberty which had come through the edict of Cyrus. To him the edict was not due to a casual impulse in the mind of a despot, nor was it the evidence of a new and saner policy for the Persian Empire : it was a renewed proof of the care God had for His people, and therefore brought a divinely given opportunity to Israel. If the people responded, they should then see the different treatment their God had meted out to Jacob and to Esau, and they should say : Yahweh is great over Israel's territory.

Instead of taking the opportunity which was thus brought within their reach, Malachi continued, the people were not even maintaining worthily their sanctuary and its services. They brought their offerings, it was true, but in perfunctory fashion. Animals which they would not have dared to present as tribute to the local satrap were reckoned adequate for the altar. Let them remember, said the prophet, that Yahweh was as great as any emperor and His demands as worthy of the best, i. 13 f. Otherwise it were better to shut up the temple altogether, rather than mock God by what they plainly considered a weariness, i. 10. The prevalent religious laxity had crept in among the priests, or the house of Levi, as Malachi called them. The men were influenced by the temper of their time, but they had an additional cause for their neglect of duty, for they were not even receiving in full measure the tithes on which they depended for their support, and they had cause to know that what reached them was given grudgingly. Their service at the altar was being rendered carelessly, and their influence in teaching among their people was lowered. Over against this condition of affairs Malachi threw up his picture of the good old days in Israel, when the divine law was in the priest's mouth and unrighteousness was not found on his lips, when he walked with God in peace and uprightness and turned many away from iniquity, ii. 6.

It is much more natural to connect this picture of the condition of the people with the time which preceded than with the time which followed the restoration of the temple. At the later date the community in Palestine had been strengthened by the accession of the returned exiles, all of whom were zealous supporters of the national faith. They had for their civil head Zerubbabel, a descendant of the

old line of David, and in his presence they could see
an evidence both of the imperial favour and of the
divine grace to the nation. The slight check from
the interference of the Samaritan satrap had only
resulted in deepening their confidence that God had
not forgotten them, for the result had been that
Darius not only confirmed the edict of Cyrus, but
ordered that the expense of the rebuilding should be
charged against the revenues of the province and
even that a grant should be made from the same
source for maintaining the daily sacrifices. It is
very difficult to explain how and why a community
which had thus reached the great desire of its heart
should have lapsed in a few years into the condition
which Malachi has represented. So great has been
the difficulty that many students, who place Malachi
after the restoration of the temple, have felt it necessary, in order to explain the sudden collapse, to
postulate a rebellion against the Empire on the part
of the people. This rebellion is supposed to have
been due to the wild hopes of the prophets who saw
in Zerubbabel the Messiah and in his arrival the
possible restoration of the Davidic kingdom. The
defeat of this rising by the Persians led to a corresponding religious collapse. Yet it must be said that
there is no support in the historical records for any
such rebellion immediately after the temple-restoration,
and there is no proof that the Jews of that date attached any Messianic character to the house of David.[1]

When, on the other hand, Malachi's oracles are
assigned to the earlier date, we are not only relieved
from the necessity for these precarious excursions

[1] Cf. pp. 192, 220 *infra.*

into history, but we are able to explain why, though the foundation-stone was laid by Sheshbazzar, the completion of the work at the temple was delayed for eighteen years. The mere fact that the Empire permitted the men to restore their temple did not in itself supply them with a motive or with the means to undertake the task. Those who were earnest about the outward forms of their religion had renewed these and secured their continuance through their pact. But the effort and the sacrifice which that entailed had strained their resources, and the conditions of the time were not propitious for launching a more ambitious scheme.

The author of the book of Ezra was right on the broad facts when he implied that without the coming of the returned exiles there would have been no temple. But, if the new temple gathered to itself the devotion of more than the men of the Return, that was partly due to the support of the three local prophets. Haggai and Zechariah stirred the zeal of the Judeans, Malachi lent his influence among his own people in Israel. But the work of Haggai and Zechariah received only a casual mention in the book of Ezra, for its author was dubious of the orthodoxy of his fellow-Judeans : as for the activity of Malachi, he ignored that altogether, since he was convinced of the heterodoxy of the Samaritans.

CHAPTER VII.

THE DATE OF THE RETURN.

THERE can be no doubt as to the attitude of the book of Ezra to the question of the date of the Return. Its editor inserted the list of returned exiles immediately after the arrival of Sheshbazzar in Jerusalem, and, when he mentioned the terms of Cyrus' edict, he was careful to include the fact that it permitted all exiled Jews to come back to Palestine. Though he denied that the foundation-stone of the temple was laid at that time, he credited " Jeshua and his brethren the priests along with Zerubbabel and his brethren " with having built the altar at Jerusalem. This act on their part is dated in the seventh month after the promulgation of Cyrus' edict, iii. 2, 6. He went on to say that the same men made preparations for the building of the temple by hiring masons and carpenters in Judah, and by making arrangements, as Solomon did at the original building of the temple, for a supply of cedar-wood from Lebanon through agents in Tyre and Sidon. The men were able to make these arrangements on such a liberal scale, because they were acting under a grant made to them for the purpose by Cyrus, iii. 7. The editor next stated that, in connection with the duties at the altar which Zerubbabel and Joshua had built, the same men appointed the service of the levites in the oversight of the temple. What this service of the levites in the future temple implied is not clearly stated. But it was not the oversight of the workmen who were busy about the material preparations, for these workmen were hired in the seventh month, as soon as the altar had been set up, while the levites were not appointed to their duties in the temple until the second month of the second year, iii. 8. Evidently the writer had in view some more permanent arrangement of the levitical functions, and one which was to concern their position in the temple. The workmen, on the other hand, who were supervised by Joshua were busy with the task of preparing for the ceremony of laying the foundation-stone, which was carried out with great solemnity, iii. 9-13. In his description of all this activity on the part of the returned exiles the writer makes no mention of the prophets, Haggai and Zechariah. That omission may be due to his conviction that the men of the Return needed no encouragement in their zeal. It is more difficult to explain his silence as to the share of the local community. So far as his account is concerned, city and country might have been unoccupied.

This feature of his narrative, however, draws attention to two other significant omissions. He ignored Sheshbazzar's part in laying the foundation-stone of the temple, stated that in the seventh month after the arrival of the exiles that stone was not yet laid, and finally described the ceremony with which the men of the Return, accompanied by a full choir of

priests and levites, carried out the act. He also ignored the existence of the altar which had been in use
during the exile, and was careful to state that the
altar which was built after the Return was alone valid
for all the sacrifices and festivals of the nation. These
major differences between his account and that of the
other sources draw attention to some minor dis-
crepancies. Thus it is remarkable that the Jerusalem
elders, in their reply to Tattenai, made no reference
to the grant for restoring the temple which, according
to the editor, Cyrus had made to the exiles. Yet it is
obvious that the men would have greatly strengthened
their case had they been able to say that Cyrus not
only permitted the rebuilding, but contributed to it.
While also Darius confirmed Cyrus' permit about the
restoration, he issued on his own authority an order
about a grant of money and defined its amount.
There is no hint, such as might have been expected,
that in this matter he was merely continuing an order
of his predecessor. It is further curious that the
records which describe the rebuilding of the temple
contain no reference to the stores of costly material
drawn from Lebanon which had been collected sixteen
years before. Instead of this, we hear of preparations
on a much more modest scale being set on foot, for
Haggai bade the people go up into the hill-country to
cut timber, i. 8, and acknowledged the poverty of
the resultant building, ii. 3.

The account in the book of Ezra is dominated
throughout by one motive. Its author was intent to
ascribe the restoration of Judaism to the returned
exiles, and he regarded any help given by the local
community as late in date and merely accessory in

character. The edict of Cyrus was accompanied by a permit to return, which was instantly taken advantage of, and the permission to rebuild the temple was combined with a grant toward the expenses. As soon as the men reached the city, they, not Sheshbazzar, laid the foundation-stone, reared an altar for the regular sacrifices, celebrated the festival of Tabernacles, collected materials for the future temple and meantime appointed the levites to their duties before the building had been erected. The new temple owed its inception to the zeal of the men of the Return, and was planned from the beginning according to their principles. But it has been necessary to point out that certain of his statements disagree with the evidence of other documents, and that in particular his remark about the foundation-stone being not yet laid directly contradicts the evidence of a document which he himself has introduced into his narrative.[1]

It was fundamental to this author's position to be able to claim that the returned exiles appeared in Jerusalem at the time of Cyrus' edict, so that the whole movement which was made possible through the royal decree fell under their control from the beginning. Hence, as has been said, he inserted the list of chapter ii. in immediate association with the arrival of Sheshbazzar. It becomes necessary to examine that list and see whether it agrees with the date to which he has assigned it.

[1] It has always appeared to me that the strongest proof of the authenticity of the documents in connection with Tattenai's intervention is that they disagree with the statements of the editor who quoted them. If the man had forged or even had recast them, he would have been more careful to bring them into agreement with his own views.

The list is said to comprise the children of the province who went up from captivity, the גּוֹלָה (the editor's technical term for the men of the Return) which Nebuchadrezzar, king of Babylon, carried captive to Babylon, and they returned to Jerusalem and Judah, everyone to his own town. The leaders of these men are stated to have been Zerubbabel, Jeshua, Nehemiah and eight others, among whom Ezra is not included. Their numbers are given as 42,360, with 7337 slaves and 200 singing men and singing women. The same list appears in two other of our authorities for the period, in chapter v. of Esdras and in chapter vii. of Nehemiah. There are slight divergences in the names as they appear in the three lists and there is a major difference in the number of singers, which Esdras and Nehemiah reckon at 245.[1]

In view of the fact that Hebrew names and numbers are peculiarly liable to suffer in transmission, these differences are not so serious as to make it doubtful that our three authorities have preserved a common original. But the three editors who have incorporated the document into their narratives have inserted it at different stages in the life of the community.

Thus, the author of the book of Ezra set the list into immediate connection with the arrival of Sheshbazzar. On the other hand, the list is introduced into Nehemiah's memoirs with an introductory statement that " my (*i.e.*, Nehemiah's) God put it into my heart to gather together the nobles and the rulers and the people that they might be reckoned by genealogies. And I found the book of the genealogies

---

[1] There is a discrepancy of greater importance, to which it will be necessary to refer later.

of them that came up at the first, and I found
written therein." Obviously such a statement supplies
no more than the reason for inserting the list in this
particular place. When it states that the list contained
the names of those who came up ' at the first,' it does
not decide the date of that early arrival. So far as
this evidence is concerned, these exiles may have
returned under Cyrus or under Darius. Finally, the
author of Esdras began with a short paragraph,
vv. 4-6, to the effect that Darius sent back under a
guard certain leaders of the Jews, and to this with
some clumsiness of expression he has appended the
list. Evidently the author of this account believed
that the list belonged, not to the period of Cyrus,
but to that of Darius. The most probable explanation of these facts is that the document in its original
form bore no indication of the date to which it was
to be assigned or to the period in the national life
to which it referred. In the same way the similar
list of those who sealed or who were sealed in Nehemiah, chapter x., beyond its mention of Nehemiah the
tirshatha bears no statement about its date. The
three writers, who have introduced the list of exiles
into their accounts, could thus feel themselves at
liberty to insert it at the period to which they believed
it to belong, and were naturally influenced in their
selection of a date by their view of the general course
of events.

It is more significant to notice that the three
writers conclude the list with a statement which
begins alike in each case, but which varies at the
conclusion. Common to them all is the statement
that " when the seventh month was come, the children

of Israel were in their towns," Ezra iii. 1*a*,[1] Neh. vii.
73*b*, Esdras v. 47. Again, the fact that all three
authorities contain this clause proves that it formed
part of the original. But, since the document bore
no precise date, the mention of the seventh month
cannot have been intended to define the exact month
in a particular year. It must have been intended
to indicate either the occasion for which the list was
originally prepared, or a special occasion in connection
with which it was used. Now the seventh month was
in itself an occasion for Jewry : it was the sacred
month *par excellence*. Hence it is significant to
notice that all our authorities have connected the
list with a sacred season, though they do not agree
in their representation of what this season was. The
writers of Ezra and Esdras proceeded to relate that
Joshua and Zerubbabel built an altar, while the
editor of Nehemiah went on to recount a public
reading of the law. They agree about the month
and even about its significance ; but they disagree
about the year, for the public reading of the law
cannot well be dated before the building of the altar.

A larger divergence appears in the description of
the place to which the people came together. The
editor of Ezra was content to say that this took place
at Jerusalem, iii. 1*b*. When he used that vague
phrase he was self-consistent, for he had connected
the list directly with the arrival of Sheshbazzar and
had made it introduce an account of the building of

---

[1] The division of the chapters here in R.V. is unfortunate, since
it produces the impression that the opening verse of chapter iii.
does not directly belong to what precedes. A reader naturally
concludes that a new subject begins with this verse in the new
chapter.

the altar. Since, according to his view, neither city nor altar had been restored before the return of the exiles, he could give no nearer indication of the place where the people gathered in the sacred month. On the other hand, the author of Nehemiah has stated that the men came together in the plaza in front of the water-gate, viii. 1*a*. He also was self-consistent, for he introduced the list after both temple and city-wall had been rebuilt, so that there was a water-gate with its plaza. Finally, the author of Esdras agrees with Nehemiah in making the concourse take place in a plaza ; but he set this plaza in front of the sacred gate or the first porch which is toward the East, v. 47. In thus making the meeting take place in front of the temple, he showed a certain consistency of view with the occasion in connection with which he introduced the list, for he spoke of the returned exiles as though they were the same whom Darius had sent home under a guard.[1]

The conclusion which can be drawn from these facts is that the original document, after having given a list of the returned exiles, stated a special occasion for which and a place to which not these men only but the children of Israel were gathered together. All our authorities mentioned the month, because it served to bring out that the gathering of all Israel was no casual event, but formed a sacred

---

[1] A ' certain ' consistency is all that can be claimed for him. For he followed this account with the record of how Zerubbabel and Jeshua built an altar and laid the foundation of the temple. But how could men have come together in a plaza in front of the temple-gate or the porch, before the temple had been founded, or even an altar had been built ? He may have used the ' temple,' as the visitors from North Israel did. That, however, is a question for students of the text and editing of the book of Esdras.

convocation. But each has taken his own way about
the place where the meeting was held ; and the place
to which the meeting was assigned reveals a different
view of its date. There are, however, certain other
features of the list which help to decide between the
three dates.

Thus, in Ezra ii. 70, before mention of the seventh
month and of the consequent public assembly at
Jerusalem, it is said that the priests, the levites and
some of the people, and the singers, porters and
nethinim were living in their towns, and all Israel
in their towns. The text is extremely puzzling. It
compels us to ask why there should be a distinction
between ' some of the people ' and ' all Israel,' what
distinguished the towns of the ' some ' from those in
which all Israel were living, and why ' some of the
people ' who were evidently laymen appear between
two bodies of the clergy. The conviction that something is wrong with the text is confirmed by the
evidence of the other authorities. For Nehemiah
vii. 73 reads : so the priests and the levites and some
of the people and the nethinim and all Israel were
living in their towns. Here matters are somewhat
simplified since there is no duplication of towns for
two groups of men, but no light is thrown on the
reason for a distinction between the two groups.
The third text, Esdras v. 46, offers another variant :
and the priests and the levites and they that were
of the country dwelt in Jerusalem and the country,
the holy singers and the porters and all Israel in their
villages. This mention of Jerusalem as being inhabited at the time offers a possible clue for the distinction between the settlements of two bodies of

men, who were composed partly of clergy, partly of
laymen. Working along purely textual lines, Bewer[1]
has reconstructed an original which ran : the priests,
levites, porters, singers, some of the people and the
nethinim were in Jerusalem, and all Israel were
living in their towns. This text has the merit of
offering good sense. The priests and other temple
officials were naturally settled in the capital in order
to be near the sanctuary where they served. Along
with them were a number of laymen who, after restoring the shattered buildings, had taken up residence
there. The rest of the people were living in the
Judean villages. Not only does Bewer's corrected
text give sense, but it agrees with another feature in
the passage, for it forms the natural introduction to
what follows in all the documents, the statement
that, when the sacred month arrived, the children of
Israel came up from the villages to attend the festival.
It also agrees with the situation in Haggai, when the
prophet addressed men who were already resident
in Jerusalem. Its picture of conditions in the city
would also suit the connection in Esdras, since the
author there connected the list and the convocation
with the return of certain exiles in the reign of Darius.
It cannot, however, be brought into agreement with
the date and the situation in the book of Ezra. What
it suggests there is a reason for the editor's omission
of any mention of Jerusalem as a place of residence
for either clergy or laity. According to him, the men
of the Return found neither altar nor population in
the capital ; there were no houses where either clergy

---

[1] ' Der Text des Buches Ezra,' *ad loc.* It is not necessary to
reproduce his reasons.

or laity could live. Nor was there immediate need for the clergy to live there, for only after the altar with its services was restored did the priests need to live near it, and as for the subordinate officials, like the porters and singers, they did not need to make their homes in the city, until after the temple itself was restored.

These conclusions, based on the final clauses in the document, are confirmed by an examination of the introduction. There all our authorities agree in describing the returned exiles as the children of the province. The expression is not very natural, when it is applied to men who had but newly arrived in Judah : it rather suggests that they had been long enough in the country to have become a constituent element in the population of the province. The statement, too, that the caravan was under no less than eleven leaders, is, to say the least, peculiar. Wherever mention is made elsewhere of a Return under Zerubbabel and Joshua, these two stand alone without coadjutors. It might be possible to explain this by saying that the full, formal list called for a detailed statement of all the leaders, such as was not necessary in other cases. But among the eleven appears the name of Nehemiah, who is thus made a contemporary of Zerubbabel, and behind that difficulty rises the perplexing question of the relation between the two governors, Sheshbazzar and Zerubbabel, even between the three, if by Nehemiah we are to understand the governor of that name.

Finally, the lists in Ezra and Nehemiah include at the end a statement of contributions toward the work of the temple which were made by certain men.

According to the document in Nehemiah, the tirshatha gave so much, some of the heads of fathers' houses gave so much, and what the rest of the people שארית העם gave was so much. In Ezra this appears in a curtailed form, and the variants are at least curious. All mention of the tirshatha and of ' the rest of the people ' has disappeared ; and, while some of the heads of fathers' houses receive full credit for their generosity, it is carefully added that these men contributed when they came to the house of the Lord at Jerusalem. The reason for omitting the gifts of the tirshatha is easily found. Since the writer set the list in immediate connection with the arrival of Sheshbazzar, the tirshatha of that time was the Persian governor. He suppressed all mention of the tirshatha, because this would have implied that a heathen had contributed to the rebuilding of the temple, in the same way as he suppressed the fact of Sheshbazzar having laid the foundation-stone. When, after the contributions of the heads of fathers' houses, he added the note that the men gave these after their return from exile, he meant to insist that these prominent men formed part of the caravan, and did not belong to the people of the land. As for his omission of all reference to the gifts of ' the rest of the people,' that is made clear by the recognition of the peculiar sense of the phrase. The original list described the temple-restoration as a joint effort on the part of the returned exiles and the remanent Judeans. Since the editor of Ezra credited the work to the men of the Return, he made the heads of fathers' houses returned exiles, and suppressed all mention of the local community. The use of the phrase, ' the rest of the people,' was peculiarly ob-

noxious to him, for it implied the claim of the remanent Judeans to be those who had been spared in
the day of the divine visitation, and who therefore
could say that they had never been, like the men from
Babylonia, driven out into an unclean land. Over
against such a claim, the editor considered the
returned exiles the true remnant, for he put into the
mouth of Ezra a prayer in which that leader acknowledged that grace had been shown from the Lord to
grant us a remnant to escape, ix. 8.

On all these grounds I am driven to the same conclusion as that which has commended itself to Bewer.
Whatever may be the date to which the list of exiles
is to be referred, that of the editor of Ezra must be
definitely rejected. Bewer has chiefly based his
conclusions on the linguistic and critical evidence.
The two lines of approach issue in the same result.

As soon, however, as it has become clear that there
are reasons in the texts themselves for rejecting the
representation of the course of events which appears
in Ezra, it becomes legitimate and even necessary to
ask whether his picture is in itself probable. It has
been pointed out that, since the date of Nebuchadrezzar's campaign, the country had had time to settle
down and for its inhabitants to resume their ordinary
life. But a country so small and poor as Judah
could not have absorbed at one time a caravan which
contained 42,000 men alone. Nor could the new
governor, who was about to take over the administration for the Empire, have permitted the entry of
a body of men who could not be sure that they were
welcome there. What may seem even more improbable is that 42,000 men were found who committed

themselves and their families to a venture in a country which most of them had not even seen. For life had not stood still during those years in Babylonia any more than in Judah. Most of the men who had been carried into exile and all their leaders were dead ; and their successors had had time, as they had had need, to take root in the place of their compulsory adoption. To these men the opportunity to return to Jerusalem meant a breach with the only world which they had ever known and in which they had grown up. They could not have launched themselves on so grave a change as the transference of their families to Judah implied without some knowledge of the conditions of the new country and the possibility of settlement there. The editor of Ezra conveys an impression of the exiles, as men who during those forty-eight years had been eagerly expecting the fulfil-ment of the prophetic message of deliverance, and who had, as it were, been sitting on their boxes in constant readiness for the arrival of that great day. The chapters in Ezekiel, which can be referred to Babylonia, give a very different picture of the attitude and temper of the exiles.

The choice, then, would appear to lie between dating the list of exiles at the stage in the life of the nation to which Esdras has assigned it—*i.e.*, in close connection with the restoration of the temple under Darius, or with Nehemiah, after the wall had been rebuilt. Yet it is not easy to decide for either alter-native. Thus it is said that Nehemiah found the book of the genealogy of them that came up at the first, vii. 5. The phrase ' at the first ' seems to imply that the list, if it formed that book, referred to a period prior to this leader's time. Yet all our sources include Nehemiah himself among the leaders in the list. It is difficult to suppose that a document which included his name could belong to the reign of Darius. For, while many scholars incline to Torrey's view that Nehemiah preceded Ezra, no one has yet ventured to suggest that he arrived about the same time as Zerubbabel and Joshua.

In view of the entire situation and of the conflicting character of the evidence, it would appear that we must fall back on a third possibility. The list may not have been drafted in order to give the names and number of the men who made up a single caravan, but to give the names of those who, at the time when it was drawn up, had arrived from Babylonia and who could prove their right to be enrolled among בני ישראל, the children of Israel. The solution is not free from difficulty, and even serious difficulty. But it serves to explain why all our authorities agree in stating that the men came up under no fewer than eleven leaders. The other caravans of which there is mention are said to have been led by Ezra alone, or by Nehemiah alone, or by Zerubbabel and Joshua. Also, wherever in the other records there is mention of Zerubbabel and Joshua, nothing is said about Nehemiah ; and *vice versa*. The proposed solution serves also to explain why the original document was undated and could therefore be referred to three different periods by the three writers who quoted it. The men who used it inserted the list where, according to their differing view of the course of events, it seemed to them appropriate. The utmost, then, which can be said about the time when the list was drawn up is that the absence of all mention of Ezra proves it prior to his time. Again, two features in our records may serve to indicate the purpose which the list was drafted to meet. All our authorities agree in connecting it with a convocation which was of a sacred character, since it was held in the seventh month : and they also agree in the statement that בני ישראל, the children of Israel were convened then. A list, which is called in Nehemiah a book of the genealogies of those who came up at the first, would serve the purpose of determining the men who had the right to take part in such an assembly. An analogy can be found in the statement which heads the pact of Nehemiah, chapter x. Those who made this solemn agreement were carefully defined as the remanent Judeans and the loyalist Israelites.

CHAPTER VIII.

THE TROUBLES WITH SAMARIA ACCORDING TO EZRA.

THE early date which the editor of Ezra assigned to the Return compelled him to discover a reason for the eighteen years' delay in the rebuilding of the temple, which followed the publication of Cyrus' edict. He was unwilling to have it supposed that, after they had laid the foundation-stone, had set up the altar, had settled the duties of the levites and had arranged for a supply of timber, the returned exiles had unaccountably done nothing more for eighteen years. There must have been a reason for this delay. Accordingly he hinted at certain troubles from ' the people of the lands ' which emerged even when the altar was built, iii. 3. But he entered into larger detail on the subject in chapter iv., where he has collected a number of cases of interference with the work of the Jerusalem community on the part of the Persian governors in Samaria. His intention in gathering these incidents into a connected narrative is plainly shown in the closing statement : then ceased the work of the house of God which is at Jerusalem, and it ceased unto the second year of the reign of Darius, king of Persia, v. 24.

The editor's method of dealing with his material was not uniform. In one case, which happened during the reign of Artaxerxes, he was able to quote the terms of a letter sent by Rehum, the chancellor, to the Persian court, setting out the governor's suspicions as to the conduct of the community at Jerusalem, and asking for instructions : he was also able to quote the reply from Artaxerxes, vv. 8-23. In another case he could only state that a similar letter was sent by certain officials in Samaria during the reign of Xerxes, but he did not quote its tenor nor mention the result, vv. 6, 7. To these, however, he prefaced a statement of his own to the effect that the Persian governors did not take action on their own initiative, but were stirred up to interfere by certain ' adversaries of Judah and Benjamin ' whom he did not definitely name.[1] According to his statement, these men were governed by religious motives in their attitude towards the Jerusalem community. So early as the reign of Cyrus they had approached Zerubbabel and Joshua, the leaders of the returned exiles, with a request to be permitted to take part in the restoration of the temple : on being refused permission, they revenged themselves for the snub by steadily fomenting the suspicions of the local governors against their adversaries. In this way the editor of Ezra not only explained the eighteen years' delay, but threw the onus for that delay on certain inhabitants of the Northern province, who were actuated by religious hatred.

[1] It deserves notice that verses 1-7, which contain the editor's own material, are in Hebrew, while the rest of the chapter is in Aramaic.

In dealing with these statements by which the editor sought to support his view of the course of events, it has seemed simplest to begin with the last, because it consists almost entirely of two documents which he has quoted. The main question there is easier to answer than where he has reported his own view of the incident. According to this Rehum, the chancellor, and Shimshai, the scribe, with some other associates, sent a letter to Artaxerxes in order to draw attention to what they considered a menacing situation which had arisen at Jerusalem. The men, from the titles they bore both in the letter and in the reply, were evidently Persian officials in Samaria and Western Syria. They reported that the Jews at the old capital were building a wall round their city, and that in their judgment the matter was sufficiently serious to deserve the attention of the imperial court. If the work was permitted to continue, the result would be to set up a dangerous centre of disaffection in the province. The court only needed to search the old records of the empire in order to discover that the Judeans had always been difficult to control and that their turbulent character had already led former rulers to dismantle the fortifications of Jerusalem. More than this does not appear to be implied by verse 15, though the last clause, " for which cause this city was laid waste," has sometimes been taken to involve a destruction of Jerusalem by the Persians later than the sack by Nebuchadrezzar. All that the statement *necessarily* implies is that the city was a strong fortress, that there had been good cause for its rulers in the past dismantling it, and that, before the restoration of the walls went further, the court ought to recognise the serious risk involved. The terms of the reply in verse 21 agree with this construction of the clause, for it was content to say that no change was to be made in conditions at Jerusalem without express authority, and that meantime the wall which had been begun was to be destroyed.

The chancellor's letter shows no evidence of animus, religious or other, against Jerusalem. What we can conclude from his conduct and from that of Tattenai is that the successive Persian governors found it necessary to keep a watchful eye on events in the old capital. Otherwise, however, his letter is very like the report which the proconsul in any border province to-day might send to the Foreign Office to say that the people in an outlying town were suspiciously busy in putting the place into a better condition for defence and that the case was more deserving attention, because the tribe was notorious for its disaffection. Indeed, from one point of view the letter is an illustration of the tight hand which the Persian court kept over its local satraps.

In one point, however, the account suggests a question, in its description of the men who were associated with the governor in his report to his court. It is said in verse 8 that Rehum and Shimshai wrote a letter against Jerusalem to Artaxerxes in this sort, but this is followed in verses 9 f. by the loose clause : then Rehum and Shimshai and the rest of their companions, the Dinaites, the Apharsathchites, the Tarpelites, the Apharsites, the Archevites, the Babylonians, the Shushanchites, the Dehaites and the Elamites and the rest of the nations whom the

great and noble Osnappar brought over and set in
the city of Samaria. The form of the sentence is
enough to prove it conflate, since Rehum and Shimshai appear twice without any reason for the repetition, and, on their second appearance with the list of
names, they have no verb. In Artaxerxes' reply
to the letter he addressed Rehum and Shimshai with
their associates in Samaria and Western Syria, v. 17,
and the same two men with their associates took
action on receipt of the royal decision, v. 23. This
in itself would not carry much weight in questioning
the originality of the list of nations, since the king
would naturally communicate with his officials who
were responsible for the peace of the province, and
need not have troubled to repeat the long list. But
those names do not appear in Esdras, which only
mentions Rehum and Shimshai and " the others who
were in commission with them, dwelling in Samaria
and other places," ii. 16, " the rest that were in
commission and dwelt in Samaria and Syria and
Phœnicia," v. 25, " the rest that were in commission
with them," v. 30.

Textually the list of the nations is gravely suspect,
and its appearance raises a further difficulty. For,
while it is easy to understand why a governor at
Samaria should have associated with himself a number
of men who were also responsible for the conduct
of affairs in Palestine—even a governor in Phœnicia,
if Esdras' text is correct—and so have sought to
strengthen his case by intimating that they agreed
with his view of the situation, it is not easy to understand why he introduced a number of nations. The

list in verse 9 cannot represent individuals who supported the Samaritan governor in his attitude toward
Jerusalem, for, while most of the names are otherwise
unknown, the mention of Babylonians and Elamites
with the closing clause " and the rest of the nations "
is enough to prove that communities at least, derived
from different peoples, are being described. It only
makes the bewilderment a little greater to find the
chancellor in such a dispatch going back into history
in order to explain how these men came to be in his province. He informed Artaxerxes that an Assyrian king
settled them there about a century before, and went
out of his way to dignify this king with honorific
titles. Was this interesting historical fact relevant
to the situation, or likely to lend any support to
his dispatch ? All this points to the list having been
intruded into the text, and it becomes legitimate to ask
whether there was a possible reason for the addition.

If, now, these two documents had stood by themselves, the question of their date would have been
comparatively easy. Rehum's letter was forwarded
to Artaxerxes, and the natural conclusion is that
the king referred to was one of the well-known later
kings of that name. Apparently, also, it was addressed
to one belonging to a dynasty which had occupied
the throne for some time, since it asked that search
be made " in the books of the records of thy fathers,"
v. 15. An Artaxerxes who was addressed in these
terms must considerably post-date the time of Cyrus.
With such a late date it also becomes natural to note
that Rehum, unlike Tattenai, had nothing to say
about the temple - restoration, but confined his

complaint to the rebuilding of the city-wall. Now, whatever may be the date of Nehemiah, it seems impossible to set a work on the city-wall earlier than the temple-restoration. Especially is this the case, since the men, whose activity at Jerusalem had roused the suspicions of the governor, were returned exiles—he referred to them as the Jews who came up from thee, v. 12. We cannot well suppose that those men turned their first attention to the city-wall, partly because their main interest in returning was the renewal of the cult and partly because they could plead the terms of Cyrus' edict as their authority for setting to work on the ruined sanctuary. The chief difficulty in connection with Rehum's dispatch has arisen out of the position into which the editor of Ezra has placed it. It was vital to his view of the course of events after the Return to find a reason for the delay in the restoration of the temple, and he found it in the opposition of the governor at Samaria. His anxiety to establish an early return under Cyrus led him into the error of pre-dating the list of exiles in chapter ii. ; his anxiety to explain the delay over the temple led him also to pre-date Rehum's dispatch. His error in each case has given rise to great confusion and difficulty. In connection with the earlier event it involved the necessity of explaining the relation between Sheshbazzar and Zerubbabel : in connection with the later it brought about the necessity of discovering an Artaxerxes between Cyrus and Darius. It cannot be said that the resultant theories, self-contradictory in some cases, rather wild in others, have been convincing. A reference to earlier studies of the period is enough to show how much desperate ingenuity has been expended on the double task.

The record of another act of interference with Jerusalem by Samaria appears in verses 6 f. Unfortunately the text is very bad, and the MT gives the impression which is reproduced in the English Versions that this is not a different case, but the same case as that of Rehum and Shimshai. Esdras, indeed, has gone further and simply telescoped verses 6-8. Following Bewer I read : and in the reign of Xerxes at the beginning of his reign Bishlam, Mithredath, Tabeel and the rest of his associates wrote an accusation against the inhabitants of Judah and Jerusalem ; also in the days of Artaxerxes, Rehum the chancellor and so on as in verse 8.[1] This records a complaint to the imperial court about which we have no information elsewhere. The information which the verses offer is extremely meagre, since they do not record where the complainants lived, in what capacity they took action, or what conduct on the part of the Southern community led them to interfere. It is further necessary to remember that the evidence is based on an amended text. Yet it is possible to draw certain tentative conclusions from the place which the editor of Ezra has given to the record, and from a comparison of the terms in which the complainants are described with those employed about Rehum and Shimshai. Thus, the fact that two of the names are good Persian

---

[1] ' Der Text des Buches Ezra.' I venture to express my admiration for the careful, scientific way in which the author has dealt with the text.

and the third is Aramaic, coupled with the other fact that the men associate with them ' the rest of their companions,' warrants the conclusion that the complaint was lodged by the local officials and was political in its character. As such, it forms an interesting illustration of the difficulties which arose for the Persian satraps, as soon as the new policy of the Empire filtered down into the minds of its subjects. The inevitable result of the liberty granted by Cyrus was to quicken the local feeling and national life of the various components of the huge Empire. It became a grave question for the satraps in each province to decide how far this sense of nationality should be permitted to go ; and the question must have been peculiarly grave wherever, as was the case in Palestine, the population was not homogeneous. In his reorganisation of the Empire Darius found it necessary to withdraw the control of the imperial forces in each province from the civil governor. The motive for this may well have been to maintain the authority of the central executive against the increasingly dangerous power of the local province. But the result of Darius' act was to increase the number of these appeals to Ecbatana, such as chapter iv. in Ezra shows for Palestine. Since the civil governor could not act on his own authority against what seemed to threaten the peace of his district, he must keep a watchful eye on everything which might produce disturbance and must refer to headquarters for decision.

The absence of all detail in the terms of the complaint and of any instructions from the court about the method of dealing with it may even be explained by the conditions which prevailed in Persia at the time. In the beginning of his reign Xerxes was planning his expedition against Greece, and the preparations for that vast enterprise may well have engrossed the attention of the officials at Ecbatana to such an extent that they could not find time to attend to what seemed a minor trouble in an outlying province. The Syrian dispatch was pigeon-holed in the Colonial Office. On the other hand, the situation was altered in the later reign, for, after the sharp set-back which the Empire received through the war with Greece, Artaxerxes did his best to stiffen the administration and to restore the weakened authority of the central power. The Jews who had hoped to profit by the weakness of the executive under Xerxes were the more sharply checked under his successor.

In view, however, of the meagreness of our information on the historical situation and the brevity of the record in verses 6 f., such suggestions cannot rank high. Only one fact remains sure : the troubles between the local satrap and the Jews at Jerusalem are definitely dated in the reign of Xerxes. They cannot, therefore, have had anything to do with the restoration of the temple. Here again the editor of Ezra has pre-dated the account in order to support his view of the delay in rebuilding the temple.

The third instance of opposition from Samaria is found in verses 1-5. The paragraph resembles the account of the complaint to Xerxes in two respects : it is written in Hebrew and it quotes no original document. The statement rests on the authority of the editor, and is related by himself. According to his account certain persons, whom he calls adversaries of Judah and Benjamin, approached Zerubbabel and the heads of fathers' houses at the time when the returned exiles were busy with the task of rebuilding the temple and requested that they should be permitted to take a share in the work. They supported their request by the claim that they also were worshippers of the God of Israel and had been in the habit of sacrificing to Him since the time when Esar-haddon, king of Assyria, brought them up here. Zerubbabel and Joshua and the heads of fathers' houses in Israel refused the request on the ground that they alone had a permit from Cyrus which empowered such an act. The consequence of this refusal was that the petitioners did all they could to hinder the two leaders, and in particular that they bribed " counsellors against them to frustrate their purpose, all the days of Cyrus, king of Persia, even until the reign of Darius, king of Persia," v. 5.

The purpose of this introductory paragraph is sufficiently clear. In it the editor of Ezra traced the opposition of the Samaritan authorities which delayed the temple-restoration for eighteen years to religious animosity on the part of a body of men in the Northern province, whom he identified with the heathen settlers planted there after Sargon's victory. The Persian officials based their complaints against the returned exiles on political grounds, but they were actually the tools of this religious party.

Certain features in his account, however, rouse suspicion. Thus the variant reading in verse 2 shows that the text was altered at an early date. The adversaries of Judah supported their request to be permitted a share in the work at the temple by the claim : we seek your God as ye do and we offer sacrifice unto Him. Some MSS. contain the reading : we do not offer sacrifice unto Him. Obviously this cannot be the original, because the insertion of ' not ' reduced the plea to nonsense. Men who asked permission to assist in the restoration of the temple would never have supported their request by the gratuitous remark that they had never been in the habit of sacrificing to the God who was worshipped there. Yet the insertion is significant. A later age has been revolted by the very suggestion that these men ever sacrificed at the beloved temple. The reading dates after the open breach between Judah and Samaria, and its insertion serves to show that the men of that time identified the adversaries of Judah and Benjamin and the heathen settlers whom Esarhaddon brought up, with the schismatic Samaritans.

But Rothstein has pointed out that the mere omission of ' not ' does not clear up the sentence.[1] The usual translation of the clause is that the men claimed to have been in the habit of sacrificing to the God of Israel since the time of Esar-haddon, king of Assyria, who brought us up hither. This translation of the final adverb is inaccurate, both in grammar and in fact. In grammar, because פֹּה always means here, not hither. In fact, because the men were supposed to be speaking in Jerusalem and Esar-haddon brought settlers to Samaria, not to Jerusalem. Further,

[1] ' Juden und Samaritaner,' p. 29.

this statement brings with it the grave difficulty of understanding how or why Assyrian settlers could have claimed to be worshippers of Yahweh, and especially to have been in the habit of sacrificing to Him. If they had done this at a sanctuary in Samaria, it is in contradiction with the statement which appears in II. Kings xvii. 29 f., according to which they erected shrines to their own gods. If, on the other hand, the men claimed to have been using the temple-site for sacrifice, this statement is in contradiction to the view of the editor of Ezra who credited the re-turned exiles with having built the altar there. All that is needed in order to make the sentence regular is to connect the troublesome adverb with ' sacrifice ' and to read : let us build with you, for we, like you, worship your God, and we have been in the habit of sacrificing here. The men who made this request were those who could urge that plea in support of their request, the loyalist Israelites who, since the days of Josiah, had been using the old altar-site for the purpose of sacrificial worship. They asked permission to take some share in the work of rebuilding the temple, as, according to the Chronicler, their ancestors had contributed to the cost of its restoration and purification under Josiah, II. Chron. xxxiv. 9. The men to whom they made this request were not merely the leaders of the returned exiles, but were Zerubbabel and the heads of fathers' houses, the same two con-stituent elements of the community who restored the temple during the reign of Darius according to Ezra, chapter v. These leaders declined the request, but did not base their refusal on any denial of the men's claim to worship the same God or to take part in the cult at Jerusalem. They merely pointed out that the terms of Cyrus' edict did not refer to any others beyond the local community. In their judgment it was more prudent to keep strictly within the limits of their powers, and so avoid anything which might rouse the suspicions of the local governor, and lead to difficulties with the imperial authorities. The caution of the Jewish leaders was shown to be justifiable and wise, since, in spite of it, Tattenai judged it necessary to inquire into their own action. That the petitioners from Samaria recognised the force of these objections and quietly accepted the decision is clear from the fact that they maintained their relations to Jerusalem and even submitted to the authority of the leaders there. For it was about the same period that they sent another deputation to ask whether they were now at liberty to discontinue their practice of fasting in the fifth month, Zech. vii. 1-3.

It is impossible to say with certainty whether the editor of Ezra was here basing on an original document, but the inconsistencies in his own account make it probable that he was employing older material. If he had been at entire liberty, he would have produced a statement which was straightforward in its terms. What influenced him in altering the older form was his suspicion of the loyalist Israelites and his dislike to the position of equality which the pact of Nehemiah, chapter x., had given to these men.[1] We can see the existence of the tension between North

---

[1] Evidence will be brought later to show that in this matter he represented the attitude of most of the men of the Return.

and South which later produced the Samaritan schism. Accordingly he inserted at verse 2 the clause which identified the loyalist Israelites with the heathen settlers in the Northern province, and at verses 9 f. the other clause which associated these settlers with the plans of the Persian governor. In both cases, it must be noted, the words employed give rise to difficulties on linguistic and other grounds. The same refusal to recognise the presence of any faithful remnant in the North, and the same deliberate desire to deny to the people there any part in the inheritance of the true Israel, appear in the paragraph which has been added to the close of chapter xvii. of II. Kings, verses 34-41. Naturally he called these men from the beginning the adversaries of Judah and Benjamin, where the use of the tribal names shows the lines along which the division of his date was supposed to run. He further made these men the *fons et origo mali*, since it was at their instigation that the local governors interfered with the men of the Return and prevented them from carrying out the pious work of rebuilding the temple, which, but for them, would not have been postponed until the reign of Darius.[1]

---

[1] A minor proof that we have to do with an older original which has received revision is to be seen in the titles given to the Persian kings : in verse 3 Cyrus is called king Cyrus, king of Persia ; in verse 5 both Cyrus and Darius appear merely as kings of Persia. There is something unnatural in the use of the title king of Persia in such a connection during the period when the Empire was still in existence. In the letters sent by local governors to the court and in the replies they received the expression is never used except at chap. v. verse 13, where Cyrus is called king of Babylon, because the writers were referring to the edict which Cyrus issued after his conquest of Babylon. In verses 5 and 24, accordingly, which are plainly editorial and late, it is not surprising to find this later usage.

The usual method of explaining the expression, ' king Cyrus, king of Persia ' in verse 3 is to suppose that the original was Cyrus, king of Persia, and to this the omission by the LXX of king before the royal name gives apparent support. Yet this fails to explain why the simpler title, which is characteristic of the earlier documents, found its way into the text. The best explanation appears to be that the original document, like other such early material, contained merely king Cyrus. The editor of the Book of Ezra, to whom we owe the description of Cyrus as king of Persia in verse 5, added the full title in his revision of the original. Finally, the Greek translators, who wrote after the time of the Persian Empire, found the title king before Cyrus' name superfluous and dropped it.

CHAPTER IX.

THE ALTAR.

IT is possible now to recognise the general character of the account of the restoration of the Jewish polity which appears in the book of Ezra. The book gives the official record put forward by the returned exiles, that party which finally obtained control of the centre of the new Jewry, the temple and the cult at Jerusalem. But this control which finally passed into their hands did not exist from the beginning. Instead of this, it was the slow result of time. What the editor has done has been to telescope his history, and to represent what was only reached by slow degrees as though it had always been.

In certain respects his history of the restoration of the Jewish polity after the exile has an interesting resemblance to the history of the conquest of Palestine in the book of Joshua. There the conquest, instead of being sporadic, effected by the separate clans under different leaders and carried out with very varied success, has been compressed into a single series of campaigns. There, too, the unity of Israel, which was only won after painful effort and with very imperfect success under the kingdom of David, was already present when Israel entered Canaan. The victory was gained under one head by a nation which was already organised for its task under elders who decided and controlled its campaigns. History has been telescoped in both Joshua and Ezra, and what was the outcome of time and much experience has been set down as though it existed from the beginning.

There are two other statements made by the editor in his representation of the work of the returned exiles which fall to be examined from this point of view. They may not be accepted in the exact form or at the precise date which he has given them, but they may yield evidence of what was done at a later time and so of the currents of thought in the community which finally resulted in setting up the new polity. The first of these was that, as soon as the seventh or sacred month arrived, the people gathered at Jerusalem, where the priests, headed by Jeshua and seconded by Zerubbabel and his brethren, built the altar of the God of Israel to offer burnt-offerings thereon, according to the law of Moses, the man of God, iii. 2. Apparently, therefore, there was no altar which answered to this description at the time of the Return, and it was the first care, because it needed to be the first care of the exiles. Also they built it without help from any other section in the community. The second feature of the account is that, even before the foundation-stone of the temple was laid, the same men took order about the place of the levites in the future building, v. 8. Later, when the stone was laid, they took equal care that the respective functions of the priests and levites should be carefully defined, v. 10. In connection with this matter, however, the arrangements were not according to that which was written in the law of Moses, the man of God, but after the order of David, king of Israel. Since the statement about the levites leads to the large and tangled question of the position of these officials in the temple, it is necessary to begin with the relatively simpler matter of the altar.

Most students of the period are now convinced that the sacrificial worship did not cease at Jerusalem during the exile, but that the altar was continued and that the exiles must have found it in use on their return. The editor of Ezra has ignored this altar, and the recognition that he deliberately passed it by draws attention to the terms in which he referred to the new altar. It is said to have been built to offer burnt-offerings thereon according to the law of Moses, the man of God, iii. 2, and it was employed at once for the תמיד, or the regular morning and evening burnt-offerings on behalf of the community, vv. 3*b*-5*a*. It was also to be employed, not only for these daily communal offerings, but for every private sacrifice which was brought by individuals, v. 5*c*. As the altar was set up in the seventh or sacred month, it became the centre for the celebration of the feast of Tabernacles, which was resumed by the returned exiles, and the regular sacrifices demanded in connection with this, the leading festival in the Jewish year, were offered there on the successive days of the feast " according to the ordinance," v. 4. Nor did it suffice to state that the altar had been employed for this sacred occasion by the exiles in the year of the Return : it was added that it must be similarly employed in connection with the new moon festivals and all the other set feasts of the community, v. 5*b*.

The statement that the new altar was built according to the law of Moses, the man of God, followed by the careful and deliberate detail of all the purposes which it was henceforth to serve in the nation, cannot be separated from the no less deliberate omission of any reference to the altar which already existed on the sacred site. The editor was clearly insisting that the only legitimate altar for the use of the community was the one which had been erected by the men of the Return. That gave his reason for ignoring the presence of the earlier altar, but it does not show the ground of his objection. It has been possible to discover a reason for his similar omission of all reference to Sheshbazzar's act in laying the foundation-stone of the temple. If Mr Gadd's suggestion as to the character of the stone laid at Ur be correct, the stone laid at Jerusalem may have been attended by circumstances which made the devout community revolt against rearing their shrine on such a base. Then we have a natural explanation for Zechariah's emphatic insistence that Zerubbabel and no other must lay that stone. The editor of Ezra has credited the act to the returned exiles immediately on their arrival, instead of dating it in the reign of Darius. In the same way there may have been something about the exilic altar or about its ritual which failed to satisfy what the men of the Return counted essential to the requirements of the law of Moses. The old altar may have been rebuilt or reconsecrated.

Now, there is a passage among the oracles of Haggai which is very puzzling, but which deals with a question as to the purity or impurity of offerings which were being presented at a certain place. The paragraph, Hag. ii. 10-14, may not be an authentic oracle of the prophet, but its inclusion among his oracles and the date assigned to it justify the conclusion that, if it was inserted, this was done by one who recognised it to belong to the period of the restoration of the temple.[1]

[1] Rothstein and Sellin have recognised that the book of Haggai differs in certain respects from some of the other prophetic collections which were made then or later, such as Malachi, Zechariah ix.-xiv. and Deutero-Isaiah. Not only have dates been supplied for the successive oracles, but an effort has been made to show the conditions in and to which the prophet spoke, and to describe the effect which he produced on his hearers. Thus, occasionally, as in i. 12-15, the original oracle, v. 13, is the nucleus round which has gathered a longer exposition. The same phenomenon appears in the book of Zechariah i.-viii., where his first oracle is better understood when it is recognised that verse 6b is no part of the original, but a curt description of its effect. When, however, Sellin makes a comparison in this respect between Haggai and Jonah, his illustration is not very happy. It is true that the book of Jonah is also thrown into the form of a narrative ; but there the narrative is of the very essence of the book ; if it be taken away, there is nothing left. On the other hand, the removal of the dates, introductions and endings in Haggai leaves the prophetic sayings more or less in their integrity.

A more useful comparison may be drawn between the way in which Jeremiah's oracles (or Ezekiel's) and those of Haggai have been treated. The book of Jeremiah contains oracles embedded in shorter or longer narratives which were intended to give the conditions to which these were addressed and the effect they produced on the prophet himself or on his hearers. But the book also contains groups of λογια or sayings which are merely strung together without comment. A similar case occurs in Zechariah, where chapter viii., in contrast with what precedes, consists of a number of oracles which were also ascribed to the prophet. The book of Ezekiel offers another illustration of the same type.

There would seem to be evidence of the practice of a species of higher criticism in the period which attended the exile. Men were not content to collect the utterances of their prophets, but, as a help to understanding these, they assigned them to their respective authors and sometimes fitted them with explanatory headings which related to the circumstances in which they were spoken. In that connection it has always seemed to me a remarkable and

According to the terms of the paragraph Haggai was instructed to address a question to the priests on a matter which was specially under their charge, since it involved a question of ritual purity. Put the case, it ran, that a man happened to be carrying holy flesh—*i.e.*, the man was carrying away the part of an offering which it was legitimate to consume beyond the temple precincts. If the skirt of his cloak, which contained the holy flesh, touched other food, would the contact render the other food holy ? The priests replied that it would not. Suppose then that a man, personally unclean through contact with a carcass, cf. Lev. xxii. 4, Num. ix. 6 f., touched any food, would this contact render the food unclean ? The priests replied that it would. The terms of the questions and answers are clear. The difficulty has always lain in tracing the connection of the discussion with the other oracles among which it stands and with the situation of prophet and community at the time.

Older interpreters tried to connect the passage with an earlier oracle of Haggai, in which the prophet bade his hearers recognise that their neglect of the duty of restoring the temple had brought upon them the divine anger and so had blighted every other undertaking to which they set their hands. The initial

significant fact that no effort was made to apply the practice to the oracles of Deutero-Isaiah and Malachi.

But it is necessary to remember that higher criticism, whether it is practised in the fifth century B.C. or in the twentieth century A.D., is not an exact science, and that its devotees may make mistakes. Men evidently knew that Haggai had been deeply interested in the restoration of the temple and had done good service in that cause. They naturally associated with his name and those of Zerubbabel and Joshua oracles which dealt with this epoch in history, but they may have included what was not his.

failure to fulfil one particular duty was like an un-cleanness which clung to the people and which tainted all their other enterprises. In the blight resting on their fields they must recognise the presence and the power of this taint. But the explanation has never been satisfying. Thus the position in which the passage stands militated strongly against it. The inquiry to the priests is dated almost four months after the rebuke which on this view it was intended to support. It has also been placed after the people, in response to their prophet's exhortation, had under-taken the work of restoration; and has even been set between two oracles which promised the divine blessing on them as a reward for pressing on the work. If his early exhortation had already produced its desired effect, what need was there for the prophet to hark back to his former reproach, and why should he have felt it necessary to enforce it by a somewhat elaborate appeal to the priests in support of his verdict?

It may be said that the separation of the two pas-sages was merely due to a mistake on the part of an editor, who gave a false date to the inquiry from the priests. But matters are not improved when the two paragraphs are read together. If the prophet's aim was to show how failure in one duty made all other faithfulness null and to strengthen this by the analogy of the transmission of ritual impurity, it was somewhat pointless to introduce a reference to whether such purity could be transmitted. Yet he not only referred to this question, he began from it. Further, the peculiar language employed in verse 14 at once demands an explanation: so is this people and so is this nation before Me, saith the Lord, and so is every work of their hands, and that which they offer unto Me there is unclean. Had the sentence closed with declaring every work of the men's hands unclean, it might have been possible to see there a reference to harvests blighted by the neglect of the temple. But the conclusion deals with the men's offerings to their God and with their offerings in one particular place.

Rothstein rejected the older interpretation and insisted that 'this people' העם הזה, especially since it is followed by 'this nation' הגוי הזה, carries with it a certain implication of contempt or blame. The words could not, therefore, be intended to describe 'the people of the land' of ii. 4, which only two months before had been assured of the divine approval in its resolve to undertake the restoration of the temple. To this it may be added that the tone in which God is said to address 'this people' contrasts strongly with the assurance of ii. 5, where the men are told that the divine spirit resteth among them. Nor can 'this people' mean 'the remnant of the people' in i. 12, 14, about whom it is said that they obeyed the voice of the Lord and listened to the exhortation of His prophet, and also that the Lord stirred up their spirit with eagerness for their task. After they had turned to obey the prophet's message, such a slighting reference to them is more than difficult.

Rothstein and Sellin, accordingly, have attempted to connect the passage with the incident mentioned in Ezra iv. 1-5, where men from Northern Israel asked to be allowed to take part in the restoration of the temple. The verses in Haggai then represent the advice given by the prophet to the leaders of the people in reply to this request. He warned them that the taint of heathenism which clung to the men from Samaria was sufficient to vitiate the whole service in the new temple, while the sanctity which attached to those who had undertaken this pious duty would not avail to counteract the evil influence of the applicants. The passage will then form another proof of early tension between the men of the Return and their Samaritan neighbours.

The interpretation has one advantage over the older. Since it does not refer ' this people ' and ' this nation ' to the community whom Haggai previously addressed, it explains the tone of contempt in the use of these words. It fails, however, to meet the difficulty presented by the peculiar language of verse 14. Sellin has recognised this, and has tried to escape from it by offering a new translation of the verse. Following Ehrlich, he has interpreted the last clause to mean, not ' that which they offer there,' but ' wohin sie sich nahen,' the place or any place to which they draw near. In support of his rendering he has appealed to Exodus xiv. 10 (to which he might have added Genesis xii. 11) for the intransitive sense thus given to the hiphil verb יקריבו. The sense of the verse will then be that the initial taint which attached to the Samaritans through their heathen origin was enough to render everything which they undertook and every place which they approached unclean.

Yet the rare use of the hiphil of קרב in the sense of approach in the two passages which can be adduced in support scarcely warrants that usage here. The paragraph in Haggai deals directly with a cult question and refers to the priests for its decision. In these circumstances it is more natural to take the word in what is its common sense as a *terminus technicus* of the cult—*i.e.*, bring near to the altar or offer. Nor does the proposed combination of the work of their hands with the place or any place which the men approach seem any more natural, apart from its awkwardness in Hebrew. Rather ' the work of their hands ' is meant for a wider and vaguer description, and ' what they are offering there ' is added to define more exactly the offensive character of this handiwork. But the principal reason which is decisive against what is otherwise an attractive explanation is that I am compelled to interpret Ezra iv. 1-5 differently from Sellin.[1] In my judgment the rejection of the request of the Northern Israelites was not on the ground that they were identified with the heathen settlers in Samaria.

Haller [2] appears to recognise the situation better when he has referred the passage to the older altar which was in use before the time of the Return. Then it ceases to be necessary to seek any unusual sense for יקריבו : the word is used in its technical sense of bringing a sacrifice to God. Haller, however, has harked back to the older interpretation, and has connected the passage with Haggai's earlier oracle. In his view the prophet meant to say that the old altar, so far as the people were being satisfied with it and were making its presence an excuse for not pressing forward with the restoration of the temple,

---

[1] Cf. p. 151.
[2] ' Die Schriften des A. Ts.': Das Judenthum, etc., nach dem Exil.

constituted the fundamental uncleanness which was vitiating all their other work. Yet the interpretation suffers under all the difficulties which have already been detailed, and it even increases them. For the prophet must then be supposed to have charged the people with carelessness about the condition of their temple in contrast with their regard for their own comfort, and to have found in this neglect a sufficient explanation of the blight on their fields. After that he proceeded to say that the men were practising a worship at their altar which was not simply invalid, in comparison with the duty of temple-restoration, but which was positively noxious. Haller scarcely does justice to the severity of the indictment which is launched against those offerings. In the earlier oracle the reproach is merely one of carelessness about the building of the temple : in the later passage the sacrifices which the people were offering were enough in themselves to taint everything else which they attempted. Nor has he recognised that, if there is a reference here to the altar which was in use before the Return, there must be some connection between the passage and the careful way in which the editor of Ezra has stated that the only valid altar at Jerusalem was the one erected by Zerubbabel and Joshua.

It is not wise to dogmatise about the precise sense of the verses, or about the reason which led to Haggai's connection with their content. Yet one may venture to say that certain conclusions with regard to them are clear. Thus the paragraph must be interpreted by itself : the attempt to connect it with Haggai's other oracles and to explain it through these leads to

nothing. When it is thus taken by itself, it becomes
equally clear that the question which the prophet was
instructed to lay before the priests was no general or
academic inquiry, but concerned a matter of practical
conduct which was troubling the minds of men at the
period when they were rebuilding the temple. Further,
it turned round a debate on ritual purity, since it was
referred for settlement to the priests, one of whose
functions was to decide between clean and unclean.
The effect of these men's decision on the general
principle was to pronounce a sentence of invalidity
against the sacrifices which certain persons were
offering at a particular place. The terms in which
those who took part in this worship are described
cannot be ignored : they are distinctly called ' this
people ' and ' this nation,' and the two expressions
cannot be counted synonyms. They might have been
so regarded had the passage been in poetical form :
but the paragraph is in prose.

Now the only form of sacrificial worship about
which we know that it was being practised at Jerusalem at the time of the restoration of the second
temple was that of the local community on the site
of the old altar. For some reason the validity of this
worship was being called in question so seriously as
to receive the condemnation of the priests. It is not
impossible to determine the party which was dissatisfied with the old form of worship, since the
attitude of the editor of Ezra helps to a decision.
He ignored the very existence of the old altar, and,
when he stated that the first task of the returned
exiles was to build an altar, he carefully added that
this altar was after the law of Moses, the man of God,

and that it alone was valid for the private and communal sacrifices of the community. When he thus represented the course of events, he followed his usual practice of pre-dating events : what was in fact the result of time and the issue of some debate was that which had been from the beginning. The paragraph in Haggai gives a glimpse into the process by which the decision was reached. It also shows the time at which the question was raised and the suitability of that time. Before men went on to build their temple, it was essential to determine the validity of the altar round which the shrine was to be raised. The account of the editor of Ezra, on the other hand, makes it clear that it was the returned exiles who had scruples about the old altar.

The ground of objection to the exilic altar is nowhere stated, but may at least be conjectured from the terms used in the passage of Haggai to describe those who worshipped there. They are called this people and this nation, so that they did not form a homogeneous body, but were composed of two parties. They are also dismissed with a like contempt, but the term employed for one of them is peculiarly severe; הַגּוֹי, by which these last are described, is generally used for a heathen people. Now the exilic altar was frequented by the remanent Judeans and the loyalist Israelites, and was served by priests from the South and the North alike, so that the use of two terms about them is readily explained. In the same way, while the tone of contempt used for both agrees with the way in which the editor of Ezra ignored the local community, the special name for one section reflects his attitude towards the Northern Israelites, whom we have already seen him identifying with the heathen settlers.

The situation which they found existing at Jerusalem seemed intolerable to the stricter party among the returned exiles. Specially offensive to them was the presence of levitical priests at the altar. To them the Northern Israelites were tainted through their admixture with the heathen settlers, and they knew nothing of the measures these men had taken to separate themselves from their neighbours. As for their priests, these were the descendants of the men who had taken part in the calf-worship of Jeroboam, the son of Nebat, who made Israel to sin.

Since, however, the ground of objection to the exilic altar is nowhere definitely stated, it may have been due to other causes. All that can be claimed for the outlined suggestion is that it explains the peculiar language of the passage in Haggai. The main thesis does not depend on its being more than a suggestion ; for the main thesis is that the old altar was rebuilt or reconsecrated, because of its having proved offensive to the scruples of the returned exiles. The newcomers were beginning to make their influence felt on the temple and the cult, to the restoration of which they had contributed so large an impulse.

CHAPTER X.

THE PRIESTHOOD.

THE question of the priesthood in the new temple is in certain respects the most perplexing problem which meets a student of the period. It involves two subjects, the relative position of priest and levite, the origin of these two bodies of clergy ; and these two subjects are so inextricably interwoven that they cannot be kept apart. Allied to it is the kindred question of the constitution of the levites into separate classes as singers and porters with the relation of the nethinim. Fortunately this subordinate problem, which developed out of the position given to the levites, can be isolated without prejudice to the more important inquiry. It has been ignored because it has no direct bearing on the character of the post-exilic polity. To discuss it here would divert attention from the first question which is fundamental to any appreciation of the new Judaism.

If the subject of the priesthood with its implications has continued to perplex students, that has not been due to any want of material bearing upon it. In varying forms it appears through all the documents which can be dated after the Exile. Both the historical books which were written after that time refer to it, though in very different fashion. Thus the editor of Ezra stated that, even before the temple was built, the men of the Return appointed the levites to their functions there, iii. 8-10. He said nothing, however, about the origin of these men or the reason for assigning them their functions at this time: he merely stated that in what they did Zerubbabel and Joshua followed the ordinance of David the king of Israel. The author of Chronicles, on the other hand, devoted a great deal of attention to the subject. What he had to say on the minor question of the connection of the levites with the choral service of the temple has been fully discussed by several scholars to the neglect of the main theme of his history. It will be necessary to devote a chapter to an examination of the peculiar attitude he took on the relation between priest and levite, and to his view of the origin of the levites. Again, references to the relative position of the two classes of clergy have been intruded into the books of Deuteronomy and Kings. A highly significant oracle, bearing on the high-priesthood, is found in Zechariah. Finally there remains the evidence of the torah. Here the evidence appears at first to be definite and uniform. In Exodus the distinction between priest and levite is sharply defined, and is set under the final authority of Moses. A supplement to the legislation appears in Numbers, where an original story of a rebellion by certain men of Reuben against the civil authority of Moses has received the addition of a revolt by one levitical clan against the peculiar privileges of the Aaronic priesthood. The anecdote was clearly intended to enforce the binding

character of the law. Yet alongside the torah must
be set a chapter in Ezekiel, which, while it purports
to be an oracle, really offers the sketch of a legislation
on the relative position of priest and levite, and which
gives a reason, based on their past history, for rele-
gating the levites to an inferior status.

The difficulty here arises from the conflicting
character of the evidence, since the witnesses do not
agree among themselves. There must be some reason
for the divergence, as well as for the resultant agreement ; and it is no real answer to water down any
part of the evidence or to relegate any inconvenient
witness to ' a later date,' which generally means
throwing it into the waste-paper basket. Do these
divergent views represent successive stages in the
development of the final arrangements in the temple ?
Since this implies that their cause must be found in
history, can we trace any historical cause behind them ?
Or is there another reason ?

Before going further, however, it is important to
ask whether there is any cause why so much attention
should have been given to the constitution of the
priesthood and to the relative position of priest and
levite in the period which immediately followed the
exile. However we may account for the divergence
of view, it is clear that the subject deeply engaged
the minds of the leaders of the new community at
the time of the restoration of the temple. There
must have been a larger reason for this than the
explanation which is generally supplied, especially
by Continental scholars. The matter has at times
been summarily disposed of, as though no more were
involved than the personal ambitions or jealousies

of two bodies of clergy in the little community, or even a somewhat squalid debate over the emoluments of office. The fact is emphasised that a large proportion of the men of the Return consisted of priests, and that a considerable number of these men must have been the descendants of those who formerly officiated in the temple. The men naturally expected to resume their place in the restored temple with the dignity and the privilege which attached to that office. But the representatives of the priests, who had not been in exile, as naturally looked to have a place assigned to them in the restored cult. Whether these men were the descendants of the priests who had officiated at the Judean high-places, or had themselves served the altar in Jerusalem during the exile, they refused to be overlooked in the new arrangements. The question of the new priesthood with the cognate question of the relation between priest and levite sprang from this situation and concerned its settlement.

That these considerations influenced some of the men concerned, it would be idle to deny. So long as it pleases God to commit the ministry at His altar to men, so long as the treasure of His grace is trusted to earthly vessels, these considerations will have weight, especially with a certain type of mind. But something larger than this is needed, in order to account for the space devoted to the subject in the documents of the Return. The men of that time were reconstituting the polity of Judaism for the future, and they would not have preserved in the records of so significant a period in their national history the account of a petty quarrel between two bodies of their priests, if it had been concerned with nothing but prestige and salary. Nor will this explanation, as will appear more clearly later, account for the remarkable variety of attitude on the subject which appears in the different documents. Ultimately the debate turned on matters of principle and involved the most pregnant and practical issues for the life of all Jewry. When the nation became a religious community, and especially when it elected to reconstitute itself round the institution of the temple-cult at Jerusalem, it became essential to determine the responsible body which was to exercise final authority at the central shrine and to issue the torah which all Israel must obey. When Josiah made the temple the only centre for the cult, the matter had not even been raised, for the sons of Zadok, who had controlled the worship there since the time of Solomon, continued in unquestioned authority. But the question could not fail to be raised and to demand an answer when the temple was rebuilt. If the services there were to be carried on with seemliness and order, they must be regulated, and therefore must be controlled by a priesthood who followed and perpetuated a tradition. The cult in Israel had grown into a complicated and elaborate ritual with sacred days and sacred seasons, each of which demanded its own sacrifices with the appropriate liturgical accompaniment. Such a service could only be conducted by trained men and in conformity with a ' use ' which was clearly laid down. The community which restored the temple must determine who were to fulfil these significant duties in it.

If the returned exiles had found at the holy city

none but their fellow Judeans who were continuing the worship at the old altar, the question could not have failed to give rise to some difficulty. The officiants were composed of the lower clergy who had not been carried into exile, recruited perhaps by priests from the disused high-places. So far as the ' use ' to be followed in the new temple was concerned, there need have been no friction, for these Judean priests would follow the old use of Jerusalem. But the men would not readily have given way to the new-comers, though those could claim descent from the line of Zadok. Not only could they urge the plea of having maintained the time-honoured ritual during the dark years of the exile, but they could urge that they had not been cut off from the means of grace, or exposed to the defilement of heathenism, as the men of the Return had been.

But the situation which the returned exiles actually found was calculated to give rise to much more serious difficulty and demanded reconsideration. The community were living according to the pact of Nehemiah, chapter x. That agreement had been made in a time of great stress, and, while it served certain large ends in maintaining the forms of religion among those who entered into it, it suffered from the defects of every hastily-made arrangement. Through it one large purpose had been fulfilled, since North and South had been able to continue the unity which had been effected under Josiah. But no effort had been made to weld the practice of the two sections, and no final authority had been instituted which might effect this. Priests and levites, whoever these may have been, were officiating together at the common altar, with

M

no determination of their respective functions : they were not even supported from the same revenues. The men who framed the pact had recognised that the new conditions demanded certain modifications of their old practice, and they had met the instant claims by levying a poll-tax for the temple and by a common regulation for the transport of their dues. But they had not attempted to form a college of priests, which might continue to issue similar regulations, such as were sure to be required in a time when much was in flux and when there was grave need for some authority to guide men. The pact had met the present need, but made no provision for the future. The men who concluded it were humble people, who provided for their own religious wants, but who did not see the full scope of the thing which they were doing. Thus they did not realise that their action in constituting themselves into a separate community based on their religion, especially when that religion became *religio licita* in the Empire, could not fail to demand a body of men who could represent their religious outlook in questions which arose between them and the local Persian governor. As little had they recognised that there was need for a college of priests with power to regulate the festivals, to determine the terms on which worshippers were admitted to a share in the worship, to decide and, if necessary, to modify the charges on the community for the maintenance of their cult, and to see that this money reached its destination. As soon as the community had resolved to restore the temple, however, the inadequacy of the old pact became patent. To ignore the necessity for order there was

to run the risk of the disintegration of what had been
so hopefully begun ; and the first necessity for good
order was to set up a sacred college with authority
to define and enforce such order. What made the
need for action greater was that the temple was now
to serve a Jewry which was wider than the Jews in
Palestine. The men who drafted the pact had thought
in terms of the Judaism which they knew, and had
been large-hearted enough to combine the two sections
of their people in a common worship, but they had
not looked beyond those limits, nor recognised that
from this time Jerusalem must think of her scattered
sons and daughters in diaspora. Some among them
may in their spiritual pride have refused to consider
the needs of those who were in the unclean lands of
the heathen. The men of the Return could not think
in these parochial terms, nor forget their kindred in
Babylon. If, however, the festivals of the temple
were to be made available for these exiled brethren,
if the sacrifices there were to have any validity for
them, some adjustment of the ritual was necessary.
Without such an adjustment a polity which had
grown up in Palestine, and which was still adapted
to the country of its origin, must fail to meet the
needs of the nation. But, if this was to be done,
if the law of Israel was still to go out from Jerusalem,
and to control the lives and guide the worship of
every observing Jew, there must be a priestly college
whose authority was recognised as final throughout
the nation.

Every institution brings with it the demand for a
controlling authority. As soon as Israel elected to
restore its polity on the basis of the temple and its

cult, it was committed to the discovery of such an authority. The question of its constitution arose, as soon as the community resolved to restore the temple. Yet it involved a readjustment of a situation which had been long enough in existence to strike roots in the habits of the people, and it was in itself a novelty on which the past could throw little light. The amount of attention which the documents of the period devoted to the problems it involved is a sufficient proof of their gravity and of the serious thought which was devoted to them.

It has already been pointed out that the editor of Ezra disposed of the whole matter very summarily. According to him, the men of the Return settled the functions of priest and levite even before the temple was restored. But this view of the situation cannot be reconciled with an item of evidence from the period of the restoration of the temple under Darius, which proves that the cardinal feature of his account, the supreme authority of Joshua in all matters connected with the cult, was seriously questioned.

The subject forms one of the visions of Zechariah, chapter iii. The scene of the vision has been laid in the courts of heaven, where Yahweh was sitting as judge with the angels for the executants of His orders : but the evident aim was to determine something on earth, even in Jerusalem. Further, the matter in debate concerned the status and authority of Joshua as high-priest, since he is not merely introduced by name, but is given his peculiar title. Also the first issue of the debate was that, after he had been exonerated of every charge which was laid against him, he was clothed in the garments which belonged to that dignity. His accuser was Satan, the angel whose function it was to bring to notice anything which might discredit a servant of God.[1] The terms of the accusation have not been reported, but something of their tenor may be gathered from the decision against them. The decision was not merely issued in the name of Yahweh, but in the name of Yahweh who had chosen Jerusalem. He who had a peculiar regard for His holy city, and who had again showed His purpose of grace toward it by the restoration of the temple, now revealed how and by whom He desired to be served there. He revealed this in consequence of an accusation against the high-priest. Further, the reason given for vesting Joshua in his official robes is stated to have been that he was a brand plucked from the burning. God had shown His mercy to the priest by intervening to rescue him from the furnace of exile, so that his return to the holy city was a sufficient proof of the divine favour to him and his like. This statement, intended to repel the charge of the Satan, shows that the gist of the accusation must be found there. Sixty-six years had passed since the year of the exile, so that none of the returned priests could ever have officiated at a sacrifice and the majority must have been born in the pollution of heathenism. Joshua himself, if he was born in Judah, must have been little more than a child when he left it, and he had spent most of his life in the unclean land. To men who held the ideas of ceremonial impurity of the period it was a real question whether such men might

[1] Cf. his function in connection with Job.

control the temple-cult. In the prophetic oracle this
central objection was seized and rebutted : the fact
of Joshua's deliverance by Him who was restoring
Israel was sufficient proof that God had blotted out
the past. Joshua was restored to every privilege
which should have been his but for the exile. Accordingly the angel was commissioned to give a charge
to the high-priest after he had been reclothed in the
garments of his office : he should judge in Yahweh's
house and keep His courts and be given a place of
access among those who stood by. He was assured
of more than a mere position in the restored temple,
for he was endowed with authority as judge there
on no other condition than that he faithfully performed the duties which were allotted to him : he
must walk in the divine ways and keep the divine
charge. Nothing in the past had any force against
him ; only a failure to fulfil his trust in the future
could be counted valid against his right.

It was not sufficient, however, to vindicate the
claims of Joshua as an individual, since the accusation
brought against him held equally against all the men
of the Return. Hence the vision continues : hear
now, O Joshua the high-priest, thou and thy fellows
that sit before thee are men of portent, for behold I
will bring forth My servant, the branch. The exact
sense of the closing promise is very obscure, but for
the present inquiry may be left in its uncertainty.
One conclusion may be drawn from it—viz., that the
prophet saw in the restoration of the temple the
promise of some greater thing which God had in
store for His people. What this end may have been

in the mind of Zechariah is left unresolved,[1] but there is such an end, and the presence of Joshua and his associates is a guarantee of its arrival. To lose them would be to lose a certain pledge for the issue which God has planned, so that the fulness of the divine promise is bound up with their presence in the temple. Since Joshua no longer appears alone, but as the leader and representative of those who sit before him, he and they constitute a party in the community. The high-priest has already been vindicated in his office and dignity on the ground that, though he has suffered in and through the exile, he has been redeemed from that calamity by God who has chosen Jerusalem. But this did not exhaust the significance which attached to him. He and his were more than a signal proof of the divine grace which had freed them and brought them back to the holy city ; they were the pledge of something greater which God was about to do for His people, and, as such, they held a peculiar place in His temple.

The vision in Zechariah is enough to prove that the authority of Joshua and his fellow-priests from the exile was not so instantly acknowledged in Jerusalem as the editor of Ezra has represented, but that it met with serious opposition.[2] It is, however,

[1] It may have been the restoration of all Israel to its own land.

[2] The majority of modern scholars accept in this matter the attitude of that editor ; to them the Jerusalem community were a feeble folk, who accepted without hesitation the leadership of the priests from Babylonia. This view of the situation appears very strongly—*e.g.*, in Herntrich's discussion on Ezekiel, *Ezechiel probleme*. To him, the remanent Judeans were socially and otherwise inferior to the exiles, and, being conscious of the fact, were at once submissive to their control. In my judgment, this position ignores the fundamental feature of the situation. That was

legitimate to draw another conclusion from the fact that such a vision was put under the authority of one of the prophets who stirred up the Judeans to undertake the restoration of the temple. Since the opposition to the claims of the exilic priests could not have come from the men of the Return, it must have had its source in the Jerusalem community, whose very existence the editor of Ezra ignored. To find a vision of this character among the oracles of Zechariah is to recognise the first stage in the settlement of the personnel of the priesthood. As soon as it was recognised that the uncleanness contracted in the exile did not incapacitate the newcomers for service at the altar, one main issue was decided. The Judean priests who had served at the altar-site and the priests from the exile could unite under Joshua as highpriest, the more readily because both bodies followed the old use of Jerusalem. The local men could acknowledge Joshua's high-priesthood, because he was a descendant of the old line uf Zadok which had exercised authority there since the reign of Solomon.

controlled, not by social considerations, but by religious conviction. In the eyes of the Judeans the exiles were the men on whom the divine anger had fallen, and who in consequence of this visitation had been living for years without the true means for maintaining their relation to their God. They needed purification. Hence, it was necessary to show at some length the peculiar sense of שאר or שארית, p. 60 *supra*. Incidentally, this view of the situation has misled these scholars in their interpretation of the oracle in Zechariah.

CHAPTER XI.

THE ATTITUDE AND AIM OF THE CHRONICLER.

By the chronicler is here meant the author of that history of Israel from the time of the foundation of the kingdom by David to the time of its collapse under Zedekiah, which appears in I. Chronicles x. to II. Chronicles xxxvi. 21.[1] This record, which forms a unity and reveals homogeneity of plan, is prefaced by nine chapters, which have no unity among themselves and are not integrally related to the rest of the book. Rothstein,[2] and more recently Von Rad,[3] seek to justify their presence on the supposition that they were intended to form a species of *Vorhalle* or porch, by which the reign of David was linked up with the past of the nation. But, without entering into detail on the subject, it must be said that, if the chapters were intended for such a purpose, they fail to fulfil it. They cannot be said to deal with any single topic, and they are not all concerned with the past. One entire

---

[1] I venture a mild protest against the vague use of the title, ' The Chronicler.' As one who has read a good deal of the literature on the Return, I have met the expression constantly, but have never found it defined—with grave loss to clarity of understanding.

[2] In Sellin's ' Kommentar.'

[3] ' Das Geschichtsbild des chronistischen Werkes.'

chapter, c. iii., is devoted to a genealogy which traces
David's descendants down to a period later than the
Exile. Another section, v. 27-41, followed one of the
levitical families as far as the time of the captivity.
The greater part of chapter ix. finds a parallel in
Nehemiah, chapter xi., and appears to deal with
conditions in Jerusalem after the Return. Verses
1-26 in chapter v. deal with the fortunes of the tribes
which settled on the East of Jordan and carry the
account down, in one case to the reign of Jeroboam II.,
in another to the Assyrian captivity. Whatever may
have been the original source of these heterogeneous
materials, and whatever the reason which led to their
having been placed before the book of Chronicles,
they were not written in order to be an introduction
or to connect David with the past of Israel. Probably
they are a collection of loose material like that which
now forms an appendix to David's life at the close of
II. Samuel ; and certainly, when they are removed,
the unity of design in the Chronicler's work becomes
apparent.

Again, the fact that the books of Chronicles end,
and the book of Ezra begins, with the same two verses
is generally taken to prove that the three books were
intended to form a continuous history and derived
from the same hand. Having related the dolorous
fate of the early kingdom, the author, it was supposed,
went on to relate the restoration of the nation through
the support of the temple and the cult. Yet the fact
of the repetition of those verses might well appear to
lead to an opposite conclusion. Men do not take the
trouble to stitch together two documents, unless they
have been originally separate. The full answer to

this position, however, can only be given through a comparison of the ideals and the attitude which dominate the two histories. Some of the characteristic traits of the author of Ezra have already been discussed, and it will be the business of the present chapter to discover those of the Chronicler. Only then will it become clear how divergent the two men were.

In seeking to determine the characteristic features of the Chronicler's narrative, it is necessary to keep in mind that his account of the history of the kingdom runs parallel to that in Kings, plus a few chapters in Samuel. Accordingly only those points where he differed from or supplemented his sources may be appealed to in evidence of his peculiar outlook. Occasionally he rearranged his material, but evidence based on such rearrangement may only be used to support conclusions which have another and surer foundation. Even his omissions must be employed with caution, since want of interest in a subject, not difference of view, may well have prompted an old - world historian to curtail his predecessor's narrative.

For the sake of clearness the attempt has been made to group the material round three main themes : the author's view of the kingdom and of the Davidic dynasty, his attitude to the temple, both its origin and its significance in the national life, and the place he gave to the Northern kingdom with his conception of the position of priest and levite in the temple-worship. The division, it must be confessed, is artificial at best, since the subjects are so closely inter-related that they run into one another. Thus the history of Judah

opens with the capture of Jerusalem by David and
closes with the destruction of the city by Nebuchadrezzar. The fact could be adduced to prove that the
centre of interest was the dynasty : it equally proves
the author's profound interest in the temple. To
write of the two separately is to run the risk of ignoring that to him Jerusalem was doubly significant, as
the city of David and the sole centre for sacrificial
worship. Yet, in dealing with the mass of detail
which must be passed under review, even a poor
division is better than none.

The emphasis which the Chronicler laid on the
Davidic kingdom reveals itself at once in the fact that
he began his history with the accession of David. All
he had to say about Saul was contained in the extract
he made from II. Samuel, which related the events of
the fatal day at Gilboa. His reason for inserting even
that brief extract is found in the two verses which he
added at its close, I. x. 13 f. The completeness of the
disaster at Gilboa proved that God had rejected the
first holder of the royal title, and threw the accession
of David into higher relief, since it was due to a
direct divine intervention. The second distinction
of the new kingdom, however, lay in the fact that
from the beginning it was accepted by all Israel.
Therefore the Chronicler omitted all mention of the
years during which David reigned at Hebron over
Judah alone, and he equally ignored the kingdom of
Ishbaal with its suggestion of opposition to David.
Immediately after Saul's death the nation recognised
the divine decision, which had not only been conveyed
in the disaster at Gilboa, but which had been directly
revealed to it by Samuel even before the death of

Saul,[1] I. xi. 1-3. What serves to show that the omission of all reference to the earlier years was deliberate is that the Chronicler has taken over from his sources a number of incidents from the early life of David which cannot be fitted into that life as he has related it. If the records in the Books of Kings had not survived, the task of dating these incidents would have been even more puzzling than they now are. The purpose of the omission of the years at Hebron is suggested by the way in which the Chronicler made a slight addition to the choice of David by his people : he related that they recognised in him the king whom God had chosen, and added that the choice was revealed to them, as it had been to Jesse, through Samuel, xi. 3. Now Samuel was an Ephraimite. The first act of the new king was to lead all Israel to the capture of Jerusalem, and so to secure the capital of the nation and the site for its future temple, xi. 4.

The divine election of David was not an act of grace toward an individual : the same choice with the divine blessing attached to it extended to the dynasty which he founded. The clearest proof of his attitude on this subject is found in the Chronicler's account of the breach under Rehoboam. In his record of the course of events during the reigns of Jeroboam and Rehoboam he followed his sources closely, and even retained the statement that a prophet, Ahijah, had supported the rebel so that the breach had the divine approval. He further retained the story of how an-

---

[1] It deserves notice that the Chronicler thus wove into his narrative the incident of Samuel's visit to Jesse, an account which is isolated in the book of Samuel.

other prophet, Shemaiah, forbade Rehoboam to fight against his rival. Evidently, in his judgment, there were good reasons for Israel having refused to endure the rule of the Judean king. But, when the breach was made final and when its consequences revealed themselves, he went on to describe in his own terms a war which broke out between Abijah and Jeroboam, II. Chron. c. xiii. ; and there he made the king of Judah say : hear me, O Jeroboam and all Israel, ought ye not to acknowledge that the Lord, the God of Israel, gave the kingdom over Israel to David for ever, even to him and to his sons by a covenant of salt ? vv. 4 f. Abijah continued that the North was withstanding the kingdom of the Lord in the hand of the sons of David, and that there were also with them the golden calves which Jeroboam made them for gods, v. 8. Apparently the initial and fundamental sin lay in the rebellion of Israel against the divinely ordained unity of the nation realised in the Davidic dynasty. The sin of erecting the golden calves is made subordinate, as though the act of having ignored the divine will by rebellion against the dynasty He had chosen brought with it inevitably a lapse from the purity of the faith. Naturally, since so great an issue was at stake, there could be only one result. In spite of the superior numbers of the Israelite army, and in spite of its king's higher military skill, the day ended in a triumph for the representative of David. Thus signally did the divine displeasure reveal itself against the man who had dared to flout the divine will. God had refrained, so long as Rehoboam was on the throne, because that unworthy scion of the race did not merit vindication ; but he did not suffer Jeroboam to come to his end without some notable evidence of the divine wrath against his conduct.

This conviction of the divine authority of the Davidic house influenced the author's attitude to the Northern kingdom in all its later course. Thus it led him to ignore the independent history of the sister kingdom. An incident which he has inserted shows his view more definitely, because the evidence it can offer is positive, and is not merely to be deduced from his silence. On one occasion, when Amaziah of Judah was at war with Edom, the king hired a number of mercenaries from the neighbouring state, but a prophet intervened and ordered the king to send the men home, because " the Lord could not be with Israel." Their presence in the camp could not fail to be disastrous. When Amaziah naturally protested against losing the money he had already paid for the men's services, the prophet replied that God would make good the loss, II. xxv. 6-11. Through casting off its allegiance to the dynasty, the Northern kingdom had practically become pagan, so that for Judah to accept help from that quarter was equivalent to reliance on the foreigner. It was true that Amaziah's obedience to the prophet in this case did not prevent him from suffering severe defeat at the hands of Joash of Israel ; but the Chronicler had his own explanation of this untoward event, for he related that Amaziah had carried away and worshipped the gods of Edom after he had defeated its king. Where the author of Kings made Amaziah's challenge to his neighbour the outcome of the Judean's arrogance after his success against Edom, the Chronicler made the king of Israel an instrument of the divine chastisement for the apostacy of the king of Judah. Even one who was little better than an alien could be such an instrument. Had not Isaiah of Jerusalem pronounced Assyria the rod in the Lord's hand ?

It is needless to multiply illustrations of the extent to which this theme occupied the historian's attention, because Von Rad [1] has already collated the evidence, and, in addition, has pointed out that, whenever the Chronicler departed from his sources in dealing with the subject, his changes and additions invariably tend to bring out that the rule of the Davidic house over a united Israel was based upon the divine purpose. Probably, therefore, it was this conviction, rather than any mere unwillingness to dwell on blemishes in the character of the national hero, which led him to omit certain incidents in David's reign, such as the betrayal of Uriah and the rebellion under Absalom. Because the Davidic kingdom was of divine appointment, the conduct of its founder must have been such as God could approve. In the freshness of its early days, also, it must have been the source of nothing except good to Israel. Men who hold such preconceptions have generally heightened the lights and ignored the shadows in an institution or movement the history of which they have undertaken to relate.

But, further, there are features in the picture of the Davidic king which appear to confer upon the dynasty something of a Messianic character. The holder of the title was endowed through his divine election with a dignity which raised him above ordinary humanity. Here also it is unnecessary to collate the evidence, since Von Rad has sifted out

[1] ' Das Geschichtsbild,' etc.

the relative passages with diligent care. Yet it is wise to recognise the clear limits set to this dignity. None of the passages, nor all of them in combination, go so far as actually to erect any member of the dynasty into Messiah. Nowhere is the line passed which marks the distinction between one who owed his signal position to the divine purpose, and one who could be entitled the actual divine representative on earth. The figure of the Davidic king, as sketched by the Chronicler, never escapes from the limits of time, or even from those of human frailty. Apart from all other evidence, one characteristic which appears from the beginning and continues throughout must be counted final on the question. When David spoke about the kingdom which God was instituting in his person and his house, he was made to say that it should endure with Solomon, if he was diligent to do the divine commandments and judgments, I. xxviii. 7 ; and the same conditional character of the promise appears in references to more than one of the later kings. The Davidic king, like all his subjects, was under the torah. Accordingly, while the Chronicler ignored many incidents which detracted from the honour of David, he had no hesitation in describing with entire frankness the errors and even the apostacy of several of his successors. The institution derived its origin from nothing less than the divine will, and continued to be the object of the divine care. So thoroughly was it founded on the purpose of God that it could survive the shortcomings of many of those who represented it. It would be legitimate to say that the Chronicler's attitude on the subject might well give rise to the view that Messiah, when He came, must be of the house and lineage of David and must be endowed with royal attributes ; but it would be an exaggeration to say more.

There was, however, another aspect of David's life and activity which bulked as largely to the Chronicler as the fact of his having been the first king over a united Israel. This was his institution of the temple and its worship. The first act of the new king, immediately after he had received the homage of the people, was to lead them to Jerusalem and wrest the site of the future sanctuary from heathen hands. After that, his interest in the temple dominated all his other activities. The historian could not and did not ignore the fact that Solomon actually carried out the building, but he has reduced the work of the son to the lowest terms and made him no more than the instrument for carrying out plans, every detail of which had already been formulated by his father. Not only did David, as in the book of Kings, conceive the idea, he collected materials for carrying it into effect. He laid down the תַּבְנִית or design of the future building, which his son must follow with exact care, I. xxviii. 11-18. The reason for Solomon being forbidden to make any change was that his father had received the design through direct divine inspiration, v. 19. Like the united kingdom under the Davidic line, the temple was no mere human institution, but owed its inception to the divine command and its form to divine guidance. Nor did the king confine himself to drafting a plan for the building : he also issued detailed instructions on the subject of the personnel of its officiants, and on the duties which many of them were to fulfil there. Even before the sanctuary had come into existence, the functions of its clergy were precisely defined by one who in these matters was acting according to divine direction.

From the time when the temple, which owed its origin and its plan to such an august source, was built in Jerusalem, it became the unquestioned centre for sacrifice in all Israel. The clearest proof of the unique place which the shrine received from the beginning is that the Chronicler ignored the scheme in which the author of the Book of Kings set his record of the kings of Judah. The writer of the earlier history judged the successive kings by their behaviour towards the high-places : they were good or bad, according as they helped or hindered the movement for centralisation of worship at Jerusalem. His very insistence on the point serves to prove that in his day the matter had not passed beyond the reach of debate. To the Chronicler, the question was finally settled. The unique sanctuary has become to him almost as much an article of faith as the demand that Israel must reserve its allegiance and its worship to Yahweh alone. Only about peculiarly sinful kings such as Jehoram and Manasseh did he mention that they built high-places. In connection with Jehoram, this sin was part of the conduct by which he walked in the way of the kings of Israel, II. xxi. 6-11. As for Manasseh, his restoration of the high-places forms part of a description of his conduct, according to which he followed the abomination of the heathen, xxxiii. 2 f. It might thus appear as though the Chronicler believed the high-places to have implied the worship of another god than Yahweh, or wished to set the use of these on the same level as apostacy.

Thus the supreme significance of David to the historian consisted in two features of his reign. He was appointed by divine election and by the choice of the nation to be king over united Israel, and so became the founder of a dynasty which had these things for its charter. He also received by divine inspiration the pattern of the future temple, the centre of worship for all Israel, and under the same guidance he laid down regulations for the worship there.[1] This attitude of the Chronicler appears again in connection with the three kings, David, Hezekiah and Josiah, whose life and activity he has related with the largest detail. The services these three rendered to their nation were double : they were all zealous supporters of the central sanctuary and they were equally eager to maintain or restore the unity

---

[1] Von Rad, *op. cit.*, p. 129, takes a different view on the latter point. According to him, " this unique significance of David in Chronicles is based upon his organisation of the levites." Now it is undoubtedly true that the Chronicler stressed the status of the levites, especially the levitical singers, in his account of David's reign. It is also true that in several later passages he carefully referred the position and the functions of the levitical order to the arrangements made by the first king. But to give *unique* significance to this side of the royal activity is to take too narrow a view, nor do the verses brought in its support bear out the contention. Thus Von Rad appeals to I. xxviii. 12-19, where David is made to claim divine authority for the plan he delivered to Solomon. Yet that plan covered much more than decisions about the temple personnel and in its reference to them described them as priests and levites without any emphasis on the peculiar rights of the levites. As for the further references to which Von Rad appeals, II. viii. 14, xxiii. 18, xxix. 24 f., these belong to later reigns, and in each case the regulations with regard to the temple-officers are merely said to follow David's pattern. In each case, also, attention is drawn, not specifically to the position of the levites, but to that of the priests and levites.

of Judah and Israel. David made Jerusalem the national capital and planned the central sanctuary there. The other two purified the temple from the defilement it had suffered under their respective predecessors, and sought to restore it to its dignity as the centre of worship for all Israel. They instituted a passover in which under Hezekiah some of, under Josiah all, the loyal elements in the Northern kingdom took their part beside Judah. The two kings showed themselves faithful to the ideal of David, for to the Chronicler the glory of the Davidic house largely consisted in its having stood for a united Israel.

When he described the past of the kingdom, the Chronicler used a large liberty in dealing with history. Thus his picture of the temple is ideal in most of its features. That sanctuary did not hold during Solomon's reign the commanding position which he assigned to it, and the elaborate arrangements for worship there, which he has ascribed to David, must be relegated to a much later date. But the recognition of this fact only serves to throw into stronger relief one commanding feature in all he had to say about the sanctuary. He remained loyal to historical realities when he set the temple solidly at a particular period in the national life. The central shrine owed its origin to the first king, and nothing resembling it had previously existed in the nation. In this respect he was more definite than the author of the Books of Samuel. All that this writer had to say on the subject was that, when David had finished with his wars, he counted it fitting to provide a more worthy shrine for the ark. He followed this by the statement that Nathan, after agreeing with the plan, returned to forbid it, II. vii. 1-7. The Chronicler included this account in I. xvii. 1-6, but he went on to relate that the plan of the future temple was due to a direct divine revelation to the king. So far from reviving an institution out of the past, David was introducing a novelty, which required a special command from God to justify it.

Any connection which the temple-building had with the past was through the ark, the famous Ephraimite emblem, about the fortunes of which the author of Samuel had much to tell. The Chronicler prefaced his account of the episode with Nathan by a long record of how David brought up the ark from its refuge in the house of Obed-Edom, cc. xiii., xv., xvi. He took the basis of his narrative from Samuel, but expanded the material in a fashion which must engage attention later. The king lodged the sacred symbol in a tent which he erected for it in the town which he had taken from the Jebusites. Our sources agree in ascribing David's purpose in building the temple to a desire to house the ark more worthily : it was not fitting that the king should occupy the house of cedar which Hiram had built for him, while the ark of God lodged behind curtains. The permanent building was to be a substitute for the mere curtains which appeared to the king unworthy of the ark's dignity and of his own. Both sources also described with some fulness the transfer of the ark under Solomon to its new resting-place, I. Kings viii. 1-11 ; II. Chron. v. 2-14. But, because this resting-place was the surrogate for the tent, neither troubled to say what was done with the curtains.

Before proceeding to relate David's preparations for the temple, the Chronicler inserted the ἱερὸς λόγος or sacred story of the divine election of the threshing-floor of Araunah as the site of the altar, c. xxi., an account which the author of Samuel had relegated to an appendix. There was a reason for this change in the position of the incident. It was necessary to show that the altar, round which the temple was built, owed its sanctity, like everything else in connection with the new structure, to the fact of the divine choice. To indicate its significance, the Chronicler added to his original that, when David first sacrificed on the sacred spot, the Lord answered him by fire from heaven upon the altar of burnt-offering, I. xxi. 26. Thus he did not leave this conclusion to be inferred from the fact that the angel sheathed his destroying sword when the smoke rose from the altar : he definitely stated that God gave approval to the place which He had chosen from all the tribes of Israel to set His name there.

But, according to our sources in their present form, there was another sanctuary besides the ark in its tent, to which David and his son resorted. This was the tabernacle at Gibeon, with an accompanying altar for burnt-offering. It suddenly appears in the neighbourhood of Jerusalem, and, except for the statement in one passage that it owed its origin to Moses, there is no hint of its connection with the past of the nation. We know nothing of its history during the years of the conquest of the land, nor of how it came to be located at Gibeon. The only time when it emerges from obscurity is at the time when David was planning and Solomon was building the temple.

After that is finished, the tent of meeting with its altar disappears as suddenly and as inexplicably as it appeared. Yet, while neither source describes its origin, both appear to acknowledge the high sanctity of the holy place. Solomon, before he built the temple, went down to offer sacrifice there, and received a divine revelation at the shrine, I. Kings iii. 4. The Chronicler appears to set the two sanctuaries of ark and tabernacle alongside each other at the close of his description of the transference of the former to Jerusalem. " David left there (*i.e.*, in the tent) before the ark of the Covenant of the Lord Asaph and his brethren to minister before the ark continually as each day's work required . . . and Zadok the priest and his brethren the priests before the tabernacle of the Lord in the high-place that was at Gibeon to offer burnt-offerings upon the altar of burnt-offerings continually morning and evening," I. Chron. xvi. 37-40. It is somewhat remarkable that the action of the king in relation to the Gibeon sanctuary is expressly said to have been done according to all that is written in the law of the Lord. It is equally remarkable that, while the levites appear here as attendants on the ark in David's city, the priests with Zadok at their head before his appointment by Solomon appear at Gibeon. Again, after the plague had been stayed by the royal sacrifice on the site of the altar in Jerusalem, it is carefully stated that the reason why David did not offer his burnt-offering at the altar before the tabernacle was that he was unable to reach it, because he was afraid of the angel's sword. Presumably the purpose of this remark was to explain why the pious king, instead of using the Mosaic altar, erected a new one : he only did it because of his reverence for the divine messenger. Yet the supposed explanation brings fresh questions as to the reason for abrogating the use of an altar which had so august an origin, and as to the fate of the Mosaic original. Was it merely deserted or pulled down, and what was done with its sacred furniture ? No such uncertainty attaches to the destiny of the tabernacle at Gibeon, for it is said at II. Chronicles v. 5 that the levitical priests brought up " the ark and the tent of meeting and all the holy vessels that were in the tent " into the temple. Evidently, therefore, while the tent for the ark was forsaken, because the temple itself had taken its place, the tabernacle was not allowed to pass out of use. But we are compelled to ask what was its use. It could not have been re-erected in one of the courts, and it surely was not dismantled and stored away in one of the chambers.[1] Also, according to the law in Exodus, the ark was one of the holy vessels in the tabernacle. Why then does it take precedence, here, of the tabernacle of which it formed part of the furniture ?

There is an artificiality about all this material dealing with tent of meeting and altar of burnt-offering which suggests that it has been added to the original narrative of the Chronicler. The original recognised that the temple was a creation of the early kingdom, and therefore traced its inception and its plan to a revelation received by David. It also linked up the new feature in the national worship

---

[1] For the perplexities to which this statement has given rise, cf. Bertheau's ' Kommentar,' *ad loc.*

with the past by making the sanctuary a surrogate
for the tent which housed the ark. The reviser who
introduced the supplementary material made the
temple no novelty, but the revival of an institution
which derived from Moses, and conceived it as a
surrogate for the tabernacle in the wilderness.

Hence the Chronicler has made the ark essential to
the temple-worship. How essential it was he has
made clear in two significant passages. When Solomon
built the temple, he built it round his father's altar,
which continued in use after its dedication through
the divine approval of the first sacrifice there. Yet
it was only when the levites brought the old symbol
to its new resting-place that the glory of the Lord
filled the house, II. v. 14, cf. vi. 11. Even more
significant is his account of the restoration and
purification of the temple by Josiah. There he made
the king command the levites " put the holy ark into
the house which Solomon, the son of David, king of
Israel, did build : there shall no more be a burden
on your shoulders : now serve the Lord and His
people Israel," II. xxxv. 3. The verse raises a series
of unanswerable questions, if it should be accepted
as sober history. Since the ark is said to have been
brought back to its place, when and why and by whom
had it been removed ? If this happened under
Manasseh, why was that sacrilegious act omitted
from the long catalogue of the bad king's deeds ?
When Josiah ordered the levites to cease from carrying
the emblem, did this mean that, during the period of
its absence from the holy of holies, it was being carried
about ? If so, what was the purpose in thus trans-
porting it ? If again Josiah ordered that from this

time the ark was to remain stationary and no longer to be carried in public processions, what prompted him to make such a change at the period of and in connection with the celebration of the united passover ? Why, also, was there such careful reference to the temple which Solomon, the son of David, the king of Israel did build ? The only way in which justice can be done to the character of the verse is to recognise in it, not the statement of a historical fact, but the expression of a conviction on the part of its author. In his judgment the ark, an Ephraimite symbol, was an essential feature of the Judean temple. Therefore he related at length how David, the founder of the Kingdom over a united nation, brought the ark into his city and how Solomon placed it in the temple, with the result that the glory of the Lord filled the house. He also inserted into the record of Josiah, the restorer of the united kingdom, the story of how he was careful to do the same.

The strong interest of the Chronicler in the maintenance of a united Israel implies that he had a certain sympathy with the men of the Northern kingdom. He entirely ignored the kingdom itself, and dropped from his history all the material bearing on it which the author of Kings had collected. But he did not include the nation in the condemnation which he thus passed upon its kings. Thus he definitely exonerated the religious guides of Israel from any share in the calf-worship. Immediately after the breach the priests and levites of all Israel resorted to Rehoboam, so that Jeroboam was compelled to appoint priests of his own for the conduct of his novel worship.

Especially faithful were the levites, for they left their ' suburbs ' and at some sacrifice to themselves refused to conform. Following the example of their religious leaders, the best of the people remained loyal to the true ritual, for from that time all in Israel who set their hearts to seek the Lord resorted to Jerusalem for sacrifice, II. xi. 13-16. Some of these laymen even forsook their country and made the same sacrifice for their faith as the levites, for it is said that Asa gathered Judah and Benjamin and those who sojourned with them from Manasseh and Ephraim. These members of the Northern kingdom fell to him in large numbers because they recognised that God was with him, II. xv. 9. How many among those who did not thus transfer themselves continued to cherish sympathy with Judah, and how practically they showed that sympathy, appear in an account of events under Ahaz. During that reign the Israelites conquered the Southern kingdom and secured many captives and much spoil. But when they had returned in triumph, a prophet rebuked the conquerors with such effect that the men of Samaria sent the captives home, even loading them with the property of which they had been deprived, II. xxviii. 8-15. Here the terms in which the prophet conveyed his rebuke are significant : ye purpose that which will bring upon us a trespass against the Lord to add unto our sins and our trespasses. For our trespass is great, and there is fierce wrath against Israel, v. 13. To the historian there were true prophets in Ephraim who counted their nation to rest under the divine anger, whether because of its rebellion against the house of David or because of its false worship, prophets too who considered the act of carrying on war against the sister people an aggravation of this initial guilt. Further, a prophet who delivered such a message was listened to and obeyed by his countrymen in their hour of victory. What makes the account more noteworthy as an indication of the attitude of the Chronicler is that he related it about a king of Judah, whose general conduct he severely censured. In his view it was enough that Ahaz was a descendant of David and king in Jerusalem : Ephraim could not fail to recognise that war against him was in itself a transgression. What he condemned in the North was the kingdom *quâ* kingdom, since it had made a schism in the unity of the nation, but this did not involve that the nation itself with its religious leaders was apostate.

So far was this from being the case that Israel could produce a prophet who rebuked a king of the house of David. For, when Jehoram, influenced by his alliance with the family of Ahab, went astray and misled his people, Elijah sent a letter with a stern threat to Jerusalem, II. xxi. 12-15. The Chronicler could even conceive it possible that a king of Samaria might be more righteous than his contemporary in Judah, for in his account of the visit paid by Ahaziah to Jehoram the son of Ahab in Jezreel he was not content to tell how ill the visitor fared, but added that the destruction of Ahaziah was of the divine will, because he had joined Jehoram in his antagonism to Jehu whom the Lord had anointed to cut off the house of Ahab, II. xxii. 7 ff. Such a view of the relation between the kings of Israel and Judah goes beyond the situation which the Chronicler described between Amaziah and Joash.[1] There the king of Israel was a mere instrument of the divine chastisement. But this implied no superiority in Joash, since even a heathen might be so used by God. Here, however, Jehu is called the anointed of the Lord, and for the Judean to oppose him was to act counter to the divine will.[2]

It is not, therefore, surprising that the historian represented the best kings of Judah as showing a lively interest in and sympathy with the sister nation. This attitude revealed itself even before the fall of the rebel State, for Jehoshaphat went out and brought back to the Lord the people from Beersheba to the hill-country of Ephraim, II. xix. 4. Naturally, however, it appeared more strongly after the actual collapse. In that catastrophe God had uttered His verdict on the schismatic and apostate kingdom. As soon as that was out of the way, there was an opportunity to restore the Davidic ideal, and the kings of Judah would have neglected their duty had they failed to bring succour to those elements in the North which had remained faithful to the worship at Jerusalem. When, therefore, Hezekiah came to the throne, he swept away all heathen images in Manasseh and Ephraim as well as in Judah and Benjamin, II. xxxi. 1. After he had purified the temple and thus made it worthy of his purpose, he instituted a passover celebration there, to which he invited the

---

[1] Cf. p. 191 *supra.*
[2] For the purposes of this study it is fortunately unnecessary to discuss the historical character of these incidents. Indeed, if they should be regarded as free constructions of history on the part of the Chronicler, they only serve to bring out more clearly his attitude to the Northern people.

men of North Israel. Josiah completed what his predecessor had begun.

The Chronicler's interest in the condition of Northern Israel runs parallel with an interest in the levites, to whom he occasionally gave the Deuteronomic title of levitical priests. By this is meant more than that he gave attention to both : he brought the two together and linked the subjects in his record. Wherever he wrote of the kings who showed sympathy with Israel or introduced mention of the restoration of the temple, he brought the levites into prominence. It is unnecessary to do more than recall how this dominates his picture of David. The founder of united Israel committed the ark to the charge of the levites when he brought it into his city, and he arranged in large detail their service in the future temple. Jehoshaphat, the first king who showed an anxiety for the faithful Israelites after the breach, showed an equal concern in the levites. He appointed in his capital a tribunal of levites, priests and laymen to supervise the מִשְׁפַּט or judgment of the Lord and to decide in controversies, II. xix. 8 ff. He also sent certain princes, nine levites and two priests throughout Judah to teach the people according to the law of God which was in their hands,[1] II. xvii. 7-9.

The levites come again into prominence in connection with the cleansing of the temple which followed the rebellion against Athaliah. Here the Chronicler has radically altered the narrative in Kings. According to the earlier account the high-priest had

---

[1] It is in Deuteronomy and in chapters viii. f. of Nehemiah that we hear of levites having for their special task the teaching of torah. The editor of the book of Ezra and the rest of Nehemiah allot them no such function.

no hesitation about bringing the Carites and a military guard into the sanctuary in order to protect the young king, II. Kings xi. 4. But the introduction of these foreigners into the sacred precincts was a grave offence in the judgment of a later age. Accordingly the Chronicler made Jehoiada issue strict orders that none except the priests and those who ministered of the levites should enter the temple, while the people must remain in the outer courts, II. Chron. xxiii. 5 f. The guard round the young king was to be composed of levites, every one with his weapons in his hand, v. 7. So far it might appear that the Chronicler had substituted levites for the foreign guards and thus relieved the high-priest from the onus of having summoned uncircumcised men into the temple. He would then be acting in agreement with the demand of Ezekiel xliv. 6 ff.[1] But the account proceeds with the statement that Jehoiada restored the conditions which had prevailed in the time of David and that, in so doing, he appointed the temple officials under the authority of the levitical priests whom David had set there to offer the burnt-offerings of the Lord according to the true Mosaic ritual with thanksgivings unto the Lord, vv. 18 f.[2] Further, in order to avoid the possibility of foreigners intruding into the sanctuary in future, he appointed porters at the gates whose business was to exclude unclean persons. The situation

[1] This was the interpretation which Wellhausen put upon the passage : cf. ' Geschichte Israels,' pp. 203 ff.

[2] To follow the LXX here in its reading ' priests and levites ' is to sin against one of the first principles of scientific textual criticism, which demands that the more difficult of two variant readings should be preferred. The Greek translator has added a waw in order to bring the text into agreement with the practice of his time.

here is entirely different from that in Ezekiel, for the levites were empowered to sacrifice and were distinct from the porters. The main feature, however, which concerns us here is that, when the priest purified the temple, he took special care of the status of the levites there.

Again, when the sanctuary was cleansed after Manasseh's lapse, Hezekiah brought together the priests and the levites, but he only addressed the latter. They were to sanctify themselves and to sanctify the house of the Lord, II. xxix. 3 ff. The men must not be careless in the matter, because the Lord had chosen them to stand before Him, to minister unto Him, serving Him and burning incense, v. 11. However the last word there, מַקְטִירִים, be translated, it implies that the levites were counted capable of fulfilling a peculiarly priestly function. After the rededication of the sanctuary they were permitted to exercise another privilege of the priests, for they stood to bless the people. Here, again, they bear the Deuteronomic title of levitical priests.[1] In his whole action in the matter Hezekiah conformed to the strict Davidic pattern, v. 2.

In his description of the work of Josiah the Chronicler largely followed the account in Kings. His alterations, however, are made more significant by this general agreement. Two of them reveal his attitude to Northern Israel.

He made the king destroy the altars, asherim, graven images and sun-images throughout the land of Israel, but he omitted all mention of the destruction of the altar at Bethel. Josiah confined his purification

---

[1] In this case LXX[B] has retained the expression.

of the holy land to the removal of heathen altars and emblems. Again, when funds were needed for the temple-restoration, the men of Manasseh and Ephraim bore their share of the burden, II. xxxiv. 9. The people of the north had their part in the pious work, and their gifts were freely offered before they had been invited to join in the celebration of the common passover. The same reason may have prompted the historian to omit all mention of the desecration of the Bethel altar : he may have desired to suggest that Ephraim surrendered it in the interests of the united sanctuary at Jerusalem. It is not necessary to enter into any detail as to the arrangements made after the temple-restoration, because these resemble so closely the situation under Hezekiah. There is the same prominent place given to the levites and their functions. Attention has already been drawn to the unique feature of the account, the command issued to the levites to restore the ark to its old resting-place. Here it is only necessary to note the position which the command occupies immediately before the passover celebration. The temple was not fit to become what it had once been, the centre of worship for the reunited nation, until the old emblem had resumed its central place there.

The appearance of the levites here, as commissioned to carry back the ark to its place, is a uniform feature of the Chronicler's history. According to him, they alone were qualified to act as porters of the sacred emblem. Thus, when he told the story of the two efforts of David to transfer the ark to Jerusalem, he took the account of the initial failure with some curious additions from Kings, but, when he came to relate the successful effort, he added that the first failure had been due to the fact that the ark had not been entrusted to its proper attendants, the levites, I. xv. 2, 13. At the second attempt everything went happily, because the work was carried out ' according to the ordinance.' Again, when Solomon brought the ark from its tent into the temple, the Chronicler assigned the privilege of carrying it to the levites, II. v. 4 f., while in Kings the porters were the priests, I. Kings viii. 1-11. The same men, who in Chronicles are called levitical priests, but in Kings priests and levites, also transferred the sacred vessels which had been in use at the old tent.[1] It is a remarkable fact that, in the picture of conditions before Solomon built the temple, the levites never appear in any reference to the Gibeon sanctuary. From the account which appears in Chronicles, it would be possible to suppose that the priests served the altar before the tent of meeting there, while the levites devoted their whole service to the ark in its tent.

But the duties of the levites in relation to the ark were not confined to acting as its porters. By the express directions of David they were appointed to be its ministers, I. xvi. 4. In the verses which follow this ministry is made to consist mainly in rendering praise to God before it. The service, however, appears in a larger form in verse 37, where it is said that David left before the ark of the Covenant Asaph and

---

[1] It has already been noted that a later hand inserted at verse 4 the tent of meeting, and so gave rise to the mistaken idea that these vessels came from the tabernacle. The same reviser continued the account with the statement that the priests brought the ark " unto its place, into the oracle of the house, to the most holy place," v. 7. According to him, only the priests could enter there.

his brethren to minister before the ark continually,
' as each day's work required.' Now sacrifice attended
the ark, as soon as it had reached its tent in safety;
and that such sacrifices were habitual ' as each day's
work required,' and formed part of the levites' service
according to the Chronicler appears from a significant
alteration he made in his account of its transfer.
While the account in Samuel stated that at each six
paces of the journey David offered sacrifices, II. vi. 13,
in I. Chronicles xv. 26 the levites, whenever God
helped them in their task, offered those sacrifices.[1]
The mention also of sacred vessels along with the ark
at the time of its transference to the temple, cf. p. 201
supra, proves that the Chronicler did not conceive of
the levitical service in the tent having been confined
to chanting before it.

Reference has already been made to the summons
which Hezekiah issued to the priests and levites after
his purification of the temple and to the charge he
then addressed to the levites, II. xxix. 3 ff. The men
must remember that the Lord had chosen them to
stand before Him, to minister unto Him, serving
Him and מַקְטִירִים, v. 11. The language used there
practically puts the levites on an equal footing with
the priests. Thus, in the law it is the priests who
stand before the Lord and minister to Him: the

---

[1] A later hand, jealous of the prominence given to the levites,
has introduced here and there mention of the priests. That the
verses have been added can be recognised from the evidence of
one case. At xv. 11 f. the text makes David summon Zadok and
Abiathar the priests as well as the levites for the task of bringing
up the ark. But, when the king instructed these men in their
duties, he addressed them as the heads of the fathers' houses of
the levites. The Chronicler did not describe the two leading
priests in the temple by such a title. Further, Zadok's promotion
to be such a leading priest dated from the reign of Solomon.

levites stand before the priests or before the congregation and minister to them. Again, the final Hebrew participle may be translated, as in the R.V., by 'burning incense' or by the alternative 'sending up the sweet smoke of sacrifice'; in either case it describes a peculiarly priestly function according to the later law. After the dedication of the temple the men stood to bless the people, another privilege which was reserved to the sons of Aaron.[1]

Again, after the celebration of the passover, Hezekiah is said to have appointed the courses of the priests and levites for burnt-offerings and for peace-offerings, to minister and to give thanks and to praise, xxxi. 2. There is no hint here corresponding to the plain statement in the intruded verses, that the function of the one set of officials was to sacrifice, that of the others to praise. Instead, the account continues that, as their duties were parallel, so were their means of support. To meet the needs of their clergy, the children of Israel gave the first-fruits of the increase of the field, the children of Israel and

---

[1] The reviser could not pass such an evident neglect of the law. Into the paragraph which related how the levites fulfilled their task of cleansing the temple, xxix. 12-19, he inserted a sentence, v. 16, to explain that the priests cleansed the holy of holies and brought out its defilement to the levites. Only the priests could enter the inner shrine. But the connection is so bad that no more is needed to prove the sentence an interpolation. He revised more drastically the description of the sacrifices which were offered after the purification, vv. 20-36. There he made Hezekiah command the priests, the sons of Aaron, to carry out the ritual described in vv. 21-24. The sole functions left to the levites were the superintendence of the praise, vv. 25-27, 30, and the flaying of some of the sacrificial victims, but even this minor duty only fell to them because the priests were too few in number to overtake the task, v. 34. It needs no more than a comparison of the two passages to recognise that we have here to do with a correction of the original.

Judah brought the tithe of all, while those who lived in the Judean towns brought the tithe of oxen and sheep, vv. 4-6.[1] Evidently the Chronicler lived at a time when there was a diversity of practice which confined the tithe of oxen and sheep to Judah, and, from the fact that he made no effort to reconcile the divergence, it may be inferred that he lived before the law on the subject was made uniform. Evidently, also, he knew nothing of the final regulation which allotted one-tenth of the tithe to the priests and left the rest to the levites. Because the provision was more than sufficient, Hezekiah instituted chambers in which the surplus was stored, setting the levites in charge of them ; and he further appointed one of that body head of a commission, whose task it was to distribute the free-will offerings and the most holy things to the ' non-resident ' priests and levites, vv. 7-19. Again, the provision for the two orders is equal, and the supervision of it is committed to the levites. Finally, when Josiah bade the levites bring the ark into the temple before the celebration of passover, he ordered them now " to serve the Lord your God and His people Israel," II. xxxv. 3. From this time the men were to take up the larger duties which had been assigned to them in connection with the ark when the temple was built. Their duties are said to be " to stand in the holy place, to kill the passover, to sanctify themselves and to prepare for their brethren," vv. 4 ff. Since the passage ignores the priests, the brethren for whom this preparation was to be made could only have been Israel, the

[1] The division of the verses which appears in LXX has been followed.

people of God whom the levites according to verse 3 were to serve.

It has been possible to point out that the Chronicler's interest in the levitical order extended to more than its part in the choral service in the temple or to the subdivisions of its classes. It has also been possible to show that this interest appears most clearly wherever he touched on the restoration of the sanctuary to its original and ideal pattern, and wherever it was made the centre of worship for the united nation. What could not be included in the protracted survey was the relation between the attention he devoted to the levites and to the priests respectively. In comparison with the space he has given to the levitical order he has practically ignored the priestly. It would, however, be as great a mistake to make too much of his silence on the one subject as it has been to neglect the nature of his insistence on the other. He may have taken the position of the priests for granted, as though it did not need to be emphasised. What he did emphasise was that the ark with its attendant levites was an essential element in the temple-worship, if and when that was to be the centre for the religion of the united nation.

There is, however, one judgment which he passed on the priests at Jerusalem which must not be ignored. He told the story of the kingdom of Judah with the temple as the centre of his interest. He related how it suffered desecration at the hands of faithless kings who ought to have been its defenders, but had been restored by kings who had honoured it. Finally it was renewed by the last great king of the Davidic line, was made the common place of worship for the reunited nation, sanctified anew when the levites brought the ark back into it, and continued thus for a time. When it and the kingdom fell together, it was because Zedekiah humbled not himself before Jeremiah the prophet. He also rebelled against king Nebuchadrezzar who had made him swear by God. Moreover all the chiefs of the priests and the people trespassed very greatly after all the abominations of the heathen and polluted the house of the Lord which He had hallowed in Jerusalem, xxxvi. 12-14. That is a verdict which is remarkable, both in what it has stated and in what it has omitted. For Jeremiah, to whom the king did not listen, did not come from Judah, and the charge of apostacy is levelled first against the chiefs of the priests.

CHAPTER XII.

THE PRIESTS AND THE LEVITES.

THE Chronicler's conception of his nation, as that has disengaged itself from his history, may be briefly summed up. His ideal was an Israel which owed its existence to its religion, and which found its centre in the two institutions of the kingdom and the temple at Jerusalem. Both of these came into existence when the nation reached consciousness of its unity after the confusion of the conquest; but both ultimately derived from God who, having elected Israel, had revealed the institutions which were to guide its outward and inward life. The historian, therefore, invested the Davidic house with a certain Messianic dignity, but he devoted peculiar attention to the pious care which its best members had exercised over the sanctuary, and described with loving interest how, after every desecration the temple suffered, a true representative of the royal line brought it back to its position as the centre of the united nation, and restored it to its original pattern. In describing what that pattern had been, he ignored the form of the building and its furniture and devoted special attention to the place and functions of the clergy who conducted its worship. There he recognised two orders, the priests and the levites, but, as between the two, he dwelt more largely on the functions of the levites. In his view this order was essential to the temple-worship, because of the relation which it held to the ark. That sacred emblem had been the first object of David's care after his capture of Jerusalem, and the temple had been planned in order to take the place of the tent which had previously sheltered it. When Solomon had finished the sanctuary he brought the ark into it with the result that with its coming the glory of the Lord filled the house ; and, when Josiah restored the house, he brought the ark back there. The place of the levites in the sacred service was guaranteed through their relation to this sacred emblem. Not only were they alone competent to handle it, but, after David had brought it into his city, he appointed the levites to minister to it. Their ministry included functions which were afterwards reserved to the priests.

In certain broad outlines the Chronicler thus agreed with the attitude of those who reconstituted Judaism after the Exile. Like them, he believed that without its religion the nation had no future : like them also he believed that this religion demanded an institution which embodied and maintained it. He was a Palestinian Jew, writing at Jerusalem. Yet he took a singularly independent attitude, which sets him apart and which makes it impossible to identify him with the author of Ezra. The purpose of that writer was to describe the final restoration of the temple and of the worship there, and thus his work might appear to link on with the work of the Chronicler who had described the varying fate of those factors in the national life. But the author of Ezra reveals no interest in the three matters which peculiarly engaged the attention of the Chronicler—the Davidic kingdom, the ark and the status of the levites. The first two he simply ignored. As for the third, he considered that the returned exiles who in his view began and carried through the entire restoration were from the beginning guided by the priests of the Aaronic line. These men at once assumed their functions at an altar which they built and allotted to the levites certain functions which consisted merely in taking charge of the work about the temple and in the service of praise, Ezra iii. 8 ff. The Chronicler's history of the kingdom from David to Zedekiah, apart from the additions which it has received, is a literary unity, and his view of the temple and its personnel has no parallel.

The difficulty which at once arises is to determine its relation to the other documents which deal with the same subjects. As has been pointed out, the question of the college of priests which was to hold final authority over the new community and to issue torah could not fail to emerge in connection with the restoration of the temple, and could not wait for an answer. Also, when a matter of such vital significance in the life of the community was once raised, it could not be left in uncertainty. Now it is one of the foregone conclusions of modern criticism that the Chronicler and his work belong to a later date than the time of the temple-restoration. I confess to have found it extremely difficult to see clearly what scholars like Sellin, Kittel and Torrey mean by ' the Chronicler,' and may therefore misrepresent their opinions in saying that they appear to hold that, if he did not actually edit the book of Ezra, he wrote with full knowledge of the content of that book. If so, it becomes extraordinarily difficult to explain how, after the relative position of the clergy in the new temple was decided, we can account for a book which does not agree with that decision, but takes up an independent attitude. How, further, can we account for such a book having been admitted to the Canon or such a writer having been allowed to edit the book of Ezra, after the torah in Exodus had pronounced the settlement Mosaic? The only writer on the subject who has been quite consistent and logical in dealing with the matter has been Vogelstein.[1] Accepting the late date of the Chronicler and recognising his peculiar attitude toward the levites, he concluded that we may find there the proof of an effort on the part of the order to improve their status and to claim equality with the priests. Then he found in the story of Korah the account of their defeat. The value of the Rabbi's work consisted in the fact that it was the logical outcome of his initial premise as to the late date of the Chronicler, and that he unconsciously raised the doubt whether that premise was so certain as he believed.

Before entering, however, on the vexed question of the relative position of priest and levite, it may be well to look at the Chronicler's high estimate of the Davidic dynasty and see whether it connects with any similar view elsewhere and so suggests any conclusion on the writer's date. Here Von Rad, like

[1] Der Kampf zwischen Priestern und Leviten.

Vogelstein before him, calls attention to Isaiah lv. 3, with its reference to the sure mercies of David, the sureness of which involved the promise that God should raise up one who was to be a leader and commander to the nations. He would, therefore, connect the Chronicler with this late prophet. Yet the resemblance is very vague and very uncertain. Clearly Deutero-Isaiah was linking up the figure which he sketched with the divine promise to David, and was probably anticipating the advent of one who belonged to the royal line. It remains, however, far from clear whether the prophet associated this royal figure with the return from exile or with the greater event of the final consummation. The fact that he spoke of the one who was to come as the leader and commander of the nations agrees better with the reference to the consummation, since the promised one was not merely to be the head of a restored Israel. In that case the prophetic figure departs from the ideal Davidic king of the Chronicler, to whom the dynasty stood for the leadership of a united Israel. The prophetic figure did belong to the lineage of David, but he was to be the divine representative in a new order which God designed for the world. As such, he was beginning to escape from those limits of time to which the Chronicler confined his similar leader of Israel. What Deutero-Isaiah expected seems to be a later development rather than a parallel.

A much closer parallel can be found in one of the oracles of Haggai, delivered during the ferment of activity and emotion which attended the restoration of the temple under Zerubbabel, a descendant of the old Davidic line. The prophet declared that Yahweh was about to make the new governor a seal on His right hand, ii. 23. In itself the utterance held nothing very remarkable. What gave it significance was its direct reference to an earlier oracle of a different character. In Jeremiah xxii. 24-30 it had been declared that, although Jehoiachin were a signet on the right hand of Yahweh, he should " be torn thence, and hurled into exile ; neither he nor any of his seed should prosper, sitting upon the throne of David and ruling any more in Judah." Now, in the fact that a descendant of the very king on whom this doom had been pronounced was restored from exile and ruling in Jerusalem, Haggai saw the proof that the fate had been reversed. God had brought back the representative of the Davidic line, and given him something of the dignity of the founder of the dynasty. He had even brought back Zerubbabel at the very time when the temple which his forerunner had planned was being rebuilt. God had not failed to remember the covenant with David, what the Isaianic oracle called the sure mercies of David. The past was blotted out in connection with Zerubbabel as in connection with Joshua, and a new era of divine favour was beginning, so that the little community might confidently expect the divine furtherance, if they were faithful in setting their hand to the work which was begun under such auspices. In the same way, Zechariah declared that Zerubbabel should finish the temple building, as no other hand than his had laid the foundation-stone. For the house of the Lord owed its renewal not to might, nor to power, but to the divine spirit, iv. 4-9. The Chronicler had said that David's plan came ultimately from divine inspiration.

The time was one which was likely to give rise to such thoughts and hopes. Already under Josiah men had conceived the idea, had even for a brief period seen the realisation of a reunited Israel under a king of the Davidic line with the temple for its centre of worship. The dream had been shattered, for the royal line had gone into captivity and the temple had suffered a like ruin. But now God had wrought a marvellous change. When a descendant of David was holding power in Judah and rebuilding the temple, a greater future was beginning for Israel. So Haggai combined with both events a prophecy of the Messianic advent, ii. 6-9, and the Chronicler set a halo round the representative of David's house. But both the prophet and the historian made the descendant of David no more than the anointed of the Lord : neither actually proclaimed him Messiah.

It serves to confirm the impression of the ferment in the mind of the community, to notice that the men were evidently not all of one mind in their view of what the future might involve, or of the way in which the situation must be met. Thus the emphasis with which Zechariah insisted that no one except Zerubbabel was to found and to complete the sanctuary more than suggests the presence of another opinion on the subject. Again the text of a later oracle, vi. 9 ff., is notoriously uncertain, but the utterance gives evidence of a certain uneasiness about the relative authority of high-priest and secular ruler. A prophet does not sketch a condition in which there should be a counsel of peace between the two representatives of the nation, unless he was conscious that the situation was likely to give rise to difficulty, even had given rise to difficulty. Nor may we overlook in that connection the forecast of the future which appears in Ezekiel. Throughout the book the centre of the community's life was the temple, and the supreme authority was lodged in the high-priest. Room was certainly found for a secular prince, but he did not bear the title of king, and his Davidic connection was not much in evidence. He has become merely a נשיא or prince, and his functions are not so much set out as they are limited ; indeed so far subordinate are they that they chiefly consist in the duty of providing the means for the sacrifices. The lay authority existed to further the temple-worship. The conditions of the time will sufficiently account for such a difference of view. What men had to consider was whether Israel was to accept the measure of liberty granted by the Persian Empire, and to use it sanely in order to consolidate itself round its religious institutions, or whether it should cherish the dream of national independence under a king of its old line and lose the golden opportunity of creating a centre for its scattered and disheartened members. The men who urged the more cautious policy were naturally the men of the Return, and, in order to explain their attitude, there is no need to insist that they were led by priests who were jealous for the prestige of their order. In Babylonia the men had had the opportunity of gauging the power and of recognising the policy of the Empire. They could realise, as their fellows in Jerusalem could not, that the appointment of Zerubbabel was a mere accident of history and that there was no guarantee that the Jewish governor should not be succeeded

by a man of a totally different character. The best
Jewry could hope for was to have a ruler who would
continue Darius' policy and supply the offerings
which that king had ordered. So far as this side of
his interest was concerned, the Chronicler took his
place beside Haggai and Zechariah, the Jerusalem
prophets.

Reference has already been made to another
general view held by the Chronicler, but it is necessary
to revert to it, because it has something to contribute
on the date of his book. While he derived the תבנית
or plan of the temple ultimately from divine authority,
he recognised that the unity of the nation must have
preceded a central shrine. So he connected the
sanctuary with the kingdom. He further linked it
to the national past by making it a surrogate for the
tent over Israel's famous palladium. David's prosperity through his successful wars made him able
to collect the needed materials, and his friendship
with Tyre provided their source and enabled his son
to secure skilled workmen. Divine though it was
in its ultimate source, the temple took its origin at
a particular stage in Israel's history, when it was
peculiarly serviceable to the people.

A very different view of the origin alike of the nation
and of its sanctuary appears in the record of events
at and after Sinai in the book of Exodus. There
Israel was a nation long before the kingdom made
it one, and, as it did not need to wait until it had
reached Palestine before attaining its unity, so it
did not need to wait for its centre of worship until
David's reign. The תבנית or plan of the tabernacle
was revealed to Moses and delivered by him to Aaron

P

the high-priest, Exod. xxv. 9, 40. The costly materials which went to its construction did not come from such a tainted source as war, far less from a heathen king : they were the free gifts of the devout people, xxv. 1-8. The workmen who carried out the divine plan were no uncircumcised foreigners : they were members of the holy community who were directly endowed by God with skill to carry out their task, xxxi. 1-11. As for the ark, it was certainly present in the tabernacle, but it held no higher place there than some of the other equally necessary vessels : it forms an item in a list which contains the table for the bread of the presence, the altar of incense and the golden candlestick, xxxi. 7-11, Num. iv. 4-12. On the day when the tabernacle was set up, not that on which the ark was brought into the temple, the cloud of the divine glory revealed itself, Num. ix. 15. The central and constant feature in the tent of meeting was the altar, and therefore the narrator made Moses command one which was portable, though this offended against the law in the Book of the Covenant, which forbade the use of any tool on an Israelite altar.

It is unnecessary to dwell on the difficulties which arise when we attempt to take this account literally, difficulties as to the source from which the fugitives so soon after the Exodus derived the costly materials, and as to how they carried the unwieldy structure during their wandering life. These have long served to prove that the record belongs to the world of religious theory, not to that of sober history. But two conclusions seem clear as soon as it is set alongside what the Chronicler had to say about the origin of united Israel and its temple. On the one hand, it departs much more widely from the basis of history than even the Chronicler, who was no precisian in these matters, has ventured to do. On the other hand, the theory of the origin of the central sanctuary is in direct disagreement with that of the Chronicler. Both in their conception of history and in their religious theory the two views differ so radically that one of them cannot have been intended to supplement the other. They are rivals. Further, the account in Exodus is homogeneous and has received no addition or correction other than in details, while that of the Chronicler has been supplemented by introducing the tabernacle at Gibeon with its altar of burnt-offering and by the assumption that the temple took the place of the Mosaic tent of meeting. Now, since the record in Exodus contains the authoritative and final judgment on the subject which came to prevail in Judaism, the obvious explanation of the situation is that the Chronicler wrote before the matter was decided. If he wrote later, he must have been protesting against the accepted view, and it becomes difficult to explain why his protest was preserved and why men took the trouble to supplement it.

It is then legitimate to suppose that the Chronicler wrote before the final torah on the arrangements at the second temple was issued. The recognition of this possibility is important in connection with his attitude to the levitical order, and here it is valuable to note again how peculiar is his estimate of it. The men appear more than once in his record as teachers of the people, and in one case are said to have exercised the gift of prophecy. They had to determine controversies, and to undertake important tasks of administration which concerned, not only the temple, but secular affairs. Certain kings are said to have appointed commissions to carry out their schemes. Some of these are entirely assigned to levites, and those are generally concerned with matters in connection with the temple. In other cases, levites, priests and laymen form the commission, and then the levites are always more numerous than the priests and are mentioned first. Inside the temple, especially in relation to the sacrifices, their specific functions are less clearly defined. But in a number of passages they appear alongside the priests on an equal footing, since no distinction is made between the respective duties of the two classes, and in one passage they have an equal claim with the priests on the gifts of the people. The equality appears most clearly in the general terms which are employed about the order. They stand before the Lord, they serve His people ; and especially they minister before the ark. Since the ark was essential in the temple, their presence was equally essential in the worship. In fulfilling their service at the ark, they did more than act as porters, for they offered sacrifice before it and afterwards blessed the people.

This view of the functions assigned to the levites must be compared, first with the legislation on the subject in Exodus and Numbers, then with a sketch of the arrangements in the future temple which appears in the book of Ezekiel.

In the legislation the levites exercise no independent functions. They do not stand before the Lord nor serve His people, since they are the substitutes for the first-born of Israel, who are set apart to serve the priests. The priests, on the other hand, derive their authority from their hereditary descent from Aaron, the high-priest since the period at Sinai. Holding such authority and forming a close corporation, these officials control the entire ritual of the sanctuary, and decide on every controversy. The lower officials could not compose a commission capable of determining any question which trenched on the law, and there is no hint that the levites were trusted to teach that law to Israel. The claims of the two bodies of officials on the temple revenues are defined, but the claims admit of no equality, and the emphasis is always laid upon the portion allotted to the priests. The only place where the levites may intromit with these revenues is in the collection of the tithes, but the first charge on these is the tenth which they must hand over to the priests.

The greatest care, moreover, is taken to shut out the levites from the right to exercise any function in direct connection with the leading sacrificial acts. Here the legislators were not content to define the relative positions of priest and levite, for they fortified their law on the question by deriving it from the express decision of Moses. They took an old account which related the rebellion of certain Reubenites against the authority of the law-giver, and transformed it into the record of a levitical rebellion against the privileges of the sons of Aaron. There the decision was given once for all on the relative positions of the two classes of clergy, since in the fearful fate which overtook the sons of Korah, Yahweh had determined " who were His and whom He would choose to bring near unto Him." Yet the fulness of detail with which the incident is related and the insistence on the finality of the decision serve to prove that there had at one time been debate on the question which was involved.

Again, as the higher status which the Chronicler gave the levites was closely related to the value he set upon the ark, so the lower dignity allotted to them in the legislation is paralleled by its attitude to that historic emblem. The ark has sunk into being no more than one of the vessels of the sanctuary, and, while the levites continue to carry it, they merely carry it as they do the tabernacle itself with all its furniture in fulfilment of their general task of taking down and re-erecting the sanctuary at each successive halting-place. In carrying out this task they dared not touch ark or shewbread-table, candlestick, golden altar or altar of burnt-offering until the priests had covered these with wrappings, Num. iv. 1-15, for, if the sons of Kohath should touch the sacred things themselves, they must die. The peculiar privilege of the levites in handling and carrying the ark has disappeared along with the peculiar sanctity of the ark itself. Again, in the wilderness journeys what had determined, according to the earlier account, the successive marches, the route and the new camping ground, had been the ark : according to Numbers ix. 15-23, it was the cloud which covered the tabernacle.

In a different connection I have pointed out that a similar attitude to ark and levites appears in two passages in the book of Deuteronomy, which on independent grounds can be proved to be late additions to the text.[1] One of these passages makes Moses issue a command that the Code of Deuteronomy, instead of being read in the hearing of the people every seventh year, was to be laid up beside the ark. There it was to serve as a testimony against the obstinate sinfulness of the nation and of their religious guides, the levites. The other passage states that the ark, instead of remaining an object of reverence in and for itself, was to become a mere box which contained the torah.[2] In the same way the later legislation ordained that the ark should become the support for the כפרת or mercy-seat, Exod. xxv. 17, 21 ; xxvi. 34, xl. 20, and that Aaron once a year, on the day of Atonement, should touch it with sacrificial blood. In Deuteronomy the ark has become a receptacle for the torah, in Exodus it has become the support for the altar-ritual : in both it has lost independent value.

There is, however, in Ezekiel, chapter xliv., a sketch of the service in the temple which develops a third view of the relative duties and position of the two bodies of clergy. According to this, the descendants of Zadok, who are called the levitical priests and who are said to have kept the charge of the sanctuary

[1] Cf. ' Deuteronomy : the Framework to the Code,' pp. 62 ff.
[2] In furtherance of the same purpose it is carefully stated in connection with the transference of the ark from David's tent to Solomon's temple that it contained nothing " except the two tables of stone which Moses put there at Horeb when the Lord made a covenant with the children of Israel," I. Kings viii. 9, II. Chron. v. 10. That the verse is an intrusion is evident, not merely from its want of connection with its surroundings, but from the fact that, both in David's tent and in Solomon's temple, levites were left to minister before the ark continually. Now, according to the later legislation, the levites were not even permitted to enter the inner sanctuary in which the ark stood.

when Israel went astray, receive the privilege of being the only priests at the altar, vv. 15 f., and they are also empowered to be the final authority in all questions of ceremonial purity and to judge in any controversy concerning the divine law, vv. 23 f. On the other hand, it allocates to the levites the inferior tasks in the service of the sanctuary, where they stand before the people to minister to them, v. 11, cf. Num. xvi. 9. Their highest duty is that they were permitted to slay the burnt-offering and the sacrifice for the people. In the broad distinction thus made between priest and levite this sketch agrees with the law, but the divergence of the two is equally marked. The first difference appears in the men who are to constitute the priestly college : in Ezekiel these were the sons of Zadok, in the law the descendants of Aaron, and in this respect the later practice conformed to the law. But a more remarkable difference appears in the attitude taken by legislator and prophet to the levites. In the law these men were the representatives of the nation, who had never exercised any of the peculiarly priestly functions at the tabernacle. Only it became necessary to emphasise the distinction between the two orders, because according to the story in Numbers, a sept of the levites claimed equality with the higher clergy. The resultant decision carried with it no degradation of the order, since the whole order had not been involved in the ambitious and novel claim ; the penalty fell on the guilty sept who thus bore their iniquity and were wiped out. On the other hand, in Ezekiel, the whole order was involved in a common sin—" they went far from Me," and it consequently suffered a common penalty

—" they shall bear their iniquity " and " they shall bear their shame and their abominations which they have committed." That penalty consisted in their degradation to fulfil tasks about the temple which had hitherto been carried out by uncircumcised aliens. The position which Ezekiel thus allotted to the levites must have been a novelty, for the men must have been fulfilling higher duties about the temple before the tasks which he committed to them could be reckoned a penalty for their iniquity.

There are three elements in the prophetic proposal which make it clear that he was dealing with an actual, a historical situation. When he referred to the presence of uncircumcised foreigners in the temple, he could not have meant to condemn a practice which belonged to the past and which had long disappeared. The mere fact that he proposed to put the levites in place of these foreigners is enough to prove that he was protesting against an existing feature in the temple-ritual which was offensive to him and to others. Again, his relegation of the levites to such offices, which was deliberately intended to punish the men for some misconduct in the tasks which they had hitherto fulfilled, shows that he was face to face with a concrete situation and was not merely theorising. Finally, his unexampled demand that the priestly duties shall be confined to the sons of Zadok—*i.e.*, to the family which had controlled the temple-worship since the reign of Solomon, bears the same character of having to do with the realities of a particular time. The only period to which I find it possible to refer such a series of concrete and definite arrangements is the time of the restoration of the temple, when it became necessary to bring order into the inchoate conditions which had hitherto prevailed at Jerusalem and especially to determine as to the men who were to hold control in the new temple, or, as Ezekiel expressed it, to judge in any controversy concerning the divine law.

Now, as between Ezekiel and the torah in Exodus and Numbers, the relations of the two are not hard to determine. The prophetic scheme represents the demand of some of the priests who returned from exile and of their adherents. To them the presence of uncircumcised aliens about the temple was peculiarly offensive, since it meant the return of an abuse which had been removed by their predecessors. To them also it was entirely natural that the supreme control of the sacrificial worship should be lodged in the hands of the men who had exercised it since the reign of the king who built the temple. As for the levites, who held some higher duties about the temple, they must be expelled from these as an order and at the utmost permitted to occupy the humble offices which had been held by the uncircumcised. Ezekiel represents the extreme conservative and reactionary element among the men of the Return, whose desire it was to see the old order of things restored.

In the torah we find a sane compromise. The wiser leaders of the community refused to ignore the claims of the Judean priests, whether these were priests at the old high-places or subordinate officials at the temple, who had maintained the altar-fire after the old ritual during the exile. They admitted these men into the priestly college, enacting that the final control should be lodged in the house of Aaron, not in the family of

Zadok. Nor is it necessary to suppose that the motive which governed this act was the desire to win over a party in Jerusalem which would have been antagonised by the other scheme. The men may have recognised the service which their brother-priests had rendered to the common cause by their loyalty to the altar and its worship, and may have further recognised that they had followed there the old Jerusalem ritual. The two bodies of clergy had a common 'use,' which they should follow in the restored temple. That the men were seeking a worthy compromise is proved by their conduct with regard to the levites. While they refused these men admission to the priestly college, they equally refused to put any stigma upon them as an order. At the utmost they condemned a party among them who claimed the higher dignity and rejected the final decision. But the order, as order, bore no iniquity and was not relegated to offices which had hitherto been performed by uncircumcised aliens. They were a special class in the community who represented the first-born in Israel and who therefore possessed a peculiar holiness as dedicated to the Lord. While, therefore, they were shut out from the highest position, they held an honoured status in relation to the worship of the nation.

But, if the matter of the priesthood is thus recognised to concern the relations between the exilic and the Judean priests, this raises acutely the question of the levites. Who formed this third body of clergy, what was their origin, and whence did they derive their claim to serve at the altar, a claim which the Ezekiel programme and the law rejected ? Now the writer in Ezekiel based his demand for the degradation of the order on the conduct of the men in their office, not on their descent or genealogy. They had, he stated, been involved in, had even been the leaders in, a national sin which amounted to apostasy.[1] There is here a definite polemic against the levitical order, but the terms of the polemic make it impossible to see in these men the priests at the Judean high-places. For the levites are accused of having taken a leading part in some national sin, so that, if the sin had been committed by Judah, the Zadokite priesthood must have been equally involved in it. The only men who will satisfy the conditions in the passage were the priests of Northern Israel, who had shared in the national guilt of the calf-worship. Then a curious feature in the chapter receives a natural interpretation. Its author stated that " the levitical priests were the descendants of Zadok." He was using the term peculiar to the Deuteronomic Code, where the phrase ' levitical priest ' is employed in the sense of legitimate priest as opposed to the untrained hedge-priests who were not descended from Levi.[2] A similar

---

[1] Kennett, in an article in the J.T.S., 1905, pp. 161-186, put his finger on these cardinal features of the Ezekiel indictment, and recognised that they demanded an explanation. Since he believed that the early chapters of Ezekiel which described the idolatrous practices in the temple were by the same man as the author of chapter xliv., he saw clearly that the levites could not have been the priests of the Judean bamoth. For if the men were to be deposed because their worship at the high-places had been idolatrous, the Zadokite priesthood at the temple, whose conduct had been worse, ought to have received the same condemnation. He further pointed out that in the generation after the Return the distinction between the two orders was entirely one of their genealogy. The questions Kennett posited are relevant, though his solution fails to carry conviction.

[2] Cf. my ' Code of Deuteronomy,' pp. 89 ff.

charge against the order appears in Deuteronomy xxxi.
24 ff., where Moses is made to command its members
to lay up their law where it might serve as a witness
against them, " for I know thy rebellion and thy
stiff neck : behold, while I am yet alive with you this
day, ye have been rebellious against the Lord, and how
much more after my death." [1] We then understand
at once why the Chronicler deliberately exonerated
the levites from any share in Jeroboam's sin, wherewith he made Israel to sin, and declared that, on the
introduction of this national apostasy, they transferred
themselves to Judah.

The situation to which the Chronicler and the author
of the chapter in Ezekiel addressed themselves was
that which faced the community in Jerusalem, as
soon as they had resolved to restore the temple. It
was essential to the new institution that it should
be under the control of some final authority which
should determine its cult and administer the law of
that cult in its relation to the faithful. It was no less
essential to have such an authority which might
speak and act in name of the faithful to the Persian
governors. The pact of Nehemiah, chapter x., under
which the local community was living, had been
framed to meet a wholly different set of conditions
and failed to supply any such ultimate authority.
The time demanded an instant settlement of the
question. On the one hand, the interference of
Tattenai had shown how vital it was to have some
central representative of the community in its relation
to the Empire ; on the other, the return of some

---

[1] Cf. my ' Deuteronomy : the Framework to the Code,' p. 63,
where on independent grounds the late date of the passage is proved.

of the exiles had brought to light that Jerusalem was the centre of a Jewry which stretched beyond Palestine.

In the extract from a prophet's oracles, in a book of history and in the torah we are able to recognise three different proposals for meeting this situation. The author of the Ezekiel programme was a conservative, whose one interest was the restoration of the past. The only priests who were fit to officiate and rule in the new temple were the descendants of Zadok who preserved the ancient traditions. As for the levites, who belonged to the rebel kingdom and the apostate nation, they must be publicly degraded from the place they had usurped. His ideal was a temple in Jerusalem, restored by a governor of the Davidic line and served by a Judean priesthood according to a Judean use. Over against this stands the Chronicler with his conception of the temple as the centre of worship for a united Israel. All Israel had united to build it under Solomon and to restore it under Josiah : all Israel should unite to rebuild it and to worship there. Therefore the levites from Israel should have an equal place with the Judean priesthood : their place in the cult was even essential to its validity, since they alone could serve the ark, that sacred symbol of Ephraim for the sake of which the temple had come into existence. Last of all came the law in Exodus, and that this was meant to be the final decision of the question at issue appears from one significant feature. All these schemes laid claim to a certain divine authority. The proposal in Ezekiel is set among the oracles of the great prophet of the exile, and could be proposed as more than a mere human plan. The Chronicler appealed in support of his position to the great name of David and to the belief that the king had received his plan of the temple through divine revelation. The legislators set their decision under the authority of Moses, and by thus carrying it back to the founder of the faith, declared that this was henceforth torah in Israel. Such a decree in Jerusalem was the equivalent of a later dictum in Christendom : causa finita, Roma locuta est.

The final decision, like all similar ecclesiastical decisions, was a compromise, but it was one which was ably and generously framed. On the one hand, it refused to limit the college of priests to the family of Zadok, and, by widening it into all the descendants of Aaron, made room there for the priests from the Judean community. It equally refused to acknowledge the equality of the levites, but, while it denied the men all access to the altar and the place in the sacred college which would have given them power to determine torah, it gave them an honoured place in the temple-service which involved no stigma on them as an order. The law occupied a middle position between Ezekiel and the Chronicler. It is even possible to recognise the principle which guided the legislators in the decision at which they arrived. What they had at heart was the creation of a uniform ritual at the temple with the corollary of a uniform guidance for all Jews who looked to Jerusalem and its cult as the centre for their life. If such a uniform ritual and observance were to be maintained, the decision of their terms must be lodged in the hands of men who had a common mind on these matters. To include in the sacred college the Judean priests who had served at the altar during the exile involved no risk of any breach with the past and brought no discordant element into the decision of questions as to Israel's practice. But the legislators hesitated to admit to authority at a critical time men who under the terms of the pact had been following the ritual of their own law. Yet they went no further, and especially they rejected the scheme of Ezekiel by which the levites were to be branded as an order for the sins of their fathers.[1] Where they felt it necessary to go further was in connection with the dangerous claims which the Chronicler had made for the levites on the ground of their peculiar relation to the ark. Attention has already been drawn to the way in which that ancient emblem of Ephraim was steadily thrust into the background in the law. It only remains to add that a late addition was made to the oracles of Jeremiah, which ran : when in these days you increase greatly in the land, men shall cease to say " the ark of the covenant of the Lord," it shall not come into their mind, or be remembered, or be sought after, or re-made. In that day men shall give the name throne of the Lord to Jerusalem, and all nations shall gather together for the sake of the Lord and shall follow

---

[1] It is possible that the story of Korah's rebellion perpetuates the memory of an incident belonging to this period. While the majority of the levites may have accepted the position assigned to them by the torah, some of them may have resisted and demanded full equality, with the result that they were expelled from the temple. Such men with the rankling sense of a grievance would be likely to become the leaders in the later breach between Samaria and Jerusalem. The importance in its earlier years of the Samaritan community makes it certain that the schism must have been due to deeper reasons than those which Josephus has supplied. But our ignorance of the later history of Palestine makes it impossible to call this more than a suggestion.

no longer their own stubborn and evil thoughts,
Jer. iii. 16 f. The disappearance of the ark in the
second temple was due to no accident.

ADDITIONAL NOTES.

I. THE DATE OF THE CHRONICLER.

To derive the Chronicler's history of the kingdom from so early
a date as the time of Darius will be apt to appear a mere eccentricity
to all who have grown accustomed to regard it as one of the latest
books in the Canon. It may lessen the shock to recognise that
even scholars who accept the unity of Chronicles and Ezra have
begun to question the reasons which led to a confident assertion
of its late date. Thus it could once be asserted that the fact of
Cyrus, Darius and other rulers being called kings of Persia was
enough to prove that the historian must have lived under a later
Empire than that of Persia. If he had been living in the Persian
period, it would have been enough to call the ruler king. In the
official communications from and to the Persian court, which are
incorporated into the book of Ezra, it was the consistent practice
to write about ' the king ' or ' the king of kings ' without any
closer definition, cf. Ezra v. 6, vi. 1-3, iv. 8, 11, vii. 11 f. Only in
the main work of the Chronicler was reference made to a king of
Persia. But it has been pointed out that the matter admits of a
ready explanation, which cannot or need not imply a later date.
In the one case we have to do with a longer history which covers
the whole period of the kingdom, and in which the author had
occasion to refer to kings of Judah and Israel, kings of Aram,
Moab and Tyre as well as to rulers of the greater Empires of Assyria
and Babylonia, cf. II. Chronicles xxxii. 1, xxxv. 20, xxxvi. 4, 6, 17 ;
Ezra ii. 1. It was accordingly natural that, as soon as he reached
the period of the Persians, he should have written of the kings of
Persia, II. Chron. xxxvi. 22 ; Ezra i. 1, iv. 5, 24, vi. 14, vii. 1, ix. 9 ;
Neh. xii. 22. The objection would have had force had we been
dealing with a contemporary pamphlet : it has no force in connection with a longer history. To one who cannot accept the unity
of Chronicles and Ezra its value is nil.

Another proof of the late date of the Chronicler was found in the
list of the descendants of Zerubbabel in I. Chronicles iii. 19-24.
This list professed to give eleven generations after Zerubbabel,
which implied that it must have been compiled much later than
the fourth century. But Rothstein has shown good cause for
questioning the text in verse 21, and for his contention that the

original genealogy contained only four names. The discovery also of the papyri at Elephantine has rendered it probable that the Anani mentioned in verse 24 is identical with the head of a council of elders who appears in Papyrus I.—*i.e.*, in 407. To one who cannot count the opening chapters of I. Chronicles an integral part of the book this argument also had no validity.

Finally, appeal used to be taken to the list of high-priests in Nehemiah xii. 10 f. 22. The Jaddua mentioned there was, on the authority of Josephus, dated in the reign of Darius Codomannus, *circa* 330. Now, however, it would appear to be more probable that he must be identified with the son of one Johanan, who is mentioned in the same Papyrus, so that Jaddua will have been the high-priest who held office *circa* 400.[1]

Even those, therefore, who hold to the original unity of the complete Books of Chronicles and Ezra have seen or are seeing cause to hesitate in the confident assertion as to the date of ' the Chronicler.'

II. Von Rad's View of Chronicles.

In connection with the attitude of the Chronicler, it was the merit of Vogelstein's contribution [2] that he recognised the divergence between the historian and the legislator on the subject of the levites to be so deep as to demand some explanation. Since, however, he was a convinced follower of Wellhausen, he took for granted that the torah was enacted at the time of the Return by Ezra, and that Chronicles must be later than this Priestly Code. In his view, the story of the revolt of Korah represented an earlier effort of the levites, after the promulgation of Ezra's law, to claim absolute equality with the priesthood on the crucial question of the right to sacrifice. This was defeated, with the result that for a time the levites were admitted only to menial duties about the temple. The books of Chronicles record a modest and successful attempt of the men to win a better status through emphasising their functions in connection with the sacred song.

Von Rad follows a similar line of approach, but has a much clearer recognition of the peculiar character of the Chronicler's history. Thus he has noted how often the historian is in close agreement with, even shows dependence on, Deuteronomy, while, on the other hand, his positions frequently diverge from, and even conflict with, those in the so-called Priestly Code. He has further noted that Chronicles is not homogeneous, but reveals another strand which closely corresponds with the later law. He has accordingly concluded to two strata in the history, but, since he

---

[1] On the question cf. Sellin, ' Geschichte,' II. p. 172, and Oesterley, ' History of Israel,' II., p. 163.

[2] Der Kampf zwischen Priestern und Leviten.

also accepts the view of its late date, he must count the stratum which diverges from the law and shows dependence on Deuteronomy the later of the two. According to him, the earlier edition of the history, which agreed with the law, was revised chiefly in the interest of the levites. Like Vogelstein, Von Rad sees in this revision evidence for a Vordringen or effort on the part of the levites in the direction of claiming, if not equality with the priesthood, at least a position higher than that which had been assigned to them.

The suggestion—it cannot be called a proof—that Chronicles contains a double strand, and that one of these is Deuteronomic in character, while the other agrees with the later law, and, I would add, with the book of Ezra, represents what has been forced upon me by this study. To establish it, however, demands a critical examination of the book from this point of view, and it has been impossible to include that here. So far as the purely critical evidence is concerned, I have needed to be content with the few illustrations which have been referred to in an earlier chapter, and especially must mark that in connection with all these the mention of the priests has patently been intruded into a narrative which dwelt on the privileges and position of the levites. But on the general question as to which of these strata represents the original Chronicler and which is the later revision, certain statements can be ventured. Thus, on the assumption that equality between priest and levite was the characteristic of the original Chronicler, his constant association of the levites with the ark, his view that the temple was the surrogate of the tent which contained the ark, his statement that when Josiah restored the temple he brought back the ark and gave the levites charge of the emblem with the right to sacrifice and to bless the people, his care to exonerate the levites from any share in the calf-worship—all these leading features in the history form a unity, for they offer the reasons on which its author based the claim to equality between priest and levite.

If, on the other hand, these belong to the later revision, it becomes necessary to find a time when the reverence due to the ark and the connection of the levites with the calf-worship were still living issues. So closely, again, are these features woven into the substance of the history and so much do they dominate the whole, that when they are removed and relegated to a later editor, they reduce the original to a mere torso. Indeed it would be no exaggeration to say that, when it is so treated, the Chronicler's history becomes a series of fragments. Besides Von Rad's theory of the relation between the two recensions makes it extremely difficult to understand why the Chronicler's work was retained in the sacred literature. That view requires us to suppose that the levites revised in the interests of their order an original history of kingdom and temple which had conformed with the regulations of the Mosaic law. They linked their conception of the status of the levites to a judgment on the ark as an essential feature of the temple worship, and they declared that David and Josiah, the two kings most honoured for their reverence for the temple, had not conformed to the law. Yet the Aaronic priesthood not only permitted this revision, but included the revised book among the sacred literature, though it traversed the actual law which governed the relations between priest and levite. On the other hand, the idea that the later men used the Chronicler's work after they had retouched it with notes which brought some of its discordant material into agreement with the later law is not only more credible in itself, but shows an analogy to what has been done in other cases. It is not necessary to look further than the Ezekiel chapter in order to find an illustration. So long as the law was not called in question, its guardians showed a singular tolerance of records which revealed how the law came to be regulative in the community.

The chief defects in Von Rad's scheme are two. He has ignored the place of the Ezekiel passage, for which Vogelstein attempted to account. He has also failed to notice the emphasis which the Chronicler laid on the ark and the way in which the law relegated it to the background. Now, if this high estimate of the ark belongs to the later stratum of the history, it becomes extremely difficult to explain why it was introduced in view of the neglect of the emblem by the law and of its acknowledged absence from the second temple. Von Rad's able book is another proof of the extent to which O.T. study is hampered by the inability of modern scholars even to call in question certain dogmas of the regnant hypothesis.

CHAPTER XIII.

THE WORK OF EZRA.

In any attempt to estimate the work of Ezra it is essential to recognise that the material on which such an estimate can be based is not homogeneous. Three documents can be readily recognised. One is the copy of an imperial rescript issued by king Artaxerxes in favour of Ezra, in which very large powers are conferred on that " scribe of the words of the commandments of the Lord and of His statutes to Israel." The second purports to be an extract from the memoirs of Ezra himself, dealing with his experiences on the way to, and after his arrival in, Jerusalem. These two documents have been combined by an editor, who added an introduction at vii. 1-11, a supplementary note at viii. 35, 36, and a conclusion in chapter x. This editor dealt somewhat differently with his two original documents. The imperial rescript he seems to have copied in its entirety, but, from the abruptness with which the extract from the memoirs begins and ends at vii. 27 and ix. 15, it is plain that he only included part of his original, and it is natural to conclude that he selected what he judged to be suitable to his purpose. At least it is certain that the memoirs contained more at the beginning, and probable that they also did not end where they now do. Yet this extract, since it is clearly more original than the narrative in which it appears, must be the starting-point for any estimate of Ezra.

According to the memoirs, Ezra was the leader of a body of returned exiles, which amounted to 1514 males, but which received an addition of 262 levites and nethinim, who joined the caravan at the leader's special request. If the editor's date in viii. 1 may be relied on, the event took place during the reign of Artaxerxes.[1] Certainly the men were acting with the full knowledge and approval of a Persian king, for Ezra began with a thanksgiving to God who had put it into the royal heart to beautify the temple and to show him favour in his enterprise, and continued that the king had even offered the protection of a body of troops on the long and dangerous journey. The danger was the greater, because the men were bringing with them gifts, both from the royal treasury and from Jews who elected to remain in Babylon. So far as the danger of these sacred offerings falling into the hands of robbers was concerned, the leader was prepared to commit them to the care of God, but he was very sensitive to another danger to which he might be exposed in connection with them. He evidently felt it possible that he might be charged with malversation of his trust, for, immediately after a list of those who made up the caravan, he stated

---

[1] We possess no data which might lead us to trust or distrust the date. But, since the editor is probably the same man who pre-dated the arrival of Zerubbabel's caravan, the statement in the text must stand.

that he selected a small number of responsible persons to whom he entrusted them. Since the gifts were intended for the use of the temple, the men he chose were all priests. This part of the memoir is closed by the statement that these priests delivered the precious articles into the charge of the temple authorities. The conclusion reads like the report of one who was anxious to prove that he had fulfilled his commission with strict fidelity. This brief introduction is followed by the story of certain events connected with the arrival of the newcomers, c. ix. Evidently some time must have elapsed since Ezra's return, for the men had had time to settle down. The chapter relates that the ' princes ' in the Jerusalem community came to the leader and reported that " the people of Israel and the priests and the levites had been contracting marriages with women from the peoples of the lands." Ezra was horrified at the news, and sat in silence with every sign of grief until the hour of the evening sacrifice, when he prostrated himself before God and uttered a prayer for pardon because of this heavy sin. There, with the same abruptness with which it began, the extract from the memoirs breaks off.

There is one question in connection with this incident on which it is necessary to be clear before going further. Dr Oesterley is of opinion that the leading men in Jerusalem turned to Ezra for help in dealing with the mixed marriages, because the exiles in Babylonia had developed a stronger sense of the necessity for segregation from the heathen than the community in Palestine.[1] This implies that the inter-marriage of which those leaders complained

[1] Cf. ' History of Israel,' II., pp. 133 f.

was prevalent among, was even confined to, the local community for which they were responsible. But this was not the case, for it is said that, when Ezra sat down astonied, there gathered to him all who trembled at the word of the Lord because of the trespass of them of the captivity. That gives the impression that the transgression was peculiar to the returned exiles, and that the leaders of the Jerusalem community were drawing Ezra's attention to a laxity among the newcomers for whom he was responsible. The prayer which Ezra offered bears out this impression, for in it he dwelt on the recent proof of the divine mercy which the men had enjoyed and on the unworthy response they were making to this favour. Obviously, such language could only be used about newcomers to the holy city, not about men who had resided there since the time of Darius, far less about those who had never been exiles. The laxity in this matter was also one into which the members of Ezra's caravan were more liable to fall, because his following, as the list shows, consisted mostly, if not entirely, of males. Further, a comparison between the prayer of Ezra and the complaint of the Jerusalem authorities serves to confirm this view of the situation. In his prayer Ezra referred to a law on the subject : now therefore give not your daughters unto their sons, neither take their daughters unto your sons, v. 12. In their complaint the Jerusalem princes said nothing about giving Jewish girls in marriage to foreigners, but confined themselves to the actual facts of the situation, that the men had taken heathen women to themselves and to their sons, v. 2. The recognition of this discrepancy brings out another weakness in

Dr Oesterley's position. He has taken for granted that the exiles in Babylonia had become conscious of the need to avoid absorption into heathenism, but he has brought no evidence to prove that they had taken measures against the danger. On the other hand, there is a good deal of evidence that, both in Samaria and in Judah, the religious leaders had not only recognised the danger, but had taken the necessary means to avoid it.[1] It cannot even be proved that there existed in the scattered colonies of exiles in Babylonia a central authority which could have promulgated such a law as that to which Ezra referred in his prayer.

In his memoir Ezra has not indicated either his authority for his acts or his status in the community. That he was the leader of the caravan is evident, for he decided the question of accepting an escort from the king, determined the date of departure, issued directions about procuring the levites, and took entire responsibility for securing the safety of the sacred gifts. After he reached Jerusalem, however, he claimed no authority and exercised none. Since he himself has stated that the scandal of the mixed marriages was a transgression of the returned exiles, it is legitimate to conclude that the local leaders turned to him, because he was recognised to have influence over these newcomers. But, when he took action in the matter, the only means which he employed was moral suasion. From his own account it cannot even be concluded with certainty that he was a priest. It is at least a remarkable fact that he did not form one of the body of priests who took charge

[1] Cf. pp. 24, 34, 74, *supra.*

of the temple gifts. Yet the omission of his own name from this committee may only be another evidence of his scrupulous care to prove his personal honour in the transaction.

These two extracts from the memoirs have been fitted with an introduction and a conclusion. At the end has been added a narrative which related the result of the complaint to Ezra on the part of the Jerusalem leaders. The community were roused to take action : and the action which they took confirms the conclusion that the mixed marriages were only prevalent among the returned exiles. For the men issued a proclamation, not to the Judeans, but to all the children of the captivity, x. 7, which required them to come to Jerusalem, with a warning that any who failed to do so should suffer excommunication. When the men came up in obedience to this order, a committee of responsible leaders was appointed to inquire into the facts and to report. The matter was investigated with care, since three months were spent in collecting evidence. The report bore that the guilty persons comprised seventeen priests, six levites, one singer, three porters and eighty-six laymen. In view of the conditions which prevailed in Judah at the period, the outstanding feature of the report is that the number of men who had contracted such marriages was so small. This is especially remarkable from the point of view of all those scholars who, like Dr Oesterley, believe that the commissioners were inquiring into the condition of all the Jews who inhabited Judah. These scholars, it must also be recognised, consider that no measures had been taken in Judah to avoid the danger of the absorption of the

Judeans into the foreign population. Yet, after a period of nearly a century, only 113 men could be found who had contracted mixed marriages. They must have comprised a very small proportion of the people.

It is a more serious omission to have ignored that both Ezra in his memoirs and the author of the closing chapter describe the lapse from strict Judaism as the trespass of the children of the captivity, ix. 4, x. 6, and that the later writer regarded the returned exiles as the men who were summoned for the purpose of having measures taken for its removal. When it is recognised that the laxity had arisen among the newcomers, it becomes easier to understand why the strict examination only produced 113 guilty persons. There are two possible explanations for looser views on the subject having been prevalent among the exilic population. The cause may simply have lain in the conditions of the time. As has already been noted, the lists of the men of the Return, and the natural probabilities of the case prove that the large proportion of the newcomers were males, who must have had difficulty in finding wives among their fellow-Jews. But it is equally possible that the men had not learned of the stricter views on the question which had been enforced among the remanent population in Samaria and Judah. Living as they did at different centres in Babylonia, they had not been brought under one central authority which could legislate on the subject, as was done in chapter vii. of Deuteronomy and in the pact in Nehemiah, chapter x.

It is not easy to decide what was the course followed in connection with the men who had contracted these

marriages, for the account, and with it the book of
Ezra, breaks off abruptly after having given their
names. We are told that five of the priests undertook
to dismiss their wives and to offer a ram in acknowledgment of their guilt, vv. 18 f., but we are not told
whether their case is mentioned as typical of what
was required from and done by all the others, or
whether they alone submitted to censure. In either
case, it is impossible to conclude from the record as it
stands that Ezra, who had been instigated to take
action by the leaders at Jerusalem, and who was
careful to guarantee that he had the support of the
community in all his acts, was compelled to sist
further procedure because of a rebellion for which
there is no evidence on the part of those who were not
prepared for such drastic measures. Since, on the
evidence of the sources, it has been shown that the
offenders were men from Babylonia, it becomes impossible to believe that 108 malcontents, who made
up no more than one-fifteenth of Ezra's caravan and
who were newcomers to Jerusalem, were able to make
headway against legislation which was set on foot
by the Jerusalem leaders, strongly supported by their
own leader, and in connection with which five of their
leading priests did public penance for their fault.

What has misled students has been that they have
taken for granted that the leaders at Jerusalem
approached Ezra in order to draw attention to the
gravity of the situation among the community for
which they were responsible. The terms, however,
of their statement do not bear this out. They spoke
about the extent to which the people of Israel had
become absorbed among the peoples of the *lands*, and

employed the term which is confined to the heathen settlers in Samaria. When, on the other hand, the Judean community gathered round Ezra, they acknowledged their transgression in having inter-married with the peoples of the country, x. 2. What the leaders in Jerusalem did was to draw Ezra's attention to a notorious example of the result which had attended laxity, but they left him to take the hint. The situation, as it appears in the documents, does not bear out the conclusion of scholars like Schäder, Sellin and Kittel, who consider that Ezra, on his arrival from Babylonia, found his co-religionists in imminent danger of absorption into the surrounding heathenism, and that, by his prompt action in introducing into Judah a law against inter-marriage which originated among the exiles, he prevented this calamity and for the first time segregated Israel. Instead of this, Ezra only took action on the initiative of the Judean community. His first act was to appoint a commission of inquiry into the actual condition of affairs, and this commission confined its scrutiny to the returned exiles. Among these only 113 persons were found who had contracted such marriages. Again, when Ezra confessed the trespass of the children of the captivity, he lamented their failure to obey the commandments of their God, which He had commanded by His servants the prophets, and especially the command against inter-marriage with the heathen of Palestine, ix. 10-12. A man who spoke in such terms was not introducing a law against inter-marriage which was wholly novel ; and the religious communion, in which an inquiry lasting for three months could only report 113 cases of such inter-marriage confined to a single class of newcomers, ran no real danger of absorption.

The extracts from the memoir have been prefaced in vii. 1-10 by a brief account the purpose of which appears to have been to state how Ezra was able to return to Jerusalem with the body of exiles whom he led, and who he was. The passage relates that he went up from Babylonia, and that the king granted him all his request. Unfortunately nothing is said which might define what the request had been. But a genealogy of the leader has been included according to which he was a priest in direct descent from Aaron through Zadok. He is further called a ready scribe in the law of Moses which the Lord the God of Israel had given, and one who had set his mind to search the law of the Lord and to do it and to teach in Israel statutes and judgments. What such a description suggests is that the man had been a zealous upholder of the demands of the Jewish law, and that he was eager to maintain these among his fellows in exile. There is no hint that he was troubled about the condition of affairs in Jerusalem, or that he was framing a law to suit those conditions. All that can be concluded from the language is that the man was likely to seize and use wisely any favour which Artaxerxes might show to his co-religionists, and that his fellow-Jews who were planning to return to Palestine would naturally make him their leader, while any of the exiles who remained would as readily trust him with their gifts to the sanctuary.

After this preamble the editor inserted a copy of a rescript which Ezra was said to have received from the Persian king, and which was presumably granted because of his request. In this official document the leader is formally described as a priest and scribe of the law of the God of heaven. On the meaning of the last term Schäder has recently published an interesting pamphlet,[1] in which he claims that this title implies that Ezra was a court-official. He points out that the reorganisation of the Persian Empire which was carried out by Darius must have brought with it the appointment at Ecbatana of bureaus, staffed by men who were conversant with the conditions in the different provinces, and able to guide the imperial authorities on any question which arose. Ezra, then, was the head of the bureau which had charge of all business in connection with the Jews, alike in Babylonia and in Palestine. Jewry was recognised in the Empire as a legalised body under its own regulations in religious matters. In this early arrangement Schäder even suggests that it is possible to see the origin of the well-known *rēsh galutha* which acted as intermediary between the Jewish community and the later Empire. Thus he finds it easy to account for the strongly Jewish character of the language of the rescript, which has always made it suspect, especially since it differs in this respect from the other similar edicts in the book of Ezra. The document will have been prepared under Ezra's supervision, may even have been written by his own hand. All that the imperial authorities had to do with it was to sign it and so give it their sanction.

This interesting suggestion, or rather series of suggestions (for it will be noted that Schäder has been

---

[1] ' Ezra der Schreiber.' He has developed a view which was suggested by Meinhold and Kittel.

led on from one hint to another), must be left for final appraisement to those who are conversant with Persian affairs at the period. One who is merely an Old Testament student cannot pretend to pronounce on such a question. Yet he may remark that, even if it should prove to be well-founded in history, it hardly carries with it the conclusion which Schäder has based upon it. For he proceeds as though, by having proved the authenticity of the title given to Ezra, he had also proved the authenticity of the entire rescript. Now the difficulties which have long been felt in connection with that document, even by students who were prepared to accept the similar edicts in chapters iv. and vi., were based upon its contents rather than on Ezra's title. It is unnecessary to repeat these difficulties here,[1] but it must be said that, even if all Schäder's contention were proved, that *might* only imply that the man to whom we owe the present form of the edict knew enough about Persian affairs to introduce a correct title.

There is, however, a more serious blot on Schäder's method of dealing with his suggestion. He has drawn from it the conclusion that Ezra was empowered to introduce and to enforce a new law in Palestine which he and some of his associates in exile had long been preparing. This was our old friend, the Priestly Code. The final law for Judaism owed its origin to a body of priests in Babylonia, and its enforcement in Palestine to a Persian edict. That requires us to believe that the Persian authorities empowered their Secretary for Jewish affairs to introduce a new law which had

---

[1] They are adequately and succinctly summed up by Dr Oesterley, *op. cit.* p. 112.

nothing directly to do with the better government of a distant province, but which involved a serious change in its people's religious practices. They could have had no special interest in meddling with the habits of worship which characterised a very peculiar people : indeed, such interference from headquarters was only likely to set up friction between the Jews and their rulers, and to do it wantonly.

The situation is not made easier when we note how badly all this agrees with the Ezra of the memoirs. The same man, who went to Jerusalem endowed with powers to remodel the practice of his fellow-Jews, and who is supposed to have made request for these powers, proudly states that he refused the offer of an escort from the king. When he reached the holy city, any law he enforced was one which concerned the conduct of the exiles he had brought back, and the means he employed for their correction was of the same nature as that in which he had trusted for their protection through the desert. Schäder has recognised the incongruity and explains that Ezra declined to employ any but moral weapons in dealing with his co-religionists. When these rejected his interference, he took no steps to coerce them, but quietly returned to Babylonia, and there wrote his memoir which was intended to form a report to the king and to the Babylonian Jews on the failure of his mission.

The situation thus sketched is interesting, but rather Gilbertian. The Persian Secretary of State for Jewish affairs has heard that matters were in a bad condition in his native country. He and his brother Jews have long been planning the introduction of a new law which they had prepared in order to put everything on a better footing. He used his opportunity as a trusted official to apply to Artaxerxes for full powers to carry out the much-needed reform, and when his request was granted, he himself drafted the terms of the imperial edict which was to confer upon him the necessary authority. Yet no sooner had he reached the capital, and opposition declared itself on the part of 108 men against a single question of practical conduct, than he made no use of the powers with which he had been careful to arm himself. Instead of exercising his authority, this imperial representative went back to Babylonia and wrote a report in which he first informed his fellow-Jews that he had delivered over their gifts to the temple and then informed his royal master that he had permitted a small group of recalcitrants in a petty province publicly to flout the imperial authority in the person of his Secretary. He did not even indicate in his report that the reason for his action was that his conscience did not permit him to use powers for which he had applied. It was not after this fashion that the Persian Empire was governed : it is not after this fashion that any empire can be governed.

It is possible, however, that Schäder and Kittel are correct when they recognise in the title given to Ezra an official designation conferred by the Persian court. Their error may consist in the conclusion they draw, that he was empowered by the rescript to introduce a new law in Palestine. To note that in his memoir he introduced no new law and that, when he enforced a measure of discipline on the returned exiles there, he made no use of the powers which the rescript is supposed to have conferred upon him, compels one to ask whether the terms of the imperial decree, which defines his functions and his powers, bear out the contention that he was sent to introduce a new law in the province. With that document must be united the two verses at viii. 35 f., which refer back to it and which relate that the newcomers delivered their commission to the local authorities in Syria.

The rescript gave Ezra permission to take with him on his journey any Jews who might desire to return to their own land, v. 13. It empowered these men to carry with them money, gifts from the imperial treasury and from other Jews who remained behind ; and it directed that these should be employed for sacrifices at the temple and for any similar purposes which were judged suitable, vv. 15-18. It gave special directions about some vessels for the temple use which had been committed to the leader, v. 19. It instructed the imperial local authorities who had charge of the fisc to meet other demands on the part of Ezra, and determined the extent of this charge, vv. 20-23. It exempted the temple officials from all imperial taxation, v. 24. All these regulations were concerned with the Palestinian Jews in their religious capacity, and gave Ezra no power to interfere with their internal discipline or habits. They rather recognised the existence of an organised community which controlled the temple and its worship. They, further, agree with the opening sentence of Ezra's memoir where the leader returned thanks to God, because He had put it into the king's mind to beautify the temple, and detailed his scrupulous care for the safe arrival of the sacred gifts. Indeed the correspondence between the two documents supports

Schäder's interesting suggestion that this part of the memoir was composed for the information of the Babylonian Jews. They only were likely to be interested in Ezra's reason for refusing to accept an imperial convoy; they, too, were likely to appreciate his full detail about the safe transmission of their gifts to the temple.

There remain, however, two verses which appear to go beyond this limited reference, and to confer larger authority on the leader. The first is verse 14 where it is said that Ezra has been sent out from the court in order to inquire concerning Judah and Jerusalem "according to the law of God which is in thine hand." If, now, the title "scribe of the law of the God of Heaven" is really a Persian title, equivalent to the Secretary for Jewish affairs, this law of God which was in his hands must be understood in something of the same sense, and be meant to define the limits of his authority. He was not granted a roving commission, which gave power to interfere with the administration of the local satraps, but was merely empowered to pursue his inquiries in connection with matters which concerned his special administration. It supports this view of the situation to notice that, in the one case where his functions trenched on the duties of the local Persian officials, the rescript ordered these men to implement his demands, but carefully set limits to those demands. Even if, however, such a view should be pronounced untenable, and if "the law of God which was in his hand" be taken to mean a new law which Ezra had framed, the sentence does not imply what has been read into it. All that it empowers is the institution of an inquiry into the condition of the community in regard to its religious affairs. The commission was one to consider and report. Whether any government would ever send out an official to consider and report in terms of a series of regulations which that official had drafted for the first time, and which were quite novel to the community on whose conduct in relation to them he was to report, may be left for decision to those who are more conversant with the habits of Government officialdom.

Again, in verse 25 Ezra was empowered to appoint judges and magistrates over the Palestinian Jews, "all such as know the laws of thy God, and teach ye him who knoweth them not." The evident intention of the statement is to restrict the authority of these new magistrates to the observing Jewish population. About this section of the population it was taken for granted that they knew and acknowledged the laws which the new magistrates were to administer. There might be some who did not know them and who needed instruction, but these were regarded as the exception. Now, if Ezra had been introducing a new law, the precise terms of which were only known to himself and to those who came from Babylonia in his company, his instructions must have been couched in wholly different terms. His first business must have been to teach the law he brought to the Palestinians, before he could appoint magistrates to administer that law. Also he must have found the new magistrates whom he appointed among his fellow-exiles, since they alone were acquainted with this law. Yet all this only throws more strongly into relief the remarkable fact that, according to his memoir, Ezra disciplined no one except his own followers and that among the defaulters there were several priests. His associates evidently did not know the law of their leader.

It must then be left to historical scholars to decide whether Ezra's title was a Persian official designation, and whether the rescript in terms of which he acted could ever have been issued to a Jew by the imperial court. What an Old Testament student must still say is that, even if such a rescript was issued to Ezra in that capacity, it does not warrant the conclusion that Ezra was the author of a new constitution for Palestinian Judaism without which it would have collapsed. The utmost extent of the power given to the leader was to inquire into the religious condition of his fellow-Jews and to appoint certain magistrates over these men in relation to the same affairs. But the magistrates who were appointed and the majority of those over whom they were appointed knew the law which the one body of men were to administer and the other were required to obey. Beyond such a view of Ezra's functions and authority, it will at once be noted, his own memoir does not go.

There is, however, mention of Ezra's activity in Nehemiah, chapter viii., where he is brought into close association with a law. The passage is, from whatever angle it is approached, one of the most baffling among all the documents which deal with the Return. It relates two incidents which took place on the first, v. 2, and on the second, v. 13, day of the seventh month. The seventh month referred to is the month which appeared in connection with the

long list of returned exiles, Neh. vii. 73 = Ezra iii. 1,[1]
so that the two incidents recorded are brought into
immediate and close relation to that historic event.
But the writer who brought them into this connection
was not the editor of the book of Ezra. For in the
book of Ezra the people gathered merely at Jerusalem,
their leaders were Zerubbabel and Joshua, and the
date followed immediately after the publication of
Cyrus' edict. In Nehemiah the people gathered in a
plaza before the water-gate, so that the walls were
restored ; the leader was Ezra ; and the date was
thus much later than the reign of Cyrus. Again,
in the book of Ezra the first task of the people was to
erect an altar, on which they offered the morning and
evening tamid, the burnt-offerings required at the
festival of tabernacles and at all the other set feasts.
In Nehemiah the first task of the people was to take
part in a public reading of the law, and their second
was to determine the right method of celebrating the
festival of tabernacles. The author who wrote
chapter viii. in Nehemiah had an entirely different
conception of the course of events from the editor of
the book of Ezra.

Further, an examination of the chapter raises a
fresh question. The account closes with the statement
that " daily, from the first day to the last, the book
of the law of God was read,[2] and the feast was kept
seven days." Plainly the reference there is to the feast
of tabernacles. But this festival took place on the

---

[1] Cf. p. 131 *supra.*
[2] So we must translate. The E.V. ' he read,' leaves the impression that Ezra was the reader. But five MSS. have ויקראו, corresponding with ויעשו הג in the second half of the verse, and so prove
that the impersonal sense was intended.

fifteenth day of the seventh month. Since, then, one of the incidents related deals with a novel method in which tabernacles was celebrated, and the other dealt with a novel method in which the reading of the law was carried out, it is a natural inference that the (first and second) days to which the two incidents are referred, really meant, not the first and second of the month, but the first and second days of the festival. Either the editor who set the incidents in their present connection made a mistake about the date of tabernacles, which is an unlikely supposition in connection with so important a festival, or he had a special reason for associating the two novel methods of celebrating tabernacles with the returned exiles, and used the seventh month of the original list for the purpose. In either case, one conclusion is clear : the chapter owes its present position to its editor. It may owe more than its position to his hand, for his association of Nehemiah the tirshatha with Ezra the scribe has led to such difficulties that it has finally been rejected. We must examine each of the incidents which he has related without reliance on the position in which he placed them.

One of these incidents, vv. 13-18, states that the lay heads of the community, the priests and the levites came to Ezra the scribe to give attention to the words of the law. They, not Ezra, found a command issued by Moses to the effect that the Israelites must live in booths during the festival of tabernacles. Accordingly, proclamation was made that the people must provide themselves with the materials for making these booths. The people carried out the injunction with the result that the city was dotted with the booths. From the description it is clear that this happened after the rebuilding of the temple and the city-wall. Then, however, it is added that this fashion of celebrating the festival was entirely novel to the men of the Return : they had not done such a thing since the days of Joshua. Finally, it is stated that the law was read daily, and that the period of the festival proper lasted for seven days with an added day of solemn assembly.

The natural sense of this passage is that it relates the adoption on the part of the whole community of a uniform practice in connection with one feature in the celebration of tabernacles—viz., the custom of living in booths. It may also record that the length of the festival was increased by the addition of an extra day. The further sense of the passage is that the practice of living in these booths was a novelty to one section of the community, the men of the Return. Not only is it expressly stated that these men made and lived in the booths, but in connection with their conduct it is added that Israel had not celebrated after this fashion since the time of Joshua. The reason for adding such an explanation was to represent this part of the ritual as the revival of an old regulation of the wilderness period which had fallen into abeyance after the entry into Palestine. Only by giving such an explanation was it possible to persuade the returned exiles to make the novel custom a permanent feature in all future celebrations : but it was they who needed the explanation.

That the practice of living in booths was a later addition to the law which governed the celebration of tabernacles appears from the festival calendar in

Leviticus, chapter xxiii. That chapter contains a list of the major and minor festivals of the Jewish year, which originally ended with a formal conclusion in verses 37 f. To this list have been appended two addenda, both of which add regulations on the method of celebrating tabernacles. These regulations appear in no other code. The first prescribes that the people must provide themselves on the opening day with fruit and branches, and must rejoice before the Lord for seven days, vv. 39-41. From the mention of these being used in the rejoicing before the Lord, it is evident that they were brought into the sanctuary. They were the *ethrog* and *lulab*, which are still brought into the synagogue at the sacred season. The regulation, therefore, has nothing directly to do with the practice of living in booths. That practice forms the theme of a second addendum in verses 42 f., and at v. 39 it is also ordained that tabernacles was to close with an extra day of solemn assembly. That the practice of living in booths was felt by those who added it at the close of the calendar to be a novelty is indicated by the fact that it is the only regulation in the chapter which is provided with a reason for its observance. The religious leaders of Israel, after their common habit, supplied to this feature in their service a motive taken from their historical religion. But the motive which they supplied, both in Leviticus and in Nehemiah, shows how difficult it was to find something which might cover the peculiar character of the rite. For the wilderness was not the place where it was easy to obtain thick branches and willows of the brook, and according to their own tradition they lived then in tents.

Evidently the festival of tabernacles was enriched at a later period by the adoption of new features. As to ethrog and lulab we know nothing more than that these appear in an addendum to the law. As to the booths, we have, besides the addendum to the law, the incident in Nehemiah which related the occasion when the entire community, laymen, priests and levites adopted it. In connection with this incident it is specially mentioned that those to whom it was a novelty were the men of the Return. The inevitable inference is that, whoever may have introduced the change, Ezra, the leader of a body of returned exiles, did not.

The chapter in Nehemiah shows that at one period there was a differing method of celebration at Jerusalem. Since the practice involved no difference in the temple-ritual, but merely in the method of celebration at home, it was possible for the two forms to continue side by side for a time. At a later date, however, it was felt to be advisable to introduce uniformity ; and a common regulation was passed which resulted in the addendum to the festival-calendar in Leviticus. In our ignorance of the full ritual of the festival it is impossible to determine the source of the custom of living in booths : but it is possible to say that, since it was novel to the returned exiles, the source was not Babylonia. As for the connection of Ezra with the incident, there appear to be three possible explanations. If Schäder's view of the title ' scribe ' be found legitimate—and he receives that title in the passage —he may have been appealed to by a deputation which consulted him to confirm the community's

decision of the question. The local leaders may have
felt it advisable to have higher authority for setting
up those booths in the open plazas of the city, where
they could not fail to be an inconvenience. Or the
editor of the account may have introduced Ezra, as
a well-known leader of returned exiles, in order to
suggest that these men were influenced by him to
accept what to them was a novel custom. The simplest
explanation is that the editor is responsible for the
introduction of Ezra's name in a passage which
originally bore no date. It serves in some measure to
support the suggestion to recognise that the verses
read more naturally, when the words אל עזרא הספר are
dropped. For it was the leaders of the community,
not he, who found the passage in the law which
decided the question, vv. 13 f.

What appears an impossible answer to the problem
is the hypothesis that the question at issue was settled
on the basis of a new law which Ezra had brought up
to Jerusalem. If the question arose before this new
law had been accepted by the community, it must
have risen because Ezra and his company were already living in booths after the regulations of his new
law. Then the priests who formed part of the deputation to him must have been the priests of the temple
before Ezra's arrival, since those who came with him
were joint authors of the new law. These men must,
therefore, have quietly accepted a decision on the
basis of a law which they did not yet know and had
not yet acknowledged. The word of Ezra that the
practice stood in a law which he had not yet promulgated was enough to decide the matter. Nor is this
all, for it is still necessary to explain why the law

about living in booths appears in Leviticus in the form of an addendum to the Priestly Code. Apparently, then, Ezra did not settle the question put by the deputation on the basis of his Code, since that in its original form contained no such regulation. He must have introduced the addendum at this time. In that case, what raised the question at all? It could not have been his followers, since they had no such custom.

If, on the other hand, Ezra had already introduced his new law and had succeeded in making it regulative in Jerusalem, matters are not greatly improved. Why did the deputation come at all, if the men knew that the question was settled by the authority of the man to whom they came on the basis of a law to which they had already given their assent? Besides, the awkward fact remains that we must explain why the custom of living in booths appears in an acknowledged addendum to the original law. That is no easier to answer on this supposition than on the other.

The final difficulty, however, which meets the supposition that Ezra had anything to do with the introduction of the practice is the need to explain why the account which deals with the matter emphasised that it was a novelty to the men of the Return.

There remains the section, viii. 1-12, which relates a public reading of the law before the assembled people on the first day of the seventh month. It has already been pointed out that the connection of this incident with what precedes it in chapter vii. is artificial and is due to a later hand. Further, the presence of such a later hand is now generally acknowledged, because of the mention of Nehemiah in his official capacity as tirshatha alongside Ezra in verse 9. The account has been revised, and revised by one who appears to have had no clear idea of the course of events. He may not have been thinking in terms of history and may have loosely used Nehemiah's name in order to say that all the leaders of the period united to hearten the people in their outbreak of distress.

To note, however, that the verse betrays the hand of an editor who was careless in his introduction of an anachronism draws attention to another peculiarity. Ezra is here introduced under the double title of priest and scribe. This might appear insignificant, were it not that he is called priest at verse 2, but scribe at verses 1 and 4. The variety of usage might be set down to mere looseness in the use of terms, were it not that the function of the priest at verse 2 in relation to the law and to the people is not the same as that of the scribe at verses 1 and 4. The priest brought the law before the assembled people and read it in their hearing during an entire forenoon. On the other hand, the people requested the scribe after this to bring the book of the law of Moses. Thereupon this scribe ascended a wooden pulpit of which there has been no previous mention. On either side of him stood thirteen coadjutors, whose function and whose composition are wholly indefinite. It is impossible to say whether they were representatives of the laymen or of the priesthood, for they remained impassive beside their leader. What is even more remarkable is the comparatively small part taken in the proceedings by that leader himself. For, while the priest had read the law for a forenoon, the scribe merely opened the book, uttered a benediction which might appear suitable as a preliminary to the priest's reading of the preceding day—and did no more. Instead of him there appear thirteen other men, whose names are not the same as the scribe's coadjutors, and the levites, who also have not been previously mentioned. About these levites it is said, not simply that they read the law like the priest, but that they read it so that the people could understand what they heard. When they so heard their law, the people broke into loud weeping. On this follows the edited verse according to which Nehemiah the tirshatha, Ezra the priest and scribe and the levites united in quieting the people. Yet this in turn is followed by another sentence which, ignoring Nehemiah and Ezra, relates that thus the levites quieted the people. The conclusion of the whole is that all the people went their way . . . to make great mirth, because they had understood the words that were declared unto them.

One thing is clear about a narrative of this character : it is not homogeneous, and the editor's hand is not confined to a single verse. The brief passage contains no less than three duplications : the law was read by Ezra and again by the levites ; those who stilled the people were Nehemiah, Ezra and the levites, and again the levites ; thirteen men accompanied Ezra without doing anything in particular, thirteen men accompanied the levites and helped them in their work about the law. There appears also a variety in the description of the leading person in the whole scene ; Ezra is priest, scribe, priest and scribe ; and there is a corresponding variety in the function he fulfilled : as scribe he merely presided over the assembly, as priest he read the law without coadjutors and without pulpit.

When there is reason to suspect revision, it is natural to look for the original in that part of the narrative which bears least evidence of such revision. At once there disengages itself an account in verses 7-12 of how on a certain occasion thirteen men with the levites caused the people to understand the law by accompanying their reading with an interpretation. The people broke out into loud weeping, but the levites, who are here called the teachers of the people, stilled their outbreak, because it was unsuited to the character of the sacred season. Thereupon the men went home in happiness because they had understood the words which had been declared unto them. In this homogeneous account the leading feature is the introduction of a novel practice of accompanying with an interpretation what was evidently a customary reading of the law. The account opens and closes with this feature. Some such arrangement must have become necessary in Judah after the exile. Nehemiah was distressed to discover that there were cases where Jewish children were unable to speak their native Hebrew. Believing that the cause was the increasing habit of intermarriage with the heathen, he tried to counteract it by tightening up the law against connubium. In reality such measures could only touch the fringe of the question, for there were forces at work which could not be checked by any law. Intercourse in business and in social relations with their heathen neighbours made it inevitable that some *lingua franca* should rise in Palestine. The conditions which finally made Aramaic the common language of the country were already operative. Instead of, like Nehemiah, cursing the men who were already beginning to forget their Hebrew, the religious leaders of the people earned the gratitude of their followers by making it possible for them to understand their law. The incident describes the tentative beginning of the use of a Targum. This was a novel feature in connection with the reading of the law, as living in booths during the seven days of tabernacles was novel to part of the community, so that the combination of the two practices in the same passage may well be original. Further, it had been the custom of the levites to read the Deuteronomic law in the hearing of the people every seventh year at that sacred season, Deut. xxxi. 9-13. Thus there was a double link of connection between the two incidents ; both were associated with the Sukkoth festival, and both were now introduced into the whole community. There was a reason for the prominence given to the levites in the original narrative, as there was a reason for the people being present on the occasion. These last had not needed to be summoned, for they were present at Jerusalem in attendance at the great festival of the Jewish year. Because of the joyous character of the celebration the levites checked the outburst of weeping among the worshippers.

The reason which prompted an editor to introduce mention of Ezra was that this novel custom, like that of living in booths, was formally accepted by the community at Jerusalem. The authorities there could not fail to recognise its usefulness : as time went on, they could not fail to recognise its necessity. But the method followed in the two cases shows a significant difference. In the one case they declared that living in booths was the revival of an old custom, which could claim Mosaic authority. Only this could justify its inclusion in an addendum to the festival-calendar in the law. Since, however, the use of a targum did not need to take its place in the torah, and since it was obviously modern in its origin, it could not be put under such an august name. Yet authority it must have, if it was to be recognised by all Jewry. Its use by the levites could confer no such recognition. The first reviser was content to give Ezra the priest and a leading representative of the men of the Return a prominent position. He read the law in its sacred Hebrew : the levites were definitely his subordinates. The second reviser, who called Ezra the scribe, was even more careful to mark that primacy. The community acknowledged Ezra's authority, for they applied to him to bring out the book of the law. He occupied the pulpit with thirteen assessors grouped round him : and he uttered the solemn benediction which preceded the reading. The initiative in the introduction of the new practice was preserved for the men of the Return.

This tentative reconstruction of one of the most confused and confusing narratives, even in Ezra-Nehemiah, departs too sharply from the current interpretation to be likely to win general acceptance. But it must be said that the current interpretation, according to which the incident relates the intro-duction by Ezra of the Priestly Code and its acceptance by the congregation, is in worse case. Except in the minor point of the mention of Nehemiah the tirshatha, it fails to recognise and explain the duplications and inconsistencies in the text, and thus ignores the evidence of later revision. It does no justice to the fact that in the first six verses Ezra occupies the leading rôle, while in the second six the levites are the actors. It does not explain how and why the levites at the period of Ezra could have held the place which is here assigned to them. Above all, it imports into the narrative two statements which are not present. There is no mention of the law which Ezra read on the first day and which the levites afterwards interpreted being new. Had it been new, it is not easy to see how the levites could with such promptitude have supplied the interpretation. Possibly the leader was anxious to add levites to his caravan in order that he might, during the desert journey, supply them with a copy in order that they might be ready for the duty ! Further, there is no mention in the narrative of the people having adopted any law, whether old or new. Their weeping as well as their later joy is definitely connected with the fact that they were able to understand the law. That is the note on which the whole narrative ends, and it has no relation to the adoption of a new law, for it is linked up with the statement that the levites had supplied an interpretation. Before it is possible to read out of the account as it stands a record of the introduction of a new law by Ezra and of its adoption by the congregation, we must read it in first.

One general consideration remains to be noted. After having examined the Ezra who appears in the memoir with its supplement and the Ezra of chapter

viii. in Nehemiah, it becomes necessary to compare the two and test whether they agree. If he was the bringer of a law which initiated and enforced a new polity at Jerusalem, and if that was the purpose which prompted him to obtain a rescript from Artaxerxes, it is a pertinent question to ask why he was entirely silent on the subject in his memoir. In that case the matter which formed the burden of his mission has been relegated to an appendix in the book of Nehemiah, and there it appears in a form which nowhere definitely states what law he introduced or describes the congregation as accepting it. It also appears in association with minor questions relating to the reading of the law with an interpretation and living in booths during the week of tabernacles. Nor is this all. In his memoir Ezra does not report that he introduced anything new in Jerusalem. Instead, at the prompting of the authorities there, he enforced a law against intermarriage among his fellow-exiles. So far from introducing new regulations, he accepted one which he found already in force, and even this he urged upon his fellows only after careful investigation into the circumstances. The contradiction between the two Ezras is strong enough to require explanation.

In attempting the reconstruction of a historical period or a historic personality, the only scientific method is to rely on the evidence of the most authentic documents. Especially is this the case where we have good reason to recognise that some of the documents of the period have been revised in the interests of a theological opinion or party. What the memoir of Ezra presents is the picture of a devoted Jew who led a caravan of returned exiles back to the beloved city and who brought with him votive offerings for the temple from his fellow-Jews who remained in Babylonia. The exiles whom he brought with him formed probably the largest contingent which had reached Jerusalem since the reign of Darius. They formed, therefore, a welcome addition to the strength of the Jewish community. But they also proved how strong was the tie which bound the diaspora Jew to the home of his race and to the centre of his faith. The gifts which the men brought were an added proof of the same fact and a means of knitting the bond more closely. More than this Ezra did not bring, and the picture his memoir presents shows that he could never have brought more. He has the tenacity, the single-ness of purpose and the limitation of the institutionalist. One recognises it in his refusal to accept the royal escort and the manifest sigh of relief with which he relates that his faith in God was justified. Evidently that decision had cost him sleepless nights in camp, and with good reason. It was the same man who scrupulously took measures to prove that he had dealt faithfully with the money with which he had been entrusted—and who wrote them all down. Again, it was the same man who learned with deep distress that the men who had returned with him were intro-ducing lax practices in relation to intermarriage into the community. His fidelity to accepted law makes him unable to ignore the facts and his own responsibility in connection with them. To under-stand the man it is only necessary to contrast his conduct with that of Nehemiah in like circumstances. The tirshatha contended with the offenders, and cursed them and smote certain of them and plucked off their hair and made them take an oath by God. Ezra rent his own garment, plucked out his own hair, confessed his share in the dishonour which had been brought on the people, and appointed a committee to inquire into the facts and to take action. If we may accept the rescript from Artaxerxes as genuine, the terms of that commission will prove how well the imperial authorities had gauged the character of their commissioner. He was given power to intromit with considerable sums of money ; and the man was incapable of dishonesty. He was also trusted with certain powers which needed delicate handling in their relation to those of the local satraps ; and he was careful not to go beyond his own sphere. Further, he was empowered to inquire and report ; there he was in his element.

The portrait with which the early documents present us is that of a devoted Jew who was the perfect administrator. It is not that of the originator of the new polity by which Jewry was to live. One can see the contentment with which the man settled down to spend the remainder of his life in the shadow of his beloved temple. It is not surprising that the editor of chapter viii. in Nehemiah, when he grouped together the two novel features in the celebration of tabernacles which came to be accepted by the whole congregation, introduced Ezra into his account. If he accepted them, they were safe. As little surprising is it that, when the author of Ecclesiasticus wrote his roll of the mighty men to whom his people owed guidance in critical hours of their history, or deeper knowledge of their peculiar genius and of their distinctive religion, he omitted the name of Ezra. For

Ezra originated nothing. He was the tenacious, loyal lover of the institutions of his people, the type which has made the stiff backbone of his nation. Judaism has bred so many of such sons that one who set himself to praise the fathers who begat us could not find time or space to mention one who was so like the rest.

CHAPTER XIV.

THE NEW POLITY.

A STUDENT who has attempted with painful care to trace the record of Israel's restoration is more conscious than anyone else can be of the uncertainty of many of his results. The utmost he may claim is that he has not ignored any of the evidence, or got rid of an inconvenient passage by merely assigning it to a late editor without seeking to explain why the editor inserted it. In the end he may reflect that he has satisfied himself at least as to the means by which a group of humble men built a house of worship in an obscure province of the Persian Empire and made it the centre for their race. Meantime great events were taking place in the history of their world. Babylon had succeeded Nineveh and given place to Persia : the Eastern world from the shores of the Aegean to the cataracts of the Nile had been united into an Empire. The stage was set for a greater upheaval and a vaster Empire, for Xerxes led his forces against the Greeks and prepared the way for the struggle between East and West. The time brought with it men who stand boldly out on the pages of history. Their very names are resonant, as though attended by a roll of drums, Sennacherib and Sargon, Nebuchadrezzar, Cyrus and Darius. In contrast with these, the work of a little group, most of whom were nameless, who piled stone on stone till their temple was finished, who wept over the meagre outcome and exulted because their eyes had seen it, may well appear insignificant.

Yet we have learned of recent years that, when the world is in the melting-pot, the result is to make some men realise with a new intensity the plot of earth on which they were born, the ideals which are their own, the dear, familiar customs which have moulded them. These people refuse to submit to fate and circumstance, and save their souls. Out of the welter of the kingdoms, which became Assyrian in one generation, Babylonian in the next and Persian in the end we have the record of one which survived. What makes the achievement in some respects more notable is that it was the work of men most of whom were nameless and none of whom can be called distinguished. Here and there a name, of a priest, a governor, a prophet, rises out of oblivion ; but his work is occasional and at best merely focuses the purpose or the hope of those for whom it was done. It was a nation which refused to acknowledge defeat ; in the best sense of the word Israel's recovery was a popular movement. No sooner had Samaria fallen than the faithful remnant began to draw together and plan resistance to the heathenism which threatened to engulf them. When Jerusalem suffered the same fate, the Judeans maintained the altar-fire and joined with their brethren to continue the cult. Among the exiles Second Isaiah was never weary in urging his fellow-countrymen to recognise the spiritual bankruptcy of the Empire which had swallowed them up : Babylonia had nothing to give to Israel, it was Israel which could teach Babylonia. Wherever we are allowed a glimpse into the life of the broken nation, we find it reacting. To notice that in every case the first actors were nameless men is an evidence that the movement was universal and spontaneous. It is as though Israel did not preserve their names, because it recognised itself in them : all they said and did was but the expression of what was in the heart of every lover of his people. At a later date there emerge the names of men who were identified with one or another outstanding feature of the work of restoration. But these men only brought to completion something which had already been begun ; behind them was the life of a nation which refused to part with the things by which men live and in which is the life of their spirit.

A movement of this character, so widespread and so spontaneous, must in the nature of the case be conservative, and runs the risk of becoming reactionary. Many documents of the period are filled with a violent revulsion against Babylonia and its alien life. The temper shows itself in the collection of oracles on that nation which has been added to the book of Jeremiah, and rises to the pitch of hatred in Psalm cxxxvii. Like all who thus react against their world, the men wished to shut themselves away from it by restoring their own peculiar life and renewing the conditions of their past, so far as the masters of the world would permit. Only among these could they feel themselves at home, and their contact with a larger world had issued in a passionate desire to win them back. As soon as Cyrus permitted the restoration of the temple and the return of the exiles, the people set themselves to make this institution the centre for Jewry. Their decision proved their strong desire to revive the past, and in turn determined the character of their future, for an institutional religion is always conservative. Accordingly, though the men rejected the extreme proposals of Ezekiel, they only modified them, for they made a descendant of Zadok head of a sacred college which included none but Judean priests, and they determined that the use at the temple must remain the old law of Leviticus, the combined manual for the priests and law for the people which was peculiar to the South. The Deuteronomic law was definitely set aside. The final rejection of the Code of Israel proper need not have been due to any animosity against the Samaritans, for a sufficient reason may be found in the character of that law-book. The Deuteronomic Code, which had been framed for the period of Israel's independence, was wholly unfitted to govern the life of a community which was now subject to Persian law. Israel was no longer free to put to death anyone who had committed the crime of man-stealing, and, even if the village communes had been permitted to continue, none of them was at liberty to deliver over a murderer to the avenger of blood. To attempt to maintain the old Code was to come continually into conflict with the local satrap. On the other hand, while the law in Leviticus did contain a few regulations on such subjects, its main interest centred round the temple and its cult.[1] The single change which the college of priests permitted in the celebration of tabernacles, the practice of living in booths, furnishes another proof of their essentially conservative outlook, for they only admitted this novel feature after they had carefully explained that it was the revival of an old Mosaic regulation which had lapsed.

Yet the most conservative ecclesiastic lives in a world which does not stand still ; and the world had not stood still since the time when the house of Zadok administered a ritual which served Judah alone. Even the author of the Ezekiel scheme intended his priests to judge in any controversy and so admitted the possibility of new questions arising which demanded decision. One notable change was that the temple with its cult had become the centre for a Jewry which was wider than Palestine. If the cult was to serve that larger community, its regulations must be adapted to meet the new conditions. The most obvious change was in connection with the three great festivals. Once it had been required of the worshippers that they appear three times in the year before the Lord, but that belonged to the time when every observing Jew lived in the holy land. The demand became impracticable with a diaspora in Egypt and Babylonia, and it has been quietly dropped from the calendar in Leviticus, chapter xxiii. Again, so long as the majority

[1] This character of the Deuteronomic Code explains why the Samaritans after the breach made no effort to revive it. They took over the Jerusalem use, because it fitted their condition, and because they had lived under it and their levites had administered it before the breach. It is an interesting illustration, however, of the tenacity of religious practice to note that they reverted to one feature in the old Deuteronomic method of celebrating passover.

of the worshippers were Jewish farmers, it was enough to date the feast of weeks "from the time that thou beginnest to put the sickle to the standing corn shalt thou begin to number seven weeks," or to say that tabernacles fell "after thou hast gathered in from thy threshing-floor and from thy wine-press." But, as soon as men resorted to Jerusalem from beyond Palestine, they needed to know the precise dates for their coming. The festivals have fixed dates for their celebration in the same calendar. Men who came from a distance on pilgrimage were also subject to the accidents of the road. They might be delayed beyond the regular period ; they might have contracted ceremonial defilement on the way and have insufficient time for the necessary purification. Provision was made for them by permitting a second celebration of passover in the second month, Num. ix. 9-14, though the first month had been solemnly decreed to be the beginning of months for Israel. The reason for confining such a regulation to passover was due to the fact that the celebration lasted only for a day. It was not necessary to make a similar law for the other festivals, because they lasted over a full week.

A profounder change, however, came over the entire sacrificial ritual, especially in its relation to the community for whose benefit it was intended. This began as soon as the temple became the only legitimate centre for sacrifice, but its influence increased with the increase of the diaspora. The worshippers were unable to be present at sacrifices, which were still offered on their behalf. This character must always have attached to such offerings as the daily burnt-offering and the bread of the presence. Day by day the temple-officials presented, on behalf of the nation, an acknowledgment of its dependence on its God, though the people were not present. But now the ritual of the major festivals was also carried on, though many of those for whom it availed were absent. Even the intimate offerings of the individual in vow or sin-offering became altered in character. Once Elkanah had gone up to Shiloh and paid his vow, and in the act recalled the occasion which had demanded it and renewed the gratitude which made it significant. Now many of the worshippers must send the money for a victim to the shrine, and be content to know that it was duly offered. The old personal relation had given place to a cash transaction, and the rest was carried out by men whom he did not know at a shrine which he had never seen, after a ritual in which he had never shared. The inevitable result of the new situation was to weaken the direct influence of the cult on the life of a large part of the community.

All this did not lead to any neglect of the temple-ritual or to a perfunctory performance of it. Rather the effect of lodging such a duty in the hands of a professional and hereditary caste was the usual one in such cases ; the men magnified their office, and elaborated the system which they administered. A detailed list of the communal offerings, corresponding to the festival calendar in Leviticus, appears in Numbers, chapters xxviii. f. The list opens with the daily burnt-offering, which now must begin and close each day. The character of the victims is defined with the cereal-offering and drink-offering which must accompany them, xxviii. 1-8. The burnt-offering, however, must be supplemented on certain holy days, such as the Sabbaths, vv. 9 f., and the first day of each month, vv. 11-15. Then follow regulations about the ritual for the great days of the year. It begins with passover, which, however, received no detailed description, since it was so largely in the hands of the worshippers. The sole concern of the priests with the service was that they slew the lamb and manipulated its blood. On the other hand, the dates and the duration of the festivals of unleavened bread and of weeks are fully stated with the sacrifices which accompanied them, vv. 16-31. Chapter xxix. is devoted to the ritual for the seventh or sacred month in the Jewish year. Its first day is marked off as a day of holy convocation with trumpet-blowing, but it is further signalised by a special series of sacrifices which were additional to the daily burnt-offering and to those offered on the first day of an ordinary month, vv. 1-6. Then followed the day of atonement with its appropriate offerings, vv. 7-11. The culmination of the month and of the year, however, was הֶחָג, the festival *par excellence*, that of tabernacles. Its significance was doubly marked. Its period was extended to an octave instead of the original seven days, and it received the largest number of sacrifices, which ran in a descending scale from thirteen bullocks on the first day to seven on the seventh, vv. 12-38.

The leading feature in this directory for the sacred year at the temple is its formal and ordered character. One has the impression of a piece of mechanism, which goes on without a hitch, because every one exactly knows his place and the duty he has to fulfil. In part this impression is due to the fact that the directory was intended to guide the priests in what had become a complicated ritual. But this merely emphasises another feature in the succession of sacrificial acts, the fact that the solemn pageant might run its stately round without the presence of any worshippers. Once, when Israel thronged to its local shrines, men did not appear before the Lord with empty hands, but there was no exact definition of that which they must bring. The sacrifices varied in amount and even in character, as the year varied in the bounty of its yield. Now the amount and character of the offering for each day have become stereotyped, so that there is no place for spontaneity.

Corresponding with this is another feature in the directory : the number of the burnt offerings has increased, while the שְׁלָמִים or ' peace-offerings ' have sunk into the background. The only mention of these last appears in a casual reference to them in verse 39. Now the peace-offerings were one of the oldest forms of sacrifice in Israel and had been peculiarly associated with the major festivals. Their characteristic feature was that, after the fat and blood were presented at the altar, the flesh of the victim which the worshipper had brought was given back to form the material for a joyous feast at the sanctuary. A well-to-do farmer invited his friends to share with him, and, according to the Deuteronomic Code, was bidden invite the poor and the levite among his guests. The sacrifice supplied the element of spontaneity, which answered to the command that no one should appear before the Lord with empty hands, though it was apt to produce the scenes which Amos censured. Yet it obviously required the presence of the worshippers. As soon as the attendance of these was no longer demanded, the peace-offerings became merely, as verse 39 proves, one of the voluntary sacrifices, and no attempt was made to regulate their amount or their method. What increased, both in number and in prominence, were the burnt-offerings, which, since they were wholly consumed on the altar, required no one except the officiating priest. They were provided from the contributions of the faithful, were determined in number and in character for the several festivals and were offered with an intention for all Israel. There was both loss and gain in the inevitable change. The services must have become more decorous, and the connection of the festivals with nature and its life was made more remote : but the element of spontaneity in men's gratitude was less, and the association of the community with the great seasons of their religious year became to many a cash-nexus.

Thus the cult became an integral part of and was subsumed under the general idea of law. The earlier codes of the nation had insisted that the true Israelite must reserve his worship for the shrines which his own God had chosen, and at which nothing was permitted except that which was according to the statutes of the God of Israel. The aim had been to prevent the similarity of the ritual from leading men into a careless use of the Canaanite shrines and so into forgetfulness of the essential difference between Yahweh and Baal. That danger had disappeared among men, some of whom had maintained their own cult during the exile, while others had returned from Babylonia in order to take part again in the worship peculiar to Israel. The new danger was that a meticulous exactness in the performance of the statutes delivered to Israel should come to be valued for its own sake. As the priests fulfilled the appointed ritual for the benefit of worshippers who could take no direct part in it, the effect could not fail to be that the service came to be considered as in itself well-pleasing to God, whose ordinance it was. Where the prophets had been able to say that obedience was better than sacrifice, the priests could now say that sacrifice was part of obedience. The cult was as much God's claim on His nation as any other part of His law. Again one may recognise that the changed attitude brought both loss and gain. It is well that men should be able to believe that, both in their moral conduct and in their religious sacraments, they seek to do the will of God. Yet it cannot be entirely wholesome when sacrifice, the fine flower of religion, which derives so much of its loveliness from its spontaneity, is construed from the side of law. The effect may not have appeared at once, but it was inevitable, and it appears in a remarkable utterance of Ben Sira. He says in general terms : he who practiseth kindness offereth a meat-offering and he who showeth mercy presenteth a thank-offering. What is well-pleasing to the Lord is to avoid evil, and the way to forgiveness is to avoid wickedness. But then, as though he had recognised the consequence of his conclusion in relation to the cult, he added : appear not in the presence of the Lord with empty hands, for all these things (are to be done) for the sake of the commandments, E.V. xxxv. 1 ff. Yet even in their crudest early form the sacrifices had once meant more than that : men had seen in them a means for maintaining and enriching their relation to God.[1]

A final feature of the directory which deserves full recognition is the larger place given in it to victims, the specific purpose of which was to secure propitiation for sin. Neither the daily burnt - offering nor the passover is associated with an offering for this purpose : but at every new moon, on the day of atonement, and on each successive day of the celebration of the festivals there is introduced a he-goat which was to be offered as a sin-offering, sometimes with the addition " to make atonement for you." What makes the fact more remarkable is that this he-goat is the only offering the purpose of which was defined, while nothing is said of the effect desired from or effected by the other offerings. It is impossible to say definitely whether any propitiatory efficacy was believed to attach during the early period to the communal offerings. We are so ill informed about the place which the cult held in the religious life of early Israel that we dare not be dogmatic on that subject. At a period when men were not making fine theological distinctions it must remain possible that, since they practised the cult as the means for maintaining their relation to God, they may also have seen in it a means for restoring that relation after it had been broken. Yet, even though this should have been the case, the fact remains that in the directory this element has obtained a new emphasis. A victim, which served to make

[1] For another illustration of the same attitude at a later date cf. Gray, ' Sacrifice in the Old Testament,' pp. 51 f.

atonement for sin, must appear in all the more important rituals.

To note this emphasis on atonement in a general list of offerings, which was concerned primarily with their amount and their constituents, directs attention in turn to the larger prominence given to propitiation in the post-exilic material. That shows itself in the effort then made to distinguish between the אָשָׁם or guilt-offering and the חַטָּאת or sin-offering. When men were making a distinction, in a way which evidently satisfied them, but which still eludes us,[1] between two forms of offering, both of which dealt with propitiation, we may conclude that the subject had won a peculiar significance in their thought. Again, scholars differ as to whether the Day of Atonement was a creation of this period, or had its roots in a much older ritual, which was original at Jerusalem, but was later extended to the whole nation. But they will agree that in the later law it reached a place in the life of Jewry for which there is no evidence in the early literature. The position it then reached has only deepened and strengthened, till it has become one of the most remarkable features in Jewish life. To recognise the date of its appearance in the festival calendar marks the extent to which the sense of the need for propitiation and of its connection with sacrifice engrossed the minds of men after the Return.

The most significant evidence, however, is the way in which the entire sacrificial system was brought into definite association with atonement for sin. As

---

[1] Even Schötz, in his suggestive and valuable 'Schuld und Sündopfer im Alten Testamente,' has not cleared up all the intricacies of that problem, at least to me.

has been noted above, we must allow for the possibility that such an association existed during the earlier period. Yet the conclusion can never reach beyond an inference. There is no need for an inference as to the post-exilic attitude, for the matter is plainly stated. It appears most clearly in certain parts of the book of Ezekiel, where the purpose, not of one or another sacrificial act, but of the entire statutory service, is declared to be " to make atonement for the house of Israel." Thus we find it broadly set down : it shall be the prince's part to give the burnt-offerings and the meal-offerings and the drink-offerings, in the feasts and in the new moons and in the Sabbaths, in all the appointed feasts of the house of Israel : he shall prepare the sin-offering and the meal-offering and the burnt-offering and the peace-offerings, to make atonement for the house of Israel, xlv. 17. Here it seems clear that most of the regular communal sacrifices had an efficacy for propitiation ascribed to them and even that this was their leading end.

It might be legitimate to say that this was merely the expression of an individual conviction or of a school of thought on the subject, were it not that the resemblance between the prophetic passage and the directory in Numbers is sufficiently close to warrant the conclusion that the same attitude to the entire cult was influencing the law. The definite inclusion of a he-goat with the mention of its purpose in so many of the public ceremonies supports it. The use, too, of the word לְכַפֵּר, to atone, in the later law offers confirmatory evidence. " This phrase is used, not only in connection with sin-offerings, but so widely that it is right . . . to recognise that the later priestly system had as a whole and in a certain measure an expiatory character, though this was intensified in connection with certain parts of it."[1] The movement of thought in this direction represented something larger than the conviction of an individual prophet.

What, however, its express appearance in the book of Ezekiel and in the later law may well suggest is that it had a natural affinity to the cult as that had been practised at Jerusalem. The connection between the cult and propitiation is emphasised in the oracles of a Judean prophet, and it colours deeply the conception of the sacrificial worship and even brings about a revaluation of some parts of it in a law which was issued after the Judean priests came into control of the temple. The ceremonial at the Day of Atonement reached a new prominence in the same law ; and certain features in its early ritual point to an original connection with Jerusalem. All these factors combine to recall that from the beginning the sacrifices at that altar were linked to propitiation for sin. The ἱερὸς λόγος of the shrine at the capital has been preserved in full because it told how Yahweh had chosen the site of His altar for the future temple in what had been a Jebusite town. But it also told that the divine election was revealed through the fact that the first offering presented there availed to turn back the divine anger from the nation. The sword of the destroying angel, already drawn to smite the city, was stayed when the smoke of the first sacrifice rose from the sacred site. In the most direct way the sacrifices offered there were given a peculiar

[1] Cf. further Gray, ' Sacrifice in the Old Testament,' pp. 82 ff.

value for the propitiation of the sins of Israel. Though Solomon's prayer at the dedication of the altar must be considered the product of a later time, the extent to which the prayer dwelt on the power of the sacrifices offered there to atone for sin, both individual and national, witnesses to the special efficacy which continued to be attached to the temple-cult.

This explains in turn why the two prophets, who derived from the Southern kingdom, paid special attention to the relation between sacrifice and propitiation. When Isaiah was troubled by the sense of his personal guilt which to him was bound up with the guilt of his nation, the conviction came to him through a vision of God in the temple ; and he found it natural to clothe his sense of forgiveness in imagery taken from the altar cult. Whatever else his language may imply, it proves that to his people there was an intimate connection between the sacrificial ritual and the forgiveness of sin. It would be unwarrantable to conclude that the prophet counted sacrifice essential to his forgiveness : it is equally unwarrantable to ignore that he used symbols which appealed to his people. In the same way Micah's reference to thousands of rams, ten thousands of rivers of oil, and to the offering of the first-born has no meaning unless the community, to whom the prophet sought to teach true religion, believed that these cult-offerings availed to atone for the sin of their souls. What makes these two references more remarkable is that there is nothing corresponding to them in the utterances of the prophets of Northern Israel. These speak often and strongly about the cult of their nation, but, except for an ambiguous phrase in Hosea iv. 8, they never associate it in the same intimate way with the craving for pardon or with the assurance of it. We seem to be conscious of a note which was characteristic of Judean piety, so that, when the men of the Return declared the entire cult valid for propitiation, they were merely bringing into special prominence a feature of that service which had always been of peculiar worth to them. Here, as elsewhere, they were essentially conservative in their standpoint.

While thus reviving the past, however, the men served the present through the new emphasis they laid on this feature of the cult. They were helping to give it a certain *raison d'être* in the life of their scattered nation. Centralisation first and the diaspora afterwards had weakened the intimate bond between the sacrifices at Jerusalem and the actual life of the people. The ritual observances were remote and had become largely professional in their character. They were urged on the loyal Jew as part of his obedience to the will of his God, and as part of what made him distinct from the heathen, rather than as the expression of his personal relation to God. As time went on and each successive generation grew up without having taken any share in this outward form of the faith, the link might have become very thin. What place did the cult fill in helping Jewry to maintain its relation to the God of the fathers ? It availed, said the law by its emphasis on propitiation, to atone for the sins of Israel. Day by day, week after recurrent week, sometimes increasing in volume but never ceasing, the smoke of the altar-fire went up to heaven. Every Israelite had his share in it, since he helped to maintain it ; and it availed for what was every man's need.

There is a sentence in Solomon's dedication prayer which might seem to have been written in order to convey the place which the constant sacrifice took now in the people's life: what prayer and supplication soever be made by any man, or by all Thy people Israel, which shall know every man the plague of his own heart, and spread forth his hands toward this house: then hear thou in heaven thy dwelling-place, and forgive, and do, and render unto every man according to all his ways, whose heart thou knowest (for thou, even thou only, knowest the hearts of all the children of men).

When the religious guides of the nation associated the sacrificial system as a whole with atonement for sin, they did not merely show the worth they conceived it to possess and the need they believed it to supply in the life of the people. They also revealed what was primary in their conception of the divine nature: to them Yahweh was the redeemer of Israel. Already the leading rituals of the nation, such as passover and tabernacles, had been supplied with rubrics, which dwelt on the historic and redemptive elements in the faith. Thus, when passover and unleavened bread were associated with the night of the Exodus in a month which was to be the beginning of months for Israel, the effect had been to bring into the foreground the nature of the God who was then worshipped. Yahweh was no mere nature-god, the giver of the new barley: He was the One who in a great historic act had intervened to save His people and to make them His own. What He had then done was the embodiment of His purpose to redeem Israel. Because this purpose was the expression of His nature, it could not be exhausted in certain acts which belonged to the past, but was still in active operation, so that Israel could be assured of the divine power and will for its restoration. The sacrificial system, which owed its origin to His direction, bore in every part the sign-manual of His purpose with His people and so had efficacy for redemption. No man in Israel need despair of restoration, for in the ritual which He had ordered was the expression of His mind. A verse in Leviticus emphasised this aspect of the Israelite ritual : for the life of the flesh is in the blood : and I have given it to you upon the altar to make atonement for your souls, for it is the blood that maketh atonement by reason of the life, xvii. 11. The verse offers no rationale of the use of blood for the purpose of propitiation. It is, indeed, a mere addendum to a law against promiscuous use of blood by the nation. What it does say is that the God against whom the Israelite has offended has provided the means of propitiation for all who choose to seek it.

In a measure this association of the cult with atonement was capable of supplying a much-needed corrective to a limitation of the divine nature which inevitably resulted from the conditions of the time. The law of centralisation could not fail to localise a deity who was only rightly worshipped at a single shrine in one city. Every man who came back from Babylonia and helped to restore the temple practically confessed that for a full relation to his God a share in this local cult was necessary. But a god who could only be worshipped aright in Palestine was himself a god of Palestine. When the cult was de-

clared to be valid for every Jew, and when its leading
worth was declared to lie in its power to restore a
broken relation between the Jew and his God, room
was made for a larger and richer conception of the
divine nature and power.

It is impossible to say more than that room was left
for such a larger conception, because the new polity
in this connection was fundamentally a compromise
between two elements which had always existed in
the faith of Israel.

The priestly college succeeded in giving the cult a
surer place in the life of their nation, when they dwelt
on its efficacy for propitiation. The temple was
also guaranteed in its lonely dignity, because of the
positive benefit it could assure men and not merely
because a rival to it was forbidden. The sacrifices
there were carefully guarded against one grave abuse,
as though they were able of themselves to atone for
sin. All their efficacy derived from God : He had
appointed them and in them had provided the means
for restoring the broken relation between Himself
and His people. But there remained the fatal ambiguity as to what constituted such a breach and with
it an uncertainty as to what was needed for its healing.
The ambiguity had always existed in the historic
faith of Israel, because the Mosaic movement was a
reform superinduced on a naïver and grosser type of
religion. The native cult, being nearer the nature-
worship of its time, conceived of sin largely as ceremonial defilement : the Mosaic and prophetic movement, to which the relation between God and man
was ethical, conceived of sin as moral transgression.
The two elements were fundamentally irreconcilable,

since they posited a different view of the divine nature, and they had lain alongside each other in the faith of the nation, confusing its religious thought.

The distinction ran deep. The idea of ceremonial impurity incapacitating a man from approach to God fatally separated between the need of repentance and the act by which a man was restored to the worshipping community. For a man could not repent of a sin which he committed involuntarily or even in ignorance. It was possible for a man to contract impurity in the performance of a religious duty, as when he performed the last rites for his dead father. Such an impurity could be contracted through physical means and could therefore be cleansed by physical means. So much was this the case that it is misleading to translate חַטָּאת in its primitive use by sin-offering, because that word inevitably brings with it our thought of sin as moral transgression. It should rather be rendered purification offering.[1] For the purpose of purgation in lighter cases lustration with water was sufficient : to cleanse a more grievous impurity the means of purification must be heightened by the addition of the ashes of the red heifer or by the blood of a victim. Since, again, the defilement could be contracted through physical means, it might attach to things as well as to persons. A vessel in a house might become unclean and so unfit for use : if it was of earthenware, it must be broken, for the impurity might have penetrated into it ; if it was of metal, it only needed lustration with water. The very altar at which atonement was effected could become un-

[1] See Kennedy's lucid and concise conspectus in the article " Sacrifice " in Hastings' single volume D.B.

clean and must therefore be ' unsinned ' every year. Here, probably because of its sacred character, its unsinning demanded the blood of a victim.

Alongside this more primitive idea of ceremonial impurity, which was naturally embedded in the cult, was the Mosaic or prophetic thought on the subject. There the relation between God and Israel was ethical, and any breach in this relation must be due to moral failure. What incapacitated a man for approach to God was his voluntary act. Therefore the first essential for restoration was repentance. The great teacher at once of the necessity and the value of true repentance was Hosea, who dwelt upon it positively, as though no more was needed. On the other hand, Isaiah and Micah developed the theme with a conscious reference to the demands of the cult. Isaiah made his demand for repentance fundamental, but he set it in definite relation to the altar and its sacrifices : Micah required for true religion that men should walk humbly with their God, but he set this over against the sacrifices which the men of his time multiplied for the relief of their troubled hearts. Both prophets, conceiving sin as voluntary and ethical, demanded repentance and posited their demand in connection with, even in opposition to, the sacrificial ritual.

It was possible to give effect to the demand for a recognition of the significance of repentance in connection with the sacrifice at the altar by the use of rubrics which were added to the ritual. In my judgment the penitential psalms, whether they were spoken by the individual or chanted in name of the community, expressed the attitude of the penitent who sought reconciliation, while the actual sacrifice embodied the unalterable purpose of God who forgave. Thus the altar became the meeting-place between the worshipper with his repentance and God with His purpose of mercy.

Yet any such revaluation of sacrifice left untouched the contradiction between the two causes of separation between Israel and God, ceremonial uncleanness and moral fault, and certain conditions of the period brought the ceremonial element into undue prominence. Thus, when the priestly college made Leviticus the use at the temple, they bound all Jewry by the Code which is most deeply influenced by this conception. That law insisted on the ethical character of the divine commands, and contains the classic pronouncement in Judaism on the duty of love toward one's neighbours ; but the regulations which bear on ceremonial impurity are more numerous and detailed, and no effort has been made to reconcile the two or to indicate their relative importance. They are simply set down alongside each other, as though they were of equal significance. Again, the men into whose hands the guidance of the people had fallen were the priests, whose specific function it had always been to distinguish between the clean and the unclean. Since the altar with its sacrifices was their peculiar care, they naturally magnified the side of the law which they administered. Nor is it difficult to realise that this conception of the relation between God and Israel fell into line with the ideal of the Jerusalem temple as the national centre. A ceremonial method of approach better agrees with a national deity worshipped at a historic shrine than the large demand for clean hands and a pure heart which could be brought

at any shrine and under any sky. Yet all this does
not fully explain why such a law with these preconceptions touched and in the end came to dominate
the life of the scattered nation. There must have
been something in the situation and the temper of
the people which made it acceptable to them. There
it is necessary to recognise that from the beginning
of the exile the Jew, whether in Palestine or in the
diaspora, was brought into close and constant contact
with heathenism. On every side he could not escape
from the sight of heathen emblems ; in his intercourse
with his world he was continually brought up against
a life which was pagan in its sanctions and in its
personal habits. It requires a real effort for men of
to-day to realise how instinctive and even physical
in its character must have been the reaction. The
devout Jew could not fail to be troubled with a continual malaise in such conditions. The man who
said, how can we sing the Lord's songs in a strange
land, expressed more than a revulsion against turning
his sacred songs into a means of amusing his neighbours. There was something revolting to him about
the use of Israel's sacred lyrics at all in that polluted
air. A similar difficulty arose in the early Church at
Corinth over the question of the use of meats offered
to idols, and it is instructive to recognise how St Paul
dealt with it. The Christian apostle was able to say
that an idol was nothing in the world and to conclude
that anything offered to it was equally impotent with
itself for good or evil. The only question which remained was the moral question of how Christian men
who saw that principle with all its consequences
should behave towards those who had scruples on the

subject. The idea of ceremonial uncleanness had no place in the Christian ethic. But the Jerusalem priests could not take that way, because ceremonial sin was embedded in their law. They must define what amount of contact did or did not defile ; they must prescribe the means by which the Jew kept himself aloof from every impure thing : they began the long series of enactments which form part of the *halakah* in the Talmud. As for those defilements which were inevitable, they taught that the cult availed to propitiate.[1]

This desire to keep Judaism aloof from the debasing and insidious influence of its heathen surroundings led to a new emphasis being laid on the outward signs which distinguished the Jew. Such practices as the observance of Sabbath and circumcision assumed a new importance. As Israel had its own thought of God and its own end for life, it must have its own

[1] On the question of sin and atonement in the later law, cf. G. F. Moore, ' Judaism,' Vol. I., Part III. The weakness of Moore's discussion is that he has not allowed for the extent to which the idea of sin as moral transgression had lodged itself in Jewish thought and has written at times as though only ceremonial impurity was recognised there. Now, in the wealth of valuable and interesting material which he has collected, especially in the Notes, Vol III., he has shown how persistently the early Rabbis discussed the value of repentance and of the sin-offering respectively in relation to voluntary sins. But he has failed to explain why this particular question continually troubled the minds of thoughtful men in Jewry. They were recognising the presence of two unreconciled elements in their ancestral faith, and thus unconsciously showed that the faith was not homogeneous in its teaching on the subject. Nor has he recognised that the distinction in the post-exilic law between sins done בשגגה or *per incuriam* and sins done ביד רמה, with the somewhat contradictory view as to whether sacrifice availed for both, proves how early the question forced itself on men's minds. Since, in my judgment, the distinction is not clearly drawn, nor is the validity of the sin-offering defined, I must conclude that the men of the Return left the fundamental contradiction unreconciled, and handed it on to their successors.

outward customs distinct from the alien world. When such things are set down in a book they leave an impression of aridity in their formal and austere demands. But no student of Church history can fail to recognise that every devout fellowship, which finds itself in a hostile world, has thrown up its own hedge of peculiar observance. Even the Friends, who submitted to no ritual in their method of worship, were once recognisable through the outward acts which they required from their members. Such a series of habits always appears to a generation which has forgotten the distinction between the Church and the world to be unnecessarily austere and more than a little arbitrary. Yet behind its shelter may blossom the scented flowers of a sincere piety, of a tender conscience and of a generous helpfulness to the brethren. Nor should it be forgotten that the circumstances of the time inevitably led to a demarcation of the community by external signs. The men of the Return were acting under Cyrus' edict which conferred liberty of worship on them, and it became necessary to distinguish those who could claim this privilege. A Persian governor needed to know beyond mistake the men who had the right to worship at Jerusalem. There inevitably arose a certain stereotyping of what was meant by Judaism, with the result that outward signs of nationality gained greater prominence, with the further result that the faith lost a little more the prophetic element of universality.

It is not therefore surprising that prophecy died out in Jerusalem. Prophecy had never quite lost its charismatic character, and this, with its sense of direct relation to the divine, is always difficult to reconcile with a formal institution. Now the new Judaism was centred round an institution, and was contracting the habit of discipline. Prophecy also, since it was primarily ethical, was inevitably universal in its outlook. But the institution was local, the cult was historic, the law with its peculiar practice was increasingly national. There are soils in which certain flowers refuse to grow, and there is an atmosphere in which the genius of the prophet was not at all at home. When, however, he sought an audience and a locus elsewhere, the resultant loss was not confined to Jerusalem. The individualist temper of the prophet had been disciplined—and no man needs discipline more—so long as he was closely allied with the actual life of a larger community of which he was an integral part. Now, too many of them, untrammelled by the wholesome realities of the world, lost their way in apocalyptic dreams.

Meantime the priestly college went their own way to guide their scattered people along the lines which have been sketched above. Their thought was engrossed in the control of the institution and in matters of its relation to the life of their nation. In much the same fashion, as soon as the Roman bishops had become the rulers of the Church, they ceased to produce theology. After the time of Ambrose what the faithful received from Rome was Canon law and Papal bulls. The torah which went out from Jerusalem was no longer that about which the prophets had dreamed that it might enlighten the world : it tended more and more to become the halakah of the Talmud.

INDEX OF SCRIPTURE PASSAGES
SPECIALLY DISCUSSED.

GENERAL INDEX.

Printed in Great Britain by
WILLIAM BLACKWOOD & SONS LTD.